Options for Risk-Free Portfolios

OPTIONS FOR RISK-FREE PORTFOLIOS

PROFITING WITH DIVIDEND COLLAR STRATEGIES

MICHAEL C. THOMSETT

palgrave
macmillan

OPTIONS FOR RISK-FREE PORTFOLIOS
Copyright © Michael C. Thomsett, 2013.

All rights reserved.

First published in 2013 by
PALGRAVE MACMILLAN®
in the United States—a division of St. Martin's Press LLC,
175 Fifth Avenue, New York, NY 10010.

Where this book is distributed in the UK, Europe and the rest of the world, this is by Palgrave Macmillan, a division of Macmillan Publishers Limited, registered in England, company number 785998, of Houndmills, Basingstoke, Hampshire RG21 6XS.

Palgrave Macmillan is the global academic imprint of the above companies and has companies and representatives throughout the world.

Palgrave® and Macmillan® are registered trademarks in the United States, the United Kingdom, Europe and other countries.

ISBN: 978–1–137–28257–6

Library of Congress Cataloging-in-Publication Data

Thomsett, Michael C.
   Options for risk-free portfolios : profiting with dividend collar strategies / Michael C. Thomsett.
     pages cm
   ISBN 978–1–137–28257–6 (alk. paper)
     1. Options (Finance) 2. Risk management. 3. Portfolio management. I. Title.

HG6024.A3T4756 2013
332.64'53—dc23
                                                     2012032632

A catalogue record of the book is available from the British Library.

Design by Newgen Imaging Systems (P) Ltd., Chennai, India.

First edition: March 2013

10 9 8 7 6 5 4 3 2 1

Printed in the United States of America.

*To the third-century BC philosopher Thales,
the earliest known options trader.*

Contents

Acknowledgments	ix
Introduction: The Quest for High Return and Low Risk	1
1. The Dividend Portfolio, an Overview	7
2. Managing and Reducing Risk with Options	33
3. The Advantage of the Covered Call	63
4. Downside Protection, the Insurance Put	89
5. The Collar: Removing All of the Risk	107
6. Rolling the Stock Positions: Turning 4% into 12%	135
7. Examples of the Basic Strategy	165
8. Modification: The Installment Collar Approach	197
9. Expanding into the Ratio Write Dividend Collar	227
10. More Expansion, Creating the Variable Ratio Write Dividend Collar	249
11. Modifying the Strategy with Synthetic Stock Positions	265
Epilogue: The Great Value in Patience	273
Notes	287
Index	291

Acknowledgments

Many thanks to all of the subscribers and members of LinkedIn groups who replied to my numerous options posts with questions and clarifications about the dividend collar. To all of those options traders struggling with the complexity of devising strategies while managing market risks, I appreciate your diligence and persistence in requiring me to be absolutely clear in my answers. To my friends at the Chicago Board Options Exchange and The Options Institute, especially Marty Kearney and Jim Bittman, thank you for the years of enthusiastic support and friendship. Special thanks for calm guidance from my agent John Willig, and also to Laurie Harting, Lauren LoPinto, and Joel Breuklander at Palgrave for guiding me through the production process.

Introduction: The Quest for High Return and Low Risk

> The market doesn't reward qualities that are not scarce.
> Mark A. Johnson, *The Random Walk and Beyond*, 1988

OPTIONS TRADERS CONTINUALLY SEEK THE BEST OF BOTH worlds—high return and low risk. A majority of the strategies they follow are not going to produce this desired result, not only in the options world but also in any market. Risk and return are two sides of the same trading coin: The higher the risk, the higher the potential for high return.

An exception does exist, however. High return and low risk can be accomplished through a strategic approach to the options market called the *dividend collar*. As options are flexible, they offer the opportunity to beat the market when used to hedge long portfolio positions; to manage your portfolio; and to take advantage of timing rules to generate exceptional but safe returns. However, options income is not the key to the dividend collar strategy; and neither is capital gains from buying and selling the underlying security. The key is that these two—options and stock—are used to eliminate risk while accelerating dividend income.

Every options trader has read all about how to get rich with covered calls, iron condors, or short puts. The "sure thing" straddle or spread sounds great on paper but falls apart if the market moves in the wrong direction. So why do options traders find themselves caught by surprise again and again? Why keep trying out new strategies or new combinations? For many, the cynical conclusion is that options just don't deliver on the promise. However, a related problem is that in addition to seeking higher than average returns, some traders are just not willing to work at it or, upon setting rules for themselves, are not willing to follow those rules based on changing valuation of the underlying elements of stock or options. They want those "fast millions" to come easily. First, they might have to settle for "fast thousands," which is more realistic. Second, nothing is all that easy.

This book presents a series of strategic ideas designed to identify opportunities to reduce risk while generating much better than average returns. Double-digit returns are not only possible but also inevitable if the discipline behind these strategies is followed faithfully. This is the key for all options traders: *Discipline.* Even a relatively safe strategy such as covered call writing works only if you stick with the program. This means, for example, that of the many possible outcomes, getting some positions exercised is one way the position may end up; and if properly constructed, that is acceptable as well. But how many have rolled out of the covered call to avoid exercise? Was it worthwhile for the small additional income but extended time in the position? Did you accept a loss on one call hoping for bigger future profits on another? Did you end self-sabotaging overlooking the initial simplicity of the position?

This is only one example. Speculators have the same problem. If they buy long calls or puts, when do they sell? If the value of the long option rises, do they hold on thinking profits will grow only next week and the week after? If the value falls, do they cut their losses or hold on hoping to get back to their original position? Time decay is going to eat away at profits even if their position is in the money (meaning the price of stock has moved above the call's strike or below the put's strike), so if they set a bail-out or profit-taking goal and then opt not to take it, their self-programming is off. It means they are programmed for losses and not for profits.

The strategies in this book are designed for traders who want to program themselves to create consistent, reliable, realistic profits. Developing these strategies demands research and analysis, but the rewards are worth the time invested. There is no such thing as a "get-rich-quick" scheme in the options market. Of course, one can get rich if one makes the right moves at the right time, but that is not always practically possible. Options traders are prone to "what if" thinking just like everyone else, but a rational trader thinks about the future and does not dwell on the past, especially if the past is littered with ill-timed entries and exits, unexpected losses, and missed opportunities.

It is prudent to learn from those mistakes and not be defined by them.

The concept underlying this series of strategies is that one can create a risk-free portfolio that yields double-digit returns. This concept goes against virtually every understanding of markets, cycles, and the nature of risk. However, it proposes an approach different from traditional equity investing or popular options strategies. In the traditional stock market approach, those companies that are exceptionally well managed (value investments) or that offer exceptional potential for growth are picked. Then begins a buy-and-hold approach until the fundamentals change. In this approach, even a conservative investor uses options to generate cash (through covered call writing), play volatility (with iron condors and spreads, or even with short options), or protect paper profits (with insurance puts).

Traditional methods such as this have not enabled traders to beat the market consistently or safely. Covered call writing can go terribly wrong if the underlying value falls and continues to fall. Volatility trades can also be conservative. But it takes only one disastrous, badly timed trade to wipe out profits on dozens of well-timed trades; insurance protects only a portion of the paper profits (intrinsic value, minus the cost of the put), and it is a limited and defensive play only.

This book rejects these traditional methods. The investment strategy of picking exceptional stocks has failed; remember, there was a day when General Motors, Eastman Kodak, and Enron were all considered "exceptional." History has convincingly shown that investors are humans with flaws and that markets contain risks, often very high risks. On the options side, conservative trading is coming to be recognized as a more sensible approach than hedge strategies or the occasional speculative play.

The strategies proposed here are "conservative" in the sense that they enable one to set up positions to generate income on short-term open positions. These positions are not based on smart stock selection or even on conservative options strategies by themselves. Instead, the "risk-free portfolio" uses the underlying stock to open a low-cost or no-cost option position designed specifically to generate a desirable end result (high return, low risk)—not from either stock or option profits but from dividends. The short-term open positions are designed to identify attractive dividend yields—*monthly* instead of quarterly. As a result, three stocks each yielding 4% per year are opened only long enough to earn a quarterly dividend. Since dividends are earned on a monthly basis, this results in an overall annual dividend yield of 12%.

The first five chapters methodically explore the features and risks of each component of the dividend collar strategy: dividends (Chapter 1), options (Chapter 2), the covered call (Chapter 3), the insurance put (Chapter 4), and the collar (Chapter 5). The purpose of devoting time to a study of the risks underlying each component is to demonstrate two seemingly contradictory observations. First, all components of the strategy contain risks, which are, at times, quite severe or invisible. Second, when these same components are combined to create a risk-free portfolio, all market risks are eliminated. Most perceptions of risk are specific to a strategy or to a market. However, the proper construction of the dividend collar works to eliminate these common market risks. Amazingly, proper application of the strategy eliminates dividend, option, and stock risks altogether, while yielding double-digit annualized returns. This is a bold claim and that is why the case is built methodically and cautiously by first examining the attributes of the components, and then providing clear examples showing how these risks are managed and eliminated.

Once the basic strategy is mastered, it can be expanded further using the installment method, ratio writes and variable ratio writes, and synthetic stock positions. Though these expansions present greater levels of risk, some traders will find them attractive. As with all market strategies, every trader needs to balance the desire for return with acceptance of risk to some degree.

This approach is the starting point for using stocks and options to generate exceptional returns and at the same time to manage market risk.

CHAPTER 1

THE DIVIDEND PORTFOLIO, AN OVERVIEW

> The easiest job I have ever tackled in this world is that of making money. It is, in fact, almost as easy as losing it. Almost, but not quite.
> H. L. Mencken, in *Baltimore Evening Sun*, June 12, 1922

DIVIDENDS ARE PERCEIVED IN MANY WAYS, SOME VERY INACCURATELY.

Traders who want to be in and out of positions short term, tend to ignore or undervalue dividends altogether. Because the dollar amount is quite small compared to a stock transaction, dividends often are viewed as nuisance factors to short-term traders. On the far end of the spectrum, value investors might ultimately pick one value investment over other choices based mainly on the dividend yield of the moment.

The point is, traders and investors cannot just buy stocks yielding higher than average dividends and expect to outperform the market. Dividend risk is one form of risk that is easily ignored or misunderstood. So while dividend yield can represent a major portion of overall yield, it has to be balanced against market risk. The dividend collar developed throughout this book is based on generating income from dividend yield, but the most crucial component of that strategy is protecting against the inherent risks that can accompany high-dividend stocks, at times to a greater extent than market risk in the overall equity market.

DIVIDEND YIELD AS PART OF OPTION RETURNS

In considering how dividends work along with long stock and long or short options positions, they cannot be ignored. Even in a more or less vanilla strategy such as the covered call, dividend yield might represent a major portion of the overall annualized return. Consider these important qualifying points:

1. If the covered call is open only a few days, but that period includes the ex-dividend date, the covered call writer's annualized yield is substantially higher due to the dividend yield than it would be if the strategy were round-tripped one week earlier or later.
2. In selecting two otherwise identically attractive underlying stocks to be used for a covered call strategy, the higher-yielding dividend may serve as a deciding factor.
3. Long-term potential growth in earnings per share as well as a potential underlying issue for options strategies might be affected by the historical and future dividend record. Those companies paying higher dividends every year for 10 years or more (so-called "dividend achievers") tend to outperform the markets over time and to be less volatile both technically (predictability of price breadth and range) and fundamentally (in terms of predictability of revenue and earnings trends).

These are significant examples of how dividend yield is related to the selection of underlying issues as well as options strategies. The covered call cannot be viewed in isolation from the dividend yield. In fact, calculating returns from covered call writing is complex, but may include dividend yield in addition to capital gains or losses on the underlying and premium income from selling the call. This method, at times called "total return," attempts to validate comparisons of net return among covered calls on a variety of stocks. These may include stocks yielding various dividend yields or offering no dividend at all. Because dividend yield changes the return (both basic and annualized), it makes sense to include the yield in the analysis of option-based return.

With this in mind, the higher the dividend yield, the better the overall return will be as well. Does this mean that selection of a covered call candidate should be limited to only those stocks yielding better-than-average dividends? No. In fact, in comparing only the covered call strategy (without considering any other hedging that might be included) the appropriate underlying stock should be selected based on sound fundamental analysis, and not on the basis of (1) richer-than-average option premium or (2) higher-than-average dividends.

Remembering that attractive yields often accrue because a company's share price has plummeted, selecting covered call candidates based solely on dividend yield is quite dangerous. Share price might have fallen due to any number of causes, including the impending demise of the company and anticipation of a further price decline in the stock. In this case, a 7% yield on a stock yielding only 1.2% a few months earlier is not likely to be a sound candidate for covered call writing.

Assuming, however, that you have narrowed down selection for covered call writing to three different companies, and also assuming that all three share the same or similar fundamental attributes, how do you know which to purchase for a covered call strategy? While you can apply a number of sensible fundamental (or technical) criteria to pick one of the three, dividend yield may certainly act as one deciding factor.

This decision is not merely a matter of opting for the highest dividend yield. Depending on your analytical standards and on the ratios and trends you follow, you are likely to prefer one company over others without consideration of the dividend level. However, as a starting point for describing any options strategy, it makes sense to analyze the components that are included; how those components affect value; and what levels of risk are caused or mitigated as a result. Dividend yield is one of those components, and traders have struggled for years to determine the role of dividends and their effect on option valuation.

THE DIVIDEND EFFECT ON OPTION VALUES

Few will doubt that dividend yield has a direct effect on both stock and option value. A higher dividend makes a company's stock more desirable than that of a company whose dividend is lower. The exception: If the yield has increased because the share price has declined, then a comparison of dividend yields is not valid. You also have to consider the reasons for changes in a stock's price, both upside and downside, before equating one dividend yield to another.

Pricing models for options have provided a dismal indicator. The most popular among these, the Black-Scholes Pricing Model,[1] is a very flawed method for identifying fair value for options, because it contains several variables and excludes many important attributes that make the model inaccurate. These include

1. *Dividends*: Exclusion of any dividend yield, with the original Black-Scholes modeling assumption based on a zero dividend. Today, with so many securities declaring and paying dividends, the model is inaccurate to the extent that it compares and estimates option valuation between companies declaring dividends and those not declaring dividends.
2. *Exercise*: Assumption of European-style exercise, even though American stocks nearly always are exercised American-style. Thus, early exercise, which occurs frequently, is not built into the assumption.
3. *Volatility*: Black-Scholes provides a factor for volatility, but is flawed because it assumes that volatility remains unchanged all the way to expiration. Every options trader knows that extrinsic value (volatility) changes continually and, in fact, provides a key timing criterion for both entry and exit of most options strategies.
4. *Interest*: The formula assumes a theoretical "risk-free" interest rate, which is a questionable assumption based on today's debt security market. If this interest rate increases,

call premium is expected to rise and put premium to decline. These effects are caused by the leverage of options in comparison to owning 100 shares of the underlying. However, in practice, when federal funds effective rates are as low as 1% or lower, the effect of risk-free interest (such as interest on US Treasury securities) is insignificant. As of 2012, the Fed effective rate was approaching zero, as shown in figure 1.1.

The complexity of how dividends and interest rates affect option valuation is not a small issue. Dividends are certainly a direct component of option and stock valuation, and interest affects the valuation of both calls and puts. It is noteworthy, however, to recognize that at the time the Black-Scholes model was devised, there was no standardized trading of puts in the US markets. In fact, even calls were available on the stock of only 16 companies.

Black-Scholes works as a pricing model in a comparative sense; however, it is so inaccurate that it provides little value in terms of

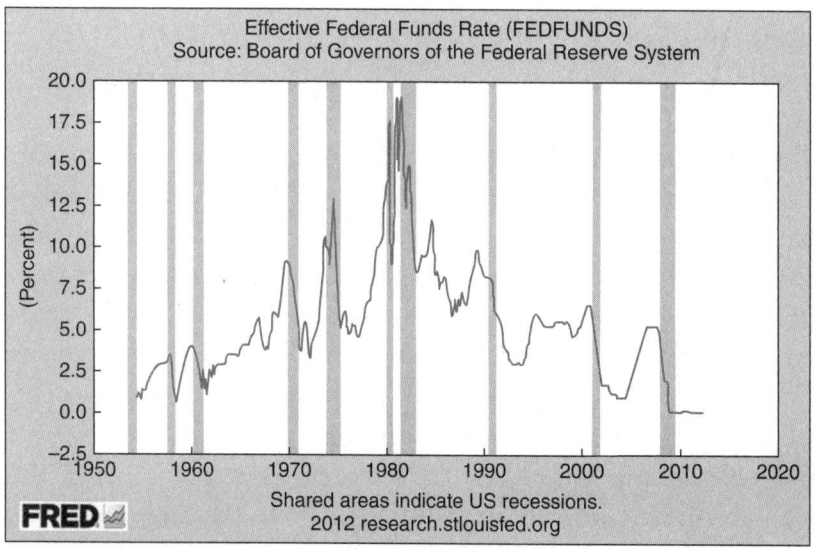

Figure 1.1   Effective federal funds rate
Source: Federal Reserve Bank of St. Louis Federal Reserve Economic Date (FRED).

changes in interest rates, and no value for dividend-paying stocks. The factor for volatility is based on assumption that the volatility level remains constant. The Black-Scholes formula is

$$c = SN(d_1) - Xe^{-rT}(d_2)$$
$$p = Xe^{-rT} N(-d_2) = SN(-d_1)$$

where

$$d_1 = \frac{\ln(S/X) + (r + \sigma^2/2)T}{\sigma\sqrt{T}}$$

$$d_2 = \frac{\ln(S/X) + (r - \sigma^2/2)T}{\sigma\sqrt{T}} = d_1 - \sigma\sqrt{T}$$

c = call
p = put
S = Stock price
X = Strike price of the option
r = risk-free interest rate
T = time to expiration (in years)
σ = volatility of the relative price change of the underlying stock price
$N(x)$ = the cumulative normal distribution function

The formula demonstrably excludes dividends, assumes unreliably about interest risk-free interest, sets volatility as a constant, and is based on European-style exercise. All of these assumptions make the model highly unreliable if applied in the "real world" of trading. It may be beneficial in an academic setting where the interest is in trying to estimate a pricing level, given the assumptions (wrong or not). But in practice, Black-Scholes is a flawed model

Among those flaws is the assumption that a risk-free interest rate exists. That is unlikely today, when even the debts of the US government have been downgraded. This does not mean they are likely to default, but it does take away the historical risk-free assumption related to Treasury securities.

Interest rates affect option values directly and also serve as a guide for when or if to exercise an option early. If interest that can be earned on the proceeds received for selling a put at a higher level than is possible from holding until expiration, then early exercise is justified, at least in theory. This assumption is based on the additional assumption that if you close out an option position, you will immediately transfer capital to an instrument yielding a more favorable net return. This is the rationale often cited in support of Black-Scholes and similar pricing models. But in the modern-day environment of very low interest rates, this comparison is not valid. When it is possible to earn as much as 4–5% or more on stock ownership, the dividend yield is a far more important measure of return than interest rates for those companies could ever expect to be.

Dividends are likely to have much greater impact on option valuation than interest rates, notably when early exercise before the ex-dividend date is compared with exercise on or after the ex-dividend date. A general assumption about dividends is that the higher the cash dividend, the lower the call premium and the higher the put premium. While there is truth in this general rule of valuation, traders will still want to time their exercise decisions to be stockholders of record two days after the ex-dividend date—and this might lead to a decision to time entry and exit, even more than the relative value of the dividend yield or *potential* yield from closing stock and option positions and investing elsewhere.

These decisions are complicated by the additional considerations of whether the option is in or out of the money, the rate of time decay, and whether in-the-money (ITM) calls are vulnerable to exercise as the ex-dividend date approaches. The day before the ex-dividend date is the second most likely time for exercise, after the last trading day. Thus, proximity of the short call to current price is a crucial factor in option valuation, meaning that dividend yield is a key factor in the overall evaluation of options. It is not just proximity but time as well as actual yield that determines the option's fair value.

PICKING DIVIDEND GROWTH STOCKS

The "dividend growth stock" is highly favored by investors as a smart way to limit the search for portfolio components. A mistake often made by investors focused on dividends is the failure to analyze price prior to selecting such stocks for inclusion in a portfolio.

If you are intent on focusing on dividend growth stocks, you should employ the same criteria that are used by fundamental investors even without considering dividend yield. The criteria beyond dividend yield include

1. *Lower than average PE (Price-Earnings) ratio.* The PE is a test of market perception of a company's value. The multiple expressed in the ratio represents the number of years' earnings per share (EPS) in the current price. So logically, a high PE on the one hand implies that the market is enthusiastic about prospects for future growth while, on the other hand, points to the stock's current price as inflated. Somewhere in between is a sensible balance.

In employing PE in any stock analysis, it makes no sense to look only at the *current* PE level. This will change each time the stock price changes, so current PE by itself is very unreliable. The earnings components may also be quite outdated today, whereas price changes from moment to moment. With this in mind, historical PE analysis is better based on long-term annual PE *range* from high to low. Traders seek consistency in this range while ignoring nonrepetitive PE spikes. Preferably, as revenues and earnings rise, analysts expect to see a corresponding reduction in the PE, both high and low each year. This range analysis provides a much more reliable indicator of market perception of a company, especially if an eight-year PE history remains consistent or declines. For example, a comparison of the eight-year ranges of PE for Wal-Mart (WMT) and Research in Motion (RIMM) demonstrates different levels of price and earnings volatility, as shown in figure 1.2.

The WMT PE range declined steadily throughout this period, revealing a low fundamental volatility that equity investors find

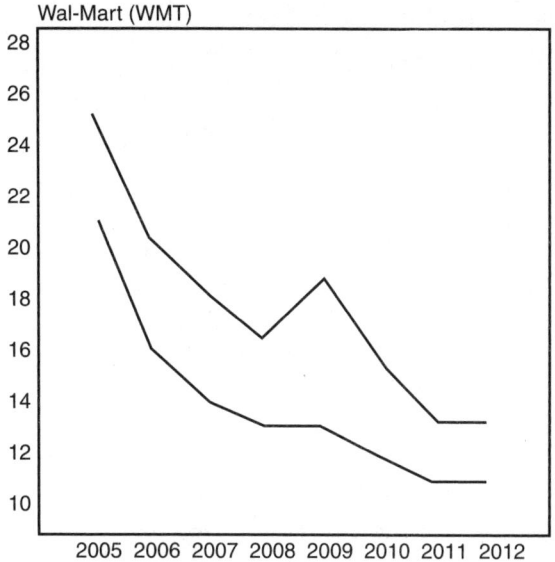

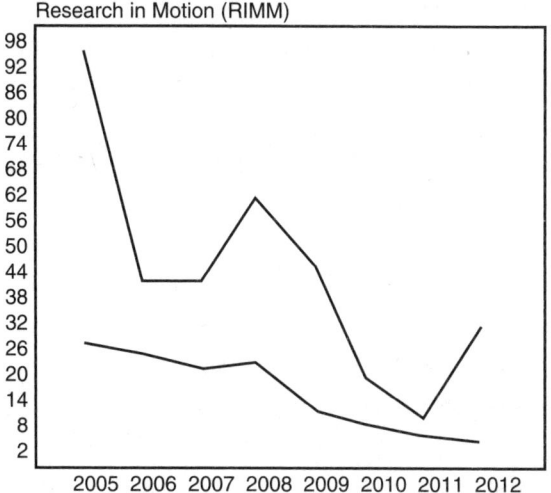

Figure 1.2 PE range, eight years
Source: Figure created by author from raw numerical data on S&P Stock Reports.

desirable. However, the RIMM history was relatively erratic. Even though the range declined, the latest year's high PE jumped into the 30s, and from this history it is quite difficult to estimate where the indicator will move next.

Investors favoring dividend growth stocks are likely to prefer issues with low PE, over those with higher or erratic PE history.

This indicates strong value and reveals that the price is likely to be reasonable. Such investors avoid overpriced stocks. However, PE also varies from one sector to another, so in making side-by-side comparisons, this has to be remembered as part of the analysis.

2. *Consistent or falling debt ratio.* The debt ratio is the best measurement of working capital trends. To compute, divide long-term debt by total capitalization (long-term debt plus total equity). The better-known current ratio (current assets dividend by current liabilities) is not reliable, since it can be manipulated easily to maintain consistency. The debt ratio reveals the truer picture, and when that debt ratio is consistent or falling, it indicates effective control by management. When debt ratio is rising, it demonstrates that in the future, less profit will be available to pay for dividends or expansion, as a larger amount must go each year toward interest on the growing debt.

For example, a comparison between AT&T (T) and Charter Communications (CHTR) shows a vast difference in the level and trend of the debt ratio. AT&T maintained its long-term debt in the 30s during the three-year period, while Charter's grew from 87.1% up to 96.9%. This means that for Charter, total capitalization consists of 96.9% debt and only 3.1% equity. These comparisons are summarized in figure 1.3

3. *High-dividend yield.* The obvious criterion for a high-dividend yield strategy is the yield itself. However, this can be deceptive. Is the yield high as a matter of competitive dividend strategy? Or is it high because the stock price has declined sharply? And if the latter is the case, what does this mean in terms of market risk and fundamental value? High-dividend yield is desirable as long as the company and its stock price are stable, but at the same—especially for unusually high yield—it might also be the result of a company's weakening fundamental indicators.

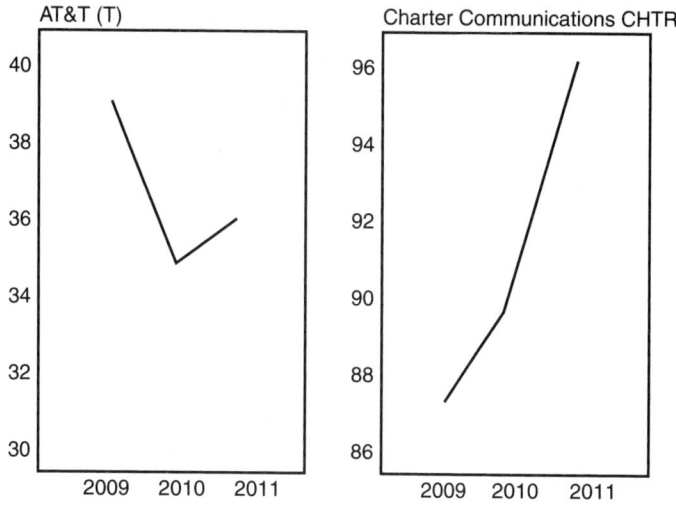

Figure 1.3   Debt ratio, three years
Source: Figure created by author from raw numerical data on S&P Stock Reports.

A second factor in studying the dividend yield is whether the stock is at risk. A high-dividend payout ratio means the price has declined, which could indicate greater market risks. Dividend yield is the calculation of yearly dividends per share, divided by EPS (or, total dividends divided by net income). Wal-Mart, for example, increased dividends during its eight-year period, from a 22% payout to the latest at 32%. However, this steady increase does not signal any danger. Wal-Mart has not missed any dividends, and its fundamental strength is reassuring for investors concerned about missed dividends.

Dividend yield can be further analyzed through two standards: limiting analysis to companies classified as dividend "aristocrats" or as dividend "achievers." The dividend achiever class includes all companies whose dividend has increased every year for at least 10 years. The aristocrats have a record of increased dividends for at least 25 years (some define aristocrats using only 5 years of increasing annual dividends).

These are important distinctions because the likelihood of missing or reducing a dividend is slim. In addition, the long-term dividend increases tend to be found among companies whose fundamental volatility is lower than average, and whose core earnings adjustments (as defined by Standard & Poor's [S & P]) also tend to be quite small. The selectivity of companies with long-term increases also defines well-managed working capital policies and annual growth in both revenues and net earnings. For these reasons, dividend achiever and aristocrat companies tend to be the strongest in their industries and the best managed.

A company paying ever-higher dividends does not necessarily fit the definition of a high-dividend company. In fact, many achievers and aristocrats pay relatively modest dividends, but annual increases are noteworthy. Many traders prefer consistent growth as a trend more important than higher-than-average yields that might not hold or that are inconsistent. And just because a company pays a higher-than-average dividend does not by itself make the investment safer.

DANGER IN HIGH-DIVIDEND PORTFOLIOS

Among the many dividend-specific strategies is the Dogs of the Dow. Under this plan, a trader purchases shares in the 10 highest-yielding components of the Dow Jones Industrial Average (DJIA) 30 industrials. These are replaced periodically as some fall off the list and are replaced by others.[2]

A problem with this systematic method for selecting stocks is that high yields are the result of many different circumstances. A company might simply pay a better-than-average dividend. For example, as of the end of May 2012, the four highest-yielding Dow components were (T), Verizon (VZ), Merck (MRK), and Pfizer (PFE). Table 1.1 summarizes their yield, S & P rating, and debt ratio.

All of these indicators are positive, and all of the companies are well capitalized and stable. However, in some cases, a company's dividend yield will rise sharply due to weak or declining earnings, loss of competitive position within a sector, or an announcement of a coming bankruptcy. These types of news would almost certainly bring a company's market value down, and thus a higher dividend yield.

Table 1.1 May, 2012 highest-yielding Dow components

Symbol	Yield	Rating	Debt ratio
T	5.23%	B	35.9%
VZ	4.84	C	26.3
MRK	4.47	B	17.6
PFE	3.90	B	22.8

Source: www.dogsofthedow.com.

For example, J. C. Penney (JCP) announced in May 2012 that it was cutting its 20-cents-per-share dividend to 10 cents. Due to a falling price in the stock (from the mid-40s in February to the mid-20s by the end of May, the 20-cent-per-share dividend represented a 3% return as of late May. This sounds like a respectable return, but the company reported losses of $163 million during the first quarter of 2012 and announced it would be writing off large restructuring charges as well.[3]

The risks associated with dividends are overlooked easily; however, that risk can be realized in many forms. The most apparent is that a high yield may be generated from a competitive policy by a company with adequate cash and profits—or as the result of a company's being in trouble and seeing its stock price decline. For example, if a company sets a dividend of $1.00 per share when the stock is at $40 per share, it is a 2.5% dividend yield (*$1 ÷ 40*). But if the stock price suddenly declines to $28 per share, the dividend yield rises to 3.6% (*$1 ÷ 28*). The investor picking stocks based solely on dividend yield can be easily misled by this, and may select stocks of companies in trouble—in terms of their fundamental weakness, losing market share, or poor management.

In other words, a "dividend growth stock" is not defined solely by the dividend yield. Some investors limit their analysis to this, at least as a starting point. However, once those high-yielding issues are identified, it requires additional research in order for an investor to avoid buying stocks in companies that are in general high risk. In that case, an attractive dividend yield is not only misleading but a negative signal as well.

A more meaningful system for identifying the true dividend growth stock is by studying the annual dividend growth rate. Even

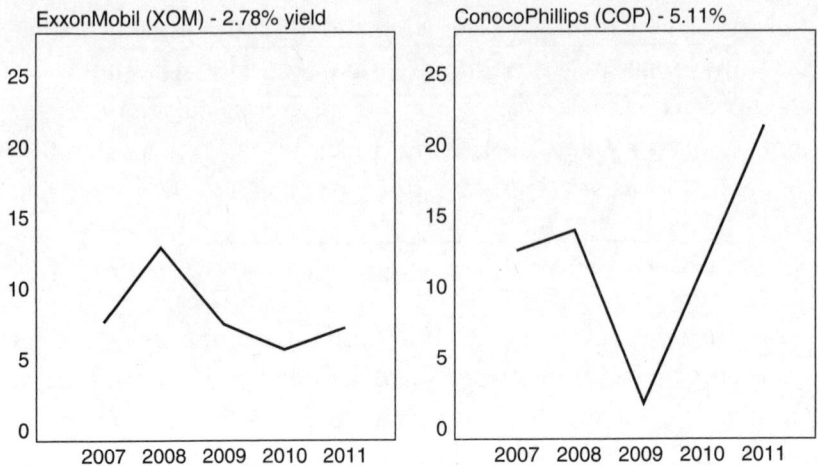

Figure 1.4 Dividend growth rate, five years
Source: Figure created by author from raw numerical data on S&P Stock Reports.

a stock with a low dividend may prove to be an attractive growth candidate if its annual dividend increase is substantial. Many dividend achievers and aristocrats meet the initial criterion of increasing dividends every year, but the increases are measured in pennies, and are not growing at the same rate as others that might not be on that selective list. Figure 1.4 compares the annual dividend growth rate between ExxonMobil (XOM) and ConocoPhillips (COP). The two are vastly different. As of the end of May 2012, XOM was paying annual dividends of 2.78%, and COP was paying 5.11%. The annual increase for XOM was lower than for COP, but COP's year-to-year change was also more volatile.

The dividend growth rate can be used to further analyze a stock's current price and determine whether it is underpriced or overpriced. The "dividend discount model" assumes that a stock's market value is set or determined by future dividend yield, to be discounted by an assumed discount rate. The formula for this is

$D \div (R - G)$.

D = dividend per share
R = discount rate
G = dividend growth rate

The problem with using the dividend discount model is that it assumes the variable of the discount rate. How do you know whether this is a fair rate or not? There are several methods for calculating this, but all are going to be estimates. It seems more reasonable to use known factors like the dividend growth rate as a means for comparison, or even the dividend yield by itself. These provide a more tangible and specific comparison of dividend yield among several companies. If the end goal is to pick investment candidates based on dividend yield (current and future), the combination of the current yield and the annual growth rate provide the most reliable comparative results. From there, traders and investors need to further study the fundamentals to select strong and well-capitalized issues (the most valuable fundamentals in this process may include trends in revenue and earnings growth, PE range, and debt ratio).

Investors who pursue dividend yield as a primary means for picking stocks may easily ignore warning signs that market risks could be correspondingly higher for high-yield stocks if and when the underlying causes of those yields are technical rather than fundamental.

Under this definition, a technical cause for high-dividend yield refers specifically to a rapidly declining price per share, which by itself drives up the dividend yield (but is likely to be accompanied by greater market risks). A fundamental cause is the declaration of a dividend given an annual growth rate, that holds up in light of the stock price and has not been caused by large changes in that price.

Investors must remember that a rapidly declining stock price will increase dividend yield (and thus may deceive investors as to the value of dividends), while a rapidly rising stock price will reduce dividend yield. So as a consequence, investors relying solely on a range of yields might easily overlook a potentially high-value investment because the dividend yield has fallen. For example, a company sets the dividend at $1 dollar per share when the stock price is $20. This is a 5% dividend yield (*$1 ÷ 20*). The stock subsequently rises to $27 per share, causing the dividend yield to fall to 3.7% (*$1 ÷ 27*).

In picking companies, if an investor sets a minimum standard of a 4% or better yield, this company would be unselected. Equally serious is the case in which there is an issue in the portfolio. If the standard is to maintain a 4% or higher yield, do you sell this stock because the yield has fallen below 4%? That would not be wise given the growth of market price, so by itself, the yield is not a reliable indicator for keeping or disposing of the stock. In addition, if you bought the stock at $20 per share, your yield remains at 5% as long as the dividend per share remains at $1. This is the yield based on the basis in the stock, regardless of current market value.

So chasing the yield is a strategy full of potential pitfalls. A wise methodology for analysis of the dividend question is to base selection on the following criteria:

1. Begin with the fundamentals. Place greater importance on growth in earnings and maintenance of working capital than on dividends alone.
2. Track yield but also pay attention to annual dividend growth rate.
3. Compare the dividend growth rate among dividend achievers and aristocrats. A very small annual growth rate qualifies a company under these definitions, but the track record of the growth rate is more important.
4. When dividend yield changes within one to two years, analyze the underlying causes to determine whether it is due to a fundamental policy by the company, or the result of a technical (price) change, either falling or rising.
5. Use the dividend growth rate to track long-term returns on initial investment as a better indicator than the basic dividend yield.

A Different Perspective on Dividend Yield

The risks associated with dividend yield point out the potential problem of pursuing yield by itself. Not knowing the genesis of the yield itself is the most dangerous starting point. In fact, even if you begin your selection process by identifying a minimum dividend yield, the results can be inaccurate. For many investors seeking the highest yield possible with some stocks, a solitary selection process like the Dogs of the Dow, while assumed to be a reliable and simple formula for improving dividend yield, may also pose a potential problem. To safely manage such a strategy, additional tests will reduce market risks. These include the basic fundamental analysis of long-term trends and ratios to ensure that the yields are fundamentally sound (versus technically caused and potentially unsound).

The perspective on dividend yield presents a dilemma for investors. In a debt-security environment yielding practically nothing on savings or money market securities, the desire for better yields invariably leads to the dividend alternative. A one-year CD yielding less than 1.5% is dismal compared to a 5% yield on some stocks. Furthermore, tying up funds for 12 months is a negative feature of a CD, compared to the flexibility of moving in and out of stock with a simple online order.

Compared to dividend yields, is the CD market as bad as that? The historical claim to great safety coming from insured accounts is a lame argument when you consider that the rates are lower than the postinflation and post-tax-breakeven point. For example, as of May 2012, the average one-year CD yield was 0.33%, and the average five-year rate was a dismal 1.13%. Even for a jumbo CD, the five-year rate was only 1.15%. At the same time, average money market account yield was down to 0.13%.[4]

In comparing money market rates to dividend yield, it quickly becomes apparent that in order for an investor to beat inflation and taxes, the money markets are not matching minimum breakeven needs. This can be demonstrated by analyzing the double effects of inflation and taxes. This calculation is:

$I \div (100 - R) = B.$

I = inflation rate
R = effective tax rate (federal plus state)
B = breakeven rate

For example, if you assume that the current rate of inflation is 2%, and your effective tax rate (the tax rate you will pay on any additional earnings after deductions and exemptions) is 20% (15% federal plus 5% state tax), your overall assumptions are very moderate. Even so, at these low assumptions, your breakeven rate is 2.5%:

2% ÷ (100 – 20) = 2.5%.

The five-year jumbo CD yielding a mere 1.15% falls short. Investing $100,000 in such a CD would yield $1,150, but your combined tax and inflation loss is $2,500. You lose $1,350 in taxes and lost purchasing power for your capital.

This undisputable analysis demonstrates why dividends are a sensible alternative to the "safe" money market and why, assuming market risks can be managed in some way, it just makes sense to prefer dividends over interest. And if your tax rate is higher and the inflation rate also rises, you need even greater yield just to break even. For example, if your combined federal and state tax rate is 38% and you assume inflation is 4%, you need 6.5% yield just to break even. Table 1.2 summarizes the breakeven rate for various rates of inflation and effective tax rates.

Until interest rates change, it is going to be very difficult to maintain purchasing power in the money market. The CD has been a long-time favorite among investors due to its one-time competitive yields and iron-clad insured value. But given current low market rates, the money market is no longer attractive to investors seeking decent returns. Dividends are the answer. But *risk* is the nagging attribute that keeps so many investors out of stocks. What is the solution?

There is a way to exploit dividend yield to create consistent and high returns, while also managing risk. The solution is to position a portfolio to forget about capital gains from stock, or premium gains from options. Both stock and options can be structured to serve as the vehicles to generate exceptionally high returns from dividends while also setting up strategies to manage risk and even to eliminate it completely.

Table 1.2 Breakeven rates

Effective tax rate (%)	Inflation rate					
	1%	2%	3%	4%	5%	6%
14	1.2%	2.3%	3.5%	4.7%	5.8%	7.0%
16	1.2	2.4	3.6	4.8	6.0	7.1
18	1.2	2.4	3.7	4.9	6.1	7.3
20	1.3	2.5	3.8	5.0	6.3	7.5
22	1.3	2.6	3.8	5.1	6.4	7.7
24	1.3%	2.6%	3.9%	5.3%	6.6%	7.9%
26	1.4	2.7	4.1	5.4	6.8	8.1
28	1.4	2.8	4.2	5.6	6.9	8.3
30	1.4	2.9	4.3	5.7	7.1	8.6
32	1.5	2.9	4.4	5.9	7.4	8.8
34	1.5%	3.0%	4.5%	6.1%	7.6%	9.1%
36	1.6	3.1	4.7	6.3	7.8	9.4
38	1.6	3.2	4.8	6.5	8.1	9.7
40	1.7	3.3	5.0	6.7	8.3	10.0
42	1.7	3.4	5.2	6.9	8.6	10.3

Source: Generated by author.

This strategy flies in the face of traditional folklore about investing. The tradition holds that smart investors seek value stocks that are bargain priced, that pay competitive dividends, and that are then bought and held for many years. This tradition has been changing in recent years, not only gradually but radically. The investing public recognizes that long-term buy-and-hold is not working, and that to beat the averages, the holding period has to be shorter, not longer. The old tradition also recommends reinvesting dividends to create a compound rate of return. That is admirable, but only if the stock value also holds or grows. And history has shown that this does not always happen. Iron-clad blue chip-quality stocks of the past (such as General Motors and Eastman Kodak) were once unquestioned and considered as safe as possible. If you had purchased shares of either company 20 years ago, you would have lost most (or all) of your capital. What good is reinvesting dividends if the stock ends up worth zero?

The long-term trend has been falling rapidly in recent years, as figure 1.5 shows.

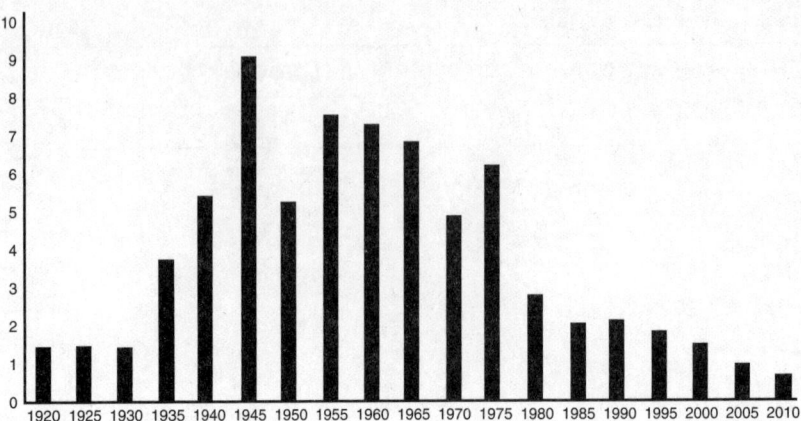

Figure 1.5 Average holding period in years, stocks
Source: Figure created by author from raw numerical data on S&P Stock Reports and New York Stock Exchange.

The causes for this trend are many. The Internet has made it possible for traders to move in and out of positions quickly and at a dramatically lower cost than in the past. The Internet made day trading and swing trading not only more convenient but faster and cheaper as well. By definition, a day trader moves in and out of positions within a single trading session, and a swing trader rarely keeps positions open longer than five days.

The Internet is only one of many causes of the dramatically changed equities market. For example, today traders can get free stock charts that include a variety of indicators online. In the past, such services were available only for a subscription fee. Charts and other technical and fundamental information are instantly available on all listed companies today, for no charge at all. This has opened the markets to many more traders and also has created an entirely different market mentality.

Another major influence on holding periods has been the options market. Popular strategies like covered call writing creates shorter holding periods due to exercise, rolling, or closing positions within a matter of months or even weeks, with little regard for long-term hold value to the underlying security.

Yet another cause of the rapidly declining hold period is the high-frequency trading (HFT) market. This includes many automated strategies for moving in and out of positions with extremely high volume and exploiting fractional changes in price. Whether this is a positive or negative aspect of the modern market is a matter of opinion, but the fact remains that HFT is a reality in today's automated, high-tech trading market.

This raises a question for every investor: Does short-term trading harm the market? Some believe that it does, but the reasons for this opinion are not all that clear.

HIGH-FREQUENCY TRADING (IN STOCK OR DIVIDENDS)—DOES IT HARM THE MARKET?

Today's markets rely institutionally on the algorithms employed in rapid and high-frequency trades. Given the cheap computing power of the modern day, it was inevitable that institutional traders would figure out how to maximize returns in this way. The algorithm, a method for calculating and then exploiting profits based on trades (including very small fractional trades on very large volume), enables the institution to produce consistent profits and exploit the otherwise inefficient pricing of securities.

This high-frequency trading has been criticized in several ways. For example, in the exchanges, 80% of trading volume is generated by a very low 2% of traders (namely, large institutional traders).[5] Some industry insiders have noted that this disparity takes place "at the expense of the average investor":

> It is now generally understood that high-frequency traders (HFTs) are dominating the equity market, generating as much as 70% of the volume... This can cause other investors to buy at a higher price, or sell at a lower price, than they would otherwise. A spike in HFT volume can cause an institutional algorithm order based on a percentage of volume to be too aggressive. A spike can attract momentum investors, further exaggerating price moves. Seeing such a spike, options traders can start to build positions, which, in turn, can attract risk arbitrage traders who believe there's potential news that could affect the stock.[6]

However, the types of fractional advantages generated by this activity are not likely to directly affect the average investor. Even though HFT algorithms provide their users with decisive advantages, the net effect on the price of stock is also going to be fractional. The consequence is likely to be measured in pennies and not in dollars.

A distinction has to be made between a true disadvantage among one set of investors compared to another (and one that is likely to create unfair advantage), versus the natural advantage institutions hold over retail investors. Even though vastly outnumbered, institutional investors do have a lot of control over the supply (and thus, the price) of equities. But this results more from the dollar volume of trades than from an inherent unfairness.

Is the advantage enjoyed by HFT strategies actually harmful to the individual investor? It probably is not, even though it might be viewed as "unfair" that a better-capitalized institution is able to take advantage of opportunities due to its ability to trade in high volume (and also to invest in automated algorithms that create those advantages). By the same logic, it is not "fair" that a wealthy person can drive an expensive car and live in a mansion, while a person with a modest income drives a cheap used car and lives in a small apartment. Does this result from some unfair advantage exploited by the rich person? While there might be cases of unfair advantage, the circumstances do not lead to such a conclusion.

The same rationale can be applied to markets. Of course institutional investors enjoy a great advantage. Volume of trades dictates incremental price movement. But this advantage does not do direct harm to the small individual traders, even while they do not enjoy those same advantages. It would be a different matter if it could be shown conclusively that in some manner, individuals are substantially harmed by the HFT activity itself.

This discussion is relevant to the topic of this book. Just as observers will complain that HFT is "unfair" because the high-volume and automated analytical tools allow institutions to take advantage of price changes, they will also point out that moving in and out of positions in stock or options also harms the market. However, the critics are not able to show how this occurs. Derivatives in general are widely criticized as being used to manipulate markets. Pundits and politicians in 2012 tried to blame rising oil prices on speculators in the commodities market, meaning of course futures and options traders. But how does any such trading affect prices or value? The truth is that these markets are dictated by ever-changing supply and demand (aggravated greatly by Organization of the Petroleum Exporting Countries [OPEC] production decisions). However, the value of futures and options are *reactions* to these economic forces, and not their cause.

A widespread lack of knowledge about how markets work (not to mention the economy) leads to these false conclusions. It is easy to set up a straw man argument and vilify options and futures rather than face the reality of how supply and demand work. In May 2012, JPMorgan Chase lost billions by investing in synthetic derivatives. The reason why anyone would take such a step is to (1) hedge risk and (2) generate profits. The synthetic derivative is an option position that includes both long and short positions, designed to replicate movement in an underlying stock, index, or future.

Because few people know what a derivative is (let alone a synthetic derivative), it is easy to blame the derivative itself. In fact, though, the real flaw is not with the product but in how and when it is used. The losses came not from the flaw in the product but in the judgment of the managers who embarked on the decision. If you buy stock in a corporation and the stock price falls, creating a loss, it does not mean the stock market is flawed; rather, it means the decision involves risks, and perhaps the managers did not truly understand the extent of that risk exposure.

Blaming the product for the bad decision is a misleading thought process. Many years ago the president of U.S. Steel commented that, "Steel prices cause inflation like wet sidewalks cause rain."[7]

You might argue that a short-term strategy will adversely affect the markets, or even the price of stock, the value of dividends, or the overall economy. But how? In this book, the strategy is proposed that you employ stock and options to move in and out of stock positions in the very short term, in order to take advantage of the rules for when dividends are earned. This strategy involves several components:

1. Buying 100 shares of stock per option position opened, timed to be recognized as stockholder or record before the current month's date.
2. Buying one put and selling one call per 100 shares of stock, timed to expire or get exercised as soon as possible after the ex-dividend date, and structured so that the net cost of these positions is at or close to zero.
3. Accepting exercise of the call or generating exercise of the long put, with the intention of closing the position as soon as possible after the ex-dividend date.
4. Repeating this strategy every month using shares with the ex-dividend in that month, and rolling in and out of positions to create *monthly* dividends in place of *quarterly* dividends.

The details are explored in later chapters. For the purpose of this discussion, the question is, Does rapid in-and-out activity somehow harm other investors or the market as a whole? If so, how? For example, when you hold stock only long enough to earn a quarterly dividend, is that destructive to anyone else? You might hold shares only a few days and yet be credited the full quarterly dividend. Does this deprive other investors? No, it does not. Anyone who wants to earn the quarterly dividend should not sell shares before the ex-dividend date. If shares are for sale at the current ask price and you buy those shares, the transaction is entered willingly by both seller and buyer. So if you earn a quarterly dividend by owning shares only a few days, that is the result of an open auction for those shares. It does not mean that the activity did any harm. The company is going to pay that dividend to the stockholder of record, and it does not change if the shares are held for three days or three years.

In embarking on the study of how dividends can be exploited to create handsome portfolio profits, you will need to struggle with a few myths. Among these is the idea that, somehow, short-term trades harm the market and other investors, using options creates unfair advantage, and earning dividends without holding shares for the full quarter is "unfair" to everyone else. If everyone decided to buy stock right before the ex-dividend date and sell stock right after, an obvious distortion would occur. The higher demand for shares would drive the price up, and the excess supply after the ex-dividend date would drive it down. And so the strategy would not work.

The concept of using stock and option positions to create risk-free, double-digit dividend income is not immoral or dishonest. It takes advantage of the rules, but it only works if traders are willing to put in the time and effort to create positions, exert the discipline to exit at the right time, and follow the same rules month after month. Any strategy goes wrong when the initial rules and guidelines are not followed, so this strategy—like all strategies—demands adherence to the discipline you set for yourself. However, in taking advantage of the rules of stock, option, and dividend positions, you are not earning an advantage at anyone else's expense. The great thing about the auction market is that you can open a position only when a willing trader exists on the other side.

The next chapter expands on this explanation with a detailed analysis of the risks of options and how those risks are best managed.

CHAPTER 2

MANAGING AND REDUCING RISK WITH OPTIONS

> To conquer without risk is to triumph without glory.
> Pierre Corneille, *Le Cid*, 1636

MOST TRADERS ACKNOWLEDGE THAT OPTIONS MARKET RISKS ARE potentially high and come in many forms, unique to that market. However, the nature of risk is widely misunderstood as well. For the options market, several key risk discussions beyond the inherent market risk and short side risk potential need to be discussed. This lays the groundwork for a majority of options strategies and may also help traders to appreciate on a deeper level the range of risk issues they face.

This range of topics includes the nature of market risk in general; stock short-selling risk (and a comparison between stock risks and alternative option strategies); differences between short calls and short puts; long option risks; spread and straddle risks; and less obvious risks of options trading.

THE NATURE OF MARKET RISK IN GENERAL

Traders usually agree on the definition of simple market risk: *The risk that portfolio values or components of the portfolio may lose value.* For the purpose of discussion relating to options, the assumed market includes underlying securities consisting of not only stocks but also indices and exchange-traded funds (ETFs as well as related exchange-traded notes, or ETNs, and exchange-traded commodities, or ETCs).

Market risk for the equity investment class on which options are written is also called equity risk, which factors in not only price but also the historical volatility, and when options are also in play as a combination strategy with equities, implied volatility is also a factor. For other nonequity markets, traders (within a portfolio as well as in consideration of derivative positioning) are concerned with interest rate risk, currency exchange risk, and commodity valuation risk. Options may apply to any and all of these, and in fact, are often used not as speculative devices but as hedging instruments, intended to reduce or eliminate common market risk as a feature of portfolio management.

Measuring market risk is elusive using stock-only measurements. Once option hedging is introduced and used as a programmed strategic measure for controlling risk, any form of statistical measurement has to be modified, revisited, or abandoned. The *Value at Risk* (VaR) method is a statistical measurement of loss risk within a portfolio of equity assets. VaR identifies a "threshold value" in the context of probability and time horizon. In this respect, VaR works well with the use of options, since both of the variables are specifically related to option pricing as well.[1]

VaR attempts to identify the maximum probability of loss within a specified time horizon, based on assumed "normal" market conditions and an absence of additional trading within the portfolio. Consequently, much like the Black-Scholes pricing model, VaR relies on assumptions that may be very unrealistic, and serves as a model and not a predictor.[2]

If you are an analytical trader, you will recognize VaR and its usage in applications beyond stock-only or stock-options portfolio valuation, including back-testing and calculations within complex technical analyses. Proponents claim that VaR helps traders to understand the extent of financial and market risk, and can then be used to justify appropriate risk management strategies. However, the application of this normally applies to equities-only portfolios that are not likely to use options as risk-hedging devices. Because VaR involves assumptions that could be inaccurate, any detailed modeling and pricing could be similarly flawed and less applicable to actual price testing than many would hope.

A benefit to VaR usage for risk analysis is that it separates the universe of risk into two distinct areas or regimes, internal to VaR limits and external. The internal statistical methods used as part of VaR are valuable because data for testing is usually more than adequate to provide confidence in the resulting estimations. The "law of large numbers" helps set probability at a reliable level using the internal and statistical modeling of portfolio risk.[3]

Externally, risk can be further studied through the application of stress tests and in a comparison between single issues and market-wide data. In this version of the risk study, there is no reliance on probability or loss-distribution studies. It is based more on the trader's or risk manager's ability to be ready to act quickly if and when losses begin to materialize.

Certain flaws or blind spots lead to criticism of VaR. Because it often presents a worst-case scenario, if losses exceed indicated VaR limits, it comes as an expensive surprise. However, this also points out the need to be concerned with losses that exceed those limits. Portfolio managers, for example, combine VaR analysis with extensive back-testing as a method of estimating the likely number of losses or the frequency of past occurrences. For traders not willing to rely on this form of modeling, a practical alternative is to find strategic alternatives through option hedging. In this manner, equity-based market risk can be mitigated and removed.

This form of modeling relies on the underlying assumption that market risk is unavoidable. Thus, it cannot be eliminated but has to be managed. So predictive modeling and probability studies are aimed at anticipating negative trends and acting before they adversely impact profitability. The dividend collar is based on a different assumption: that market risk is not inevitable and that it can be not only managed or mitigated but eliminated. This claim will be challenged by many market observers who, based on tradition, *know* that risk is a constant and that the most common form of risk—*market risk*—is here to stay. However, with the properly constructed options strategy, it is possible to cap risk and eliminate it below a fixed point. If such a position can be created cost-free (and it can), that troublesome market risk is, in effect, eliminated from the picture.

Traders are frustrated in attempts to understand or predict market risk, usually because they assume that risk cannot be eliminated, but only managed. The great concern, invariably, is to estimate the potential loss or maximum loss within a portfolio. The accuracy of any system aimed at measuring the future extent or frequency of market risk is flawed. No set of assumptions is reliable enough to comfort a trader whose concern extends beyond the speculator's "iron hand" and willingness to live with risk at very high levels. Here again, various arbitrage-type options strategies provide an elegant solution by setting up positions in which the loss on one side (a long portfolio or component of the portfolio) may be offset by intrinsic growth in the other side (short calls or long puts, or combined strategies synthetically duplicating an offsetting price direction).

This offsetting strategy based on options may involve collars (out of the money [OTM] short call and long put with stock value in between) or synthetic short stock positions (long put and short call opened at the same strike, intended to increase in value as the stock price falls beneath the strike). These measures are not mitigation measures, but risk removal devices. In both the collar and the synthetic stock position, the net cost of the options is at or close to zero, so that any downward price movement creates an offsetting zero loss at no added cost. The upside risk associated with the short call adds no market risk since in both instances, the trader is assumed to own 100 shares of stock for each short call opened.

So, in spite of the many formulations and simulations of risk management, the easiest and most effective may prove to be options strategies in which market risk is either offset point for point, or just eliminated. In both the collar and synthetic stock positions, a drastic decline in the underlying value is offset by profitable sale of the put, or done away with by exercise of the put. In both cases, no losses occur. As a result, the concern with market risk is managed effectively with the options strategies, a far superior and reliable method compared to the probability approach. Traders can only rely on the law of averages in favor of not experiencing a loss, *on average*; however, this is far from reassuring because losses are not individually mitigated. With options positions, there is no such probability. The elimination of long equity market risk is removed for as long as the option positions remain open. This difference is profound, and this comparison demonstrates why in growing numbers, traders are recognizing the value of options as risk reduction and portfolio management devices, and not merely as high-risk speculative products.

This method of using options to eliminate market risk is a starting point for seeing how options are most effectively employed: not for speculation but to manage risk in a long equity portfolio. This fits perfectly into the theme of identifying risk-free strategies that not only eliminate risk but also build attractive and consistent profits. In a majority of risk-reduction strategies, the complete removal or capping of risk is also accompanied by similar capping or limitations on profits. This unsatisfactory offset is avoidable, however, with the proper construction of strategies like the dividend collar. Even sensitivity to changes in premium levels may be turned to an advantage when put-call parity momentarily favors the opening of a position designed to create a breakeven or small credit in the open options.

Specific to options, the *delta* is widely used to judge the sensitivity of premium to price changes in the underlying security. This is the most reliable method for comparison between option volatility on different underlying issues. So the higher the call's positive delta value, the more it is likely to rise per point rise in the underlying. For example, if delta is 0.60, you expect to see increases of 0.60 for every $1.00 the stock rises. All call delta valuation is positive. Puts express delta in the negative. As stock values rise, puts lose value based on delta. Thus, a delta of -0.70

would mean the put is expected to lose 0.70 per 1.00 point rise in the underlying. These conclusions are based on long positions, so short position calls and puts are expected to change in value in the opposite direction. Thus, a short call loses more as the delta rises, and a short put gains more as the delta rises.

Delta tends to rise as options move further in the money (ITM), and to decline as options move further out of the money (OTM). When an option is at the money (ATM) or very near the money (NTM), delta of a call is 0.50 and delta of a put is -0.50. This is due to the 50% chance of a particular option moving either in or out of the money (based solely on random likelihood of direction and ignoring other price and volatility factors).

When time to expiration is short, the odds grow that options will remain where they reside (in or out of the money), and the longer the time remaining to expiration, the more uncertainty concerning whether options will remain at their moneyness or not.

The option risk as expressed by delta is summarized in figure 2.1.

Another factor influencing option valuation as expressed via delta is the rate of change likely to occur. The closer to the money,

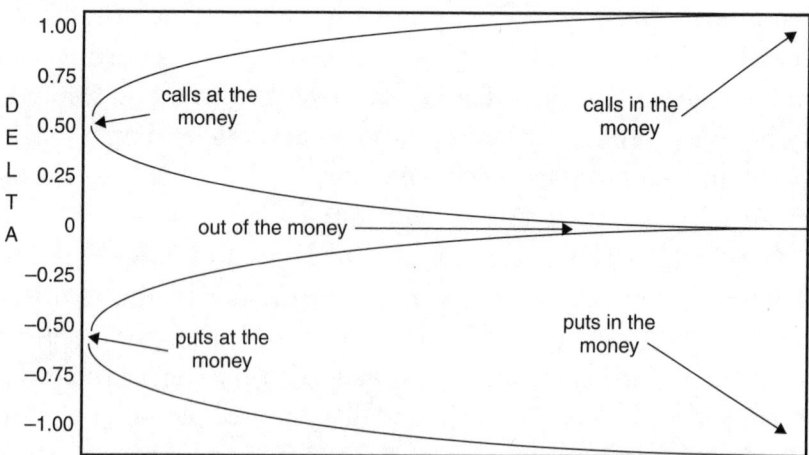

Figure 2.1 Delta relationship to the money
Source: Figure created by author from raw numerical data.

the greater the acceleration of delta toward a maximum value of 1.00 (for calls) or −1.00 (for puts). *Gamma* is the measurement of this acceleration; delta and gamma are the only two of the Greeks directly related to each other.

Option risk can be measured in terms of delta and its related gamma, especially in timing strategies. Delta expresses the probability of an option ending up either in or out of the money by expiration. At the maximum, delta of 1.00 (for calls) or −1.00 (for puts) signals a 100% probability of the option ending up ITM by expiration. By the same statistical argument, delta of 0.50 (calls) or −0.50 (puts) have a 50% chance of expiring ITM.

Because delta is a precise measurement of option value movement relative to the price movement of the underlying security, it measures risk probabilities. There are numerous mathematical and statistical systems to measure and "prove" risk, but delta (along with gamma) is one of the more reliable and easiest to track. The use of numerous free online calculators makes this task even easier than calculations performed by hand. One of the easiest enables calculations of all of the Greeks in a single fill-in worksheet, and that is provided by the Chicago Board Options Exchange (CBOE). Go to www.cboe.com and then link to "tools," and from there to "option calculator." The worksheet asks for a trading symbol, style (American or European), price, strike, expiration date, dividend amount, and value of both the call and the put.

As a general rule, delta values are going to follow these levels:

Status	Delta
At the money	0.50
Nearest ITM options	0.75
Next deeper ITM options	0.90
Deep ITM	1.00
Far OTM options	0.25
Next further OTM options	0

Underlying security valuation can also be calculated using the Greeks. VaR is the statistical method for quantifying underlying risk, while *beta*—also termed elasticity or relative volatility—is a more accessible way to identify underlying risk as expressed via volatility (the most reliable measurement of risk). A comparison is made between the underlying security and a benchmark to which it is compared. A popular benchmark for measuring stock beta is the Standard & Poor's (S & P) 500, for example.

When the asset is at the extreme of moving independently from the market (the benchmark), its beta approaches or resides at zero. A positive beta value implies that the asset tracks overall market in terms of degree of movement and direction. While upper beta has no specific limits, attaining beta of 4 would indicate extremely high-volatility underlyings. If beta turns negative, it tells you the asset's value is likely to move opposite the overall market direction. It is inversely correlated to the market. The simplicity of beta, notably in comparison to VaR, is appealing for the purpose of tracking market risk.

The level of beta as measurements of volatility is shown in figure 2.2.

In theory, a particular underlying might be very volatile in comparison to the benchmark of the overall market, and the greater the volatility, the higher the beta value. When beta is negative, it reveals that the underlying is inversely correlated to the market or at least unresponsive to the market's movements. This implies

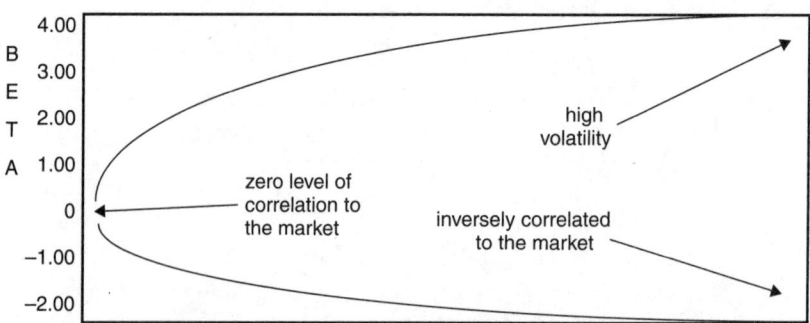

Figure 2.2 Beta as a measurement of underlying security volatility
Source: Figure created by author from raw numerical data.

that the price is likely to move opposite benchmark trends. A zero beta often is misunderstood to reveal a zero risk. This is not the case. A zero beta only reveals that there is no correlation between the underlying security and the benchmark. Risk is present, but not in terms of a measurement of volatility (beta). In that respect, a zero beta is not reassuring, but troubling. How do you measure risk when beta is at zero?

The beta measurement tracks sensitivity of a stock or other asset to the market, thus identifying the form of risk that cannot be mitigated through diversification. The risk is specific to the nature of the asset, but this also provides clues for options traders. When a stock is more volatile than other stocks, the tendency is for this condition to directly affect the implied volatility of the option as well. So for options traders, this creates an opportunity as well as a problem. For short sellers, for example, higher beta creates higher implied volatility, and that means richer option premium. At the same time, though, it also goes back to the underlying, whose market risks are correspondingly higher. If "market risk" is equated with "volatility," as it most accurately would be, the options trader has the dilemma of needing to select between a range of underlying issues and options. On one extreme are highly volatile underlying issues with highly volatile options; on the other end are low volatility underlying issues whose options provide very low implied volatility. If a strategy requires substantial movement in value, the higher volatility is desirable but contains greater risks, and the lower-volatility issues are safer but less likely to move into profitable zones.

Any system designed to measure market risk has to be viewed as potentially inaccurate. Most modeling is going to be based on long-term price trends and probabilities, but options tend to be very short term in comparison. Because time decay is an unforgiving aspect of option pricing, a departure from the pricing model is unlikely to recover and correct before the expiration of the option. Thus, traders must rely not so much on the attributes of beta and other risk models, but on the creation of strategies designed to hedge risk by offsetting long and short, whether intra-option or between option and underlying assets.

The observation that beta and other market risk models might not be reliable was supported by a paper about beta, which pointed out the flaw in relying solely on any singular measurement:

> I find it preposterous that a single number reflecting past price fluctuations could be thought to completely describe the risk in a security. Beta views risk solely from the perspective of market prices, failing to take into consideration specific business fundamentals or economic developments... Beta fails to allow for the influence that investors themselves can exert on the riskiness of their holdings through such efforts as proxy contests, shareholder resolutions, communications with management, or the ultimate purchase of sufficient stock to gain corporate control and with it direct access to underlying value. Beta also assumes that the upside potential and downside risk of any investment are essentially equal, being simply a function of that investment's volatility compared with that of the market as a whole. This too is inconsistent with the world as we know it. The reality is that past security price volatility does not reliably predict future investment performance (or even future volatility) and therefore is a poor measure of risk.[4]

Options traders contend with the conflict between levels of implied volatility (and thus, option premium) versus market risk and how to measure it. They seek continuously to figure out strategic methods for managing or eliminating risk while maximizing short-term profits. Relying on statistical pricing and risk models, or allowing risk assessment for short-term positions to be determined by long-term risk analyses, are flawed approaches to managing these risks. Equally flawed is the back-testing of option trends, simply because pasty volatility existed at a moment in time and is rarely a fixed attribute of a security or its options.

In managing or predicting risks from options trading, the only possible solutions are to accept higher risks (which is not a reliable alternative for moderate or conservative investors) or to rely on strategies designed to conservatively hedge long portfolio positions, or even to replace reliance on long equity positions, using options-based strategies. As long as such strategies outperform the long equity portfolio, they are highly desirable. If a strategy is designed to create exceptional returns while eliminating market risk, it solves the entire problem. This reality is what has led to the development of dividend-based and options-based risk-free portfolio management.

Stock Short-Selling Risk and Options-Based Alternatives

Among the many traditional strategies traders and investors employ, short selling of stock is one that predates options by many years. However, this is a high-risk, awkward, and expensive strategy. Stock is borrowed from the brokerage firm (meaning interest has to be paid to the broker for as long as the short position remains open). The market risk is as severe as uncovered call risks, in the sense that if the stock price rises, losses in the shorted stock track that movement dollar for dollar. A mandatory 150% of the short stock value has to be maintained on margin, compared with 75% (or 50% in some hedged long put positions).

Options can solve part of the problem related to shorted stock. The use of long calls, for example, is a form of an "insurance call" when a trader holds shorted stock. If the stock price rises above the strike of the call, the call's intrinsic value grows point for point with the stock. The call's profit offsets the 100-share loss on the short stock.

The entire strategy may not be necessary most of the time, however. A less risky and cheaper alternative for those desiring to adopt a bear position is to employ long puts. The long put, like shorted stock, gains value if the underlying security market value falls. And if the market value rises, the long put cannot lose more than the relatively low original cost of that put. So while the profit potential is equal to shorting stock, the maximum loss is limited to the cost of the long put. This is a considerable difference, a demonstration of how options can provide superior portfolio management and timing advantage over traditional stock-based strategies.

The problem with short stock goes beyond this, however. When shorting activity is exceptionally high, it distorts the market. If the price of the underlying falls as expected, short sellers enter purchase orders to close short stock. To the inexperienced investor or trader, the high volume of buy orders takes on the appearance of buying pressure, indicating that the stock price is likely to rise. However, that buying activity is not demand for shares, but short cover, a vastly different activity with very different significance.

In 2011, the Securities and Exchange Commission (SEC) adopted a new Rule 201, also called the Alternative Uptick Rule. This set a newly revised price test on short-sale orders. It requires that trading centers set up and enforce written policies intended to prevent execution of a short sale equal to or below the current "best bid" based on additional criteria. The rule aims at curtailing manipulative short-selling practices including intentionally driving down a stock's price in order to artificially generate profits at the expense of other traders.

The regulatory attempt to control short selling and prevent manipulation points out the flaw in this strategy (from a purely regulatory point of view). Volumes of opinions, revisions, analyses, and procedures have been drafted to prevent abuse of the system. On a practical level, short selling can create very inefficient markets. For example, a short squeeze is created when the stock's price rises due to high buying activity. This may be a combination of actual buying demand plus very high-volume short covering. Due to the sharp price increase, short sellers close positions to prevent further losses and to satisfy margin calls, and this artificially distorts the supply-and-demand picture.

Equally troubling is so-called "naked" short selling, banned in the US markets, in which the trade is entered without borrowing stock from the brokerage. This transaction includes a promise to deliver stock in the future, a practice referred to as hypothecated shares. If the seller is unable to deliver shares based only on the promise, the transaction fails and would have to be unwound.

Another variation on short selling involves options. A reverse conversion is a combination of a short put and a long call at the same strike, which sets up a synthetic long stock strategy. At the same time, the trader sells short 100 shares of the underlying. Since the synthetic long stock strategy mirrors movement in the underlying stock, the shorted stock hedges the option-based position. This is advantageous only when the marginal price difference between put and call (parity) is favorable and creates a profit. However, the strategy is a marginal one, and hedges that accomplish the same end result could be set up without having to sell stock and pay interest to the brokerage firm.

Given the very limited advantages of short selling and its related high risks, the potential advantages are difficult to justify. Regulatory authorities continually try to curb manipulation and the creation of artificial or inefficient markets. The disorder at times created by short selling brings into question whether the strategy is a positive force or a negative one.

The simple and obvious solution is to avoid the risky, expensive, and highly regulated short sale of stock, while accomplishing the same market position with long puts. Thus, activities like insider trading with short stock would not be prevented, but might be more easily recognized when options are used in place of short equity positions.

For a majority of traders interested in adopting a bearish position in a particular underlying security, long puts offer a viable alternative. For regulators, the troublesome burden of regulation and the not entirely successful desire to control manipulation might also be more easily accomplished using long puts in place of short stock. For those professional traders and institutional managers using short stock positions as hedges against portfolios during volatile markets, most situations would not be affected adversely by replacement of short stock with long calls.

The debate concerning the regulatory problems and market disruption risks of short stock point out yet another method under which options solve many problems. Notably as a hedging instrument, long puts often are more efficient than short stock, but the price movement and hedging efficiency are identical.

Long options used as replacement of short stock solve several problems, including the expense of borrowing stock and paying interest on it; the exceptionally high market risk of short stock positions (compared to very limited long put risks); elimination of a good portion of the regulatory concern related to insider trading and price manipulation; and further removal of the condition in which combined buyer demand and short covering create a shortage of shares, making the market inefficient.

This alternative, like so many hedging ideas based on options in place of long positions in securities, is cheaper, lower risk, and less likely to create regulatory headaches. As the, low-risk and no-risk strategies that follow demonstrate, the use of puts in the capacity of insurance or hedging instruments is quite efficient and solves many problems found in older, less efficient strategic methods. Using short stock as a play in anticipation of a bear market is one example.

Differences between Short Calls and Short Puts

Traders exhibit a tendency to identify risks in options strategies as a feature that cannot be changed. Realistically, however, a strategy initially considered high-risk may see reducing risk threat as expiration approaches, and an initially low-risk strategy may turn high-risk for the same reasons. But in spite of historical methods for defining options in terms of risk, the truth is more elusive. Option risks are not specific to strategies, but to the timing of those strategies and based on a time/proximity and volatility/probability analysis. An excellent example is the comparative analysis of risks between short calls and puts. Risk levels, given identical attributes, are quite different for calls and for puts on the short side.

As a first observation, option-based risk is not always specific to a strategy. On the contrary, the timing of a strategy and specific choices made by a trader determine the actual market risks to which they are exposed. For example, a basic covered call strategy is widely considered a "safe" trade or even highly conservative. However, if a trader's basis in the stock is $39 and a covered call is opened with a 35 strike and with premium of only one point, the risk is considerable. Exercise creates an automatic net capital loss of $300 (four points between strike and the higher basis, minus one point for the option premium received). This is clearly a high-risk strategy, notably because the premium is small compared to the negative point spread between strike and basis.

The profit and loss zones of this strategy are summarized in figure 2.3.

The same situation is further aggravated if the underlying stock pays no dividend or a very small dividend. The potential risk is further increased if the short call is ITM and the current ex-dividend date is impending and will occur prior to the option expiration date. The underlying will probably be called away on or immediately before the ex-dividend date, thus creating (1) a

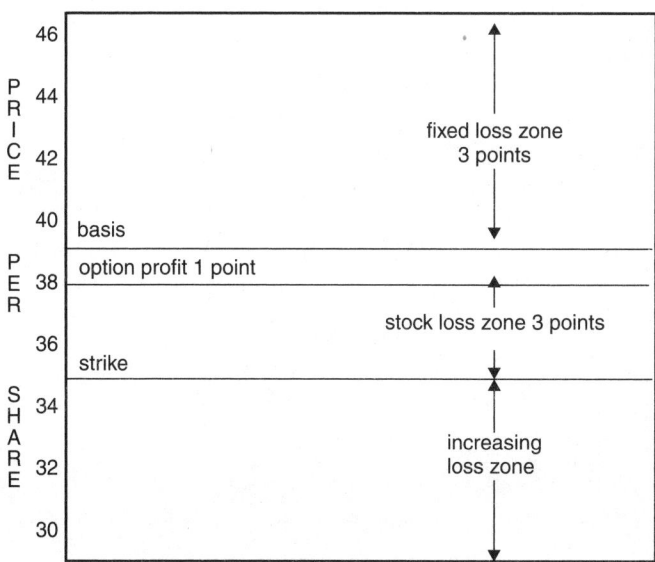

Figure 2.3   Covered call strike lower than basis
Source: Figure created by author from raw numerical data.

net capital loss on the stock and (2) closure of the stock position without earning the current dividend.

Even without the negative factors of strike below basis and lost dividend, a covered call strategy is likely to be high risk if the underlying is a highly volatile company. If the stock's market value does decline rapidly, it will result in a paper loss. For example, a trader bought 100 shares at $39 and sold a covered call with a 40 strike, receiving a premium of 5. In this case, the breakeven on the downside is $34 per share ($39 basis, minus 5 points received for selling the option). If the stock declines below that level, the net outcome is in the loss zone. On the upside, exercise produces a profit of $600 ($500 received for selling the call, plus one point capital gain). So this situation presents a limited profit on the upside with potentially unlimited loss on the downside. Thus, the highly volatile issue presents market risks that cannot be ignored by traders. Covered calls do not ensure profits in every case.

The profit and loss zones for this strategy are summarized in figure 2.4.

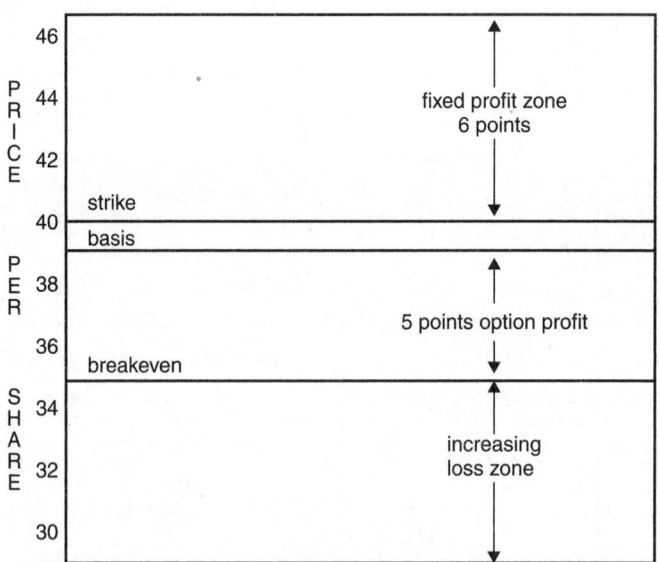

Figure 2.4 Covered call strike higher than basis
Source: Figure created by author from raw numerical data.

The example of a covered call positioned as a high-risk strategy makes the point that risk is not strategy-specific but relies on the attributes and on proximity between basis and strike. By the same argument there are situations in which an uncovered call will be considered as a conservative strategy.

One example is when the naked call is combined with other, covered calls as part of a ratio write or variable ratio write. In these strategies, traders are able to track the overall position and also watch movement in the underlying. Exercise can be avoided by closing one or more of the uncovered portions, covering it with stock or long calls, or rolling it forward (or forward and up to a higher strike).

Even simple short calls may be conservative relative to other short and uncovered calls when the probability is factored in. For example, a short call with probability above 80% is quite conservative, especially when implied volatility is also at a maximum. However, such positions require continual monitoring to avoid unexpected price movement and the possibility of exercise and a net loss. If traders consider "low risk" to mean the assured net profit even without needing to monitor a position, that is an unrealistic expectation. Options traders need to monitor in order to act quickly if and when underlying price changes occur in a negative direction.

Risk, even for uncovered calls, based on high probability trading strategies, may be quite low. As a first step, focusing on calls expiring within one month or less reduces risk due to accelerated time decay during the option's final month. From there, uncovered calls can be selected based on a combined analysis of implied volatility and probability (based on standard deviation, for example). The probability, quantified by proximity and time to expiration, may be 80% or more, making this a conservative criterion. It means there will be an 80% chance of a successful trade. As the probability level begins to decline due to changing underlying price, the position is closed to avoid exercise and net loss.

The uncovered call opened without concern for time or proximity, but only to augment the premium level, is far more likely to represent a very high-risk strategy, notably if (1) it is deep in the money or (2) time to expiration is further out. In either of these cases, the overall risk is far greater than is a more selective process based on proximity and time, and also with the position timed to coincide with favorable implied volatility and probability.

The uncovered put contains much lower risks than the uncovered call. Although both of these options may be defined in terms of risk based on implied volatility and probability, proximity between strike and current underlying price, and time until expiration, there is more. The short put is less risky because risks are finite.

An uncovered call may contain unknown levels of risk because the underlying could rise to unknown levels. Practically speaking, the supply and demand of the market limits the potential rise in price, but the ceiling cannot be known. For this reason, market risk of uncovered calls is undefined, and thus potentially unlimited.

An uncovered put is finite and more easily defined in terms of risk. An underlying price can only fall so far, so at first glance it appears that zero is the maximum risk level. A stock currently worth $30 per share has a maximum short call risk of 30 points. Based on this, higher-priced stocks have greater short put risk than lower-priced stocks. However, this is not accurate.

The true maximum risk for an uncovered put has to be defined more specifically. It is the difference between the strike of the put and the tangible book value per share, minus the premium received for selling the put. For example, you sell a 30 put and receive 2.50. The underlying stock's tangible book value per share is $13. The maximum risk is:

$$(30-13) - 2.50 = 14.50 \text{ points } (\$1,450).$$

This example is summarized in figure 2.5.

Because 14.50 is the *maximum* risk, the realistic level of risk may be much smaller. The way to judge short put risk is by asking the question: Is the breakeven value considered a good value

Managing and Reducing Risk with Options 51

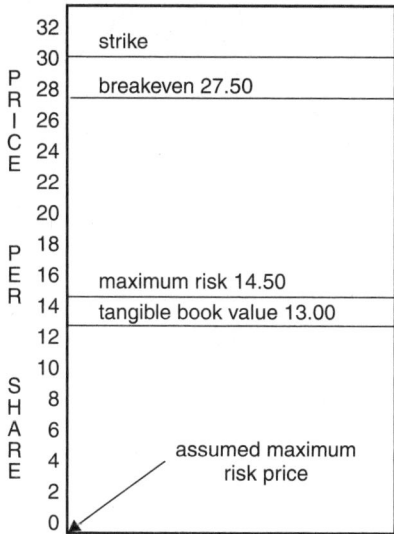

Figure 2.5   Uncovered put net risk
Source: Figure created by author from raw numerical data.

for shares of this company? In the example, breakeven is 27.50 (30–2.50). If you believe this represents a fair value for stock of the underlying, that is a starting point in selecting a short put. From there, it makes sense to analyze implied volatility and probability to best time the sell-to-open order (and later also to time the buy-to-close order). This risk analysis is assisted by a study of the recent price volatility of the underlying, including identification of price behavior at or near support level.

LONG OPTION RISKS

Most traders have heard the report that 75% of all options expire worthless. However, this is not entirely accurate. The actual statistic is that 75% of all options *held until expiration* will expire worthless. That is a key distinction. A high volume of long options traded are closed prior to expiration. Traders owning long options may close at a profit or at a loss (with the intention of accepting a small loss to avoid a complete loss later). These traders also have the right to exercise the long option and acquire 100 shares of stock at the strike.

The difference between long calls and puts cannot be applied universally. The level of worthless expiration is determined largely by the price trend of the underlying. A long call is likely to be closed at a profit when the underlying price has moved well above strike, just as the long option is more likely to be closed at a profit when the underlying price has fallen well below strike. In both of these cases, exercise of long options is also influenced by price direction. An OTM option will not be exercised, but traders will exercise ITM options when doing so fits with their overall strategy, and buying shares (via exercise of a call) or selling shares (via exercise of a put) is likely when the options are ITM.

For example, exercise fits perfectly with the dividend collar introduced in coming chapters. One purpose to this strategy is to move into and then out of long stock positions in a very short term. So traders accept exercise as sellers of calls if the stock price rises. However, if the price falls, traders will exercise their long puts to dispose of shares at the strike. This is the essence of market risk elimination as a key benefit to the strategy, and is one example of how long options (in this case, puts) are used not solely for speculative positioning but as part of a more complex strategy.

With this in mind, the argument against buying calls or puts is narrow. Long option positions serve as hedges to other positions or as an offset to a risk reduction strategy, and this translates to sensible reasons for buying options. The case against options based on a misread of the 75% claim does not address the use of long options as portions of other strategic applications.

Another method in which long options play important roles is swing trading or day trading. If traders employ options in place of stock, they accomplish considerable leverage due to the low cost of long options relative to 100 shares of stock. This further reduces risk, as the maximum loss is limited to the cost of the option. In addition, using long puts at the top of a price swing allows traders to eliminate the risks specific to shorting stock. In the swing trading strategy, the market risk of long options is not significant in comparison to the same strategy but with shares of stock. In this case, options are more practical as the vehicle for the trade, especially if limited to those contracts due to expire in one month or less. (During this period, time value is mostly gone from the position, and using ATM or ITM options is mostly likely to produce point-for-point intrinsic value change, tracking the stock as closely as possible to make the swing trade successful.)

Spread and Straddle Risks

The risks specific to long and short combined strategies cover a broad range. For both long spreads and long straddles, the maximum loss is the sum of premiums paid to acquire both sides of the position. The maximum gain is the degree of point movement above or below the strike of either side, minus the cost of opening the position. There is no exercise risk since traders are long on both sides of the position.

For short spreads and straddles, the maximum loss is the ITM exercise level, minus the premium received by the trader for opening the position. Maximum gain is limited to the premium received, and this is realized only when options end up OTM at ATM, or are closed prior to expiration at a profit.

Both long and short combined strategies can be constructed in dozens of possible variations. However, the risk issues limited to spreads and straddles as stand-alone strategies are only a small part of the broader risk picture. In practice, both spreads and straddles may be employed as part of a broader play. For example, the dividend collar that is the subject of this book is based on constructing a collar (long put, short call, 100 shares) or a synthetic stock position in which 100 shares of the underlying are owned as well. Because this is designed to eliminate market risks, the collar should not be judged in terms of its specific risks, but rather in how it mitigates or eliminates risks inherent in stock and option positions. Although the strategy is not designed to generate profits from either, it does enable traders to achieve double-digit returns from dividends without the attendant stock or option risks.

This demonstrates that with long or short positions comprised of spread or straddle strategies, it is not necessarily the isolated risk of each position that matters, but how these are employed in a broader strategy. The hedging advantages of both spreads and straddles can be built so that risk levels are controlled quite specifically. This does not mean that market risks reveal the entire risk scenario for spreads or straddles by themselves.

Less Obvious Risks of Options

Market risk is the best known among all risks. However, options traders are able to offset market risk with well-designed hedging, synthetic, and insurance strategies. This does not mean that all risk is avoided or eliminated. Options traders face greater risks than most, in fact, due to the variations and forms of risk they face.

Margin and collateral risk is a limiting form of risk, and all options trades are required to be made through margin accounts (and the restrictions that come with margin trading). Margin requirements define the dollar value of cash or securities that must be held in the account based on the type of trade. Margin varies based on the type of trade, but the end result is that you are limited in the number of open options contracts allowed at any time.

A valuable margin calculator is provided free by the CBOE and can be accessed on their site at http://www.cboe.com/tradtool/mCalc/default.aspx—and this enables you to enter a variety of different strategies to make the calculation. Margin varies by the level of exposure, time until expiration, and long versus short.

A special set of rules applies to day trading. The "pattern day trader" is defined as anyone who transacts a boy/close within a single trading session. Margin requirements are calculated as of end-of-session balances, so one of the strategic advantages to day trading is the ability to circumvent this rule—and the risk-reduction features that limit risk exposure—by closing out all open position in that single session. In theory, a day trader could be exposed to unlimited levels of risk, and as long as open positions were closed by session's end, there would be no margin requirement. This was changed with the rule governing the pattern day trader.

This is any trader who conducts open/close transactions on the same security four or more times within five business days and when the sum of those trades exceeds 6% of the individual's total trading activity over the same period. If a trader exceeds these limits, the rule states that no less than $25,000 of equity has to be kept in the account before any further trading is allowed. If the level is exceeded, the broker will issue a day trading margin call requiring the trader to bring the equity up to $25,000 before any further trading is allowed.

Option trade margin requirements are different from the requirements for stock trading and are also more complex. Some strategies, such as covered call writing, have no added requirements beyond margin on the underlying security, since by its nature the position does not add to margin risk. In the event of exercise, the long stock serves as collateral and is sold at the strike.

Options traders thus face two specific types of margin risk. First is the requirement to maintain required minimum margin requirements, which restricts the number of open contracts allowed. Second is the danger that a high frequency of trades might change the status to that of a pattern day trader. In this case, trading will be restricted until equity is brought up to the minimum level of $25,000. If that cannot be accomplished, further activity in the account is limited to a cash basis only.

Knowledge risk is specifically the risk that a trader may be qualified to execute specific trades but does not really understand the exposure involved. Although traders are required to complete an options application and submit it to the broker, the claims made on that application are not exhaustively verified by the broker. The application serves as a protective device as much as a prequalification to execute specific types of trades. Based on the claims made by a trader in terms of knowledge and options trading experience, the broker sets an appropriate trading and risk level. This defines the types of trades allowed.

The knowledge risk is not merely the risk involved with various types of trades and the potential lack of knowledge about the risk and mechanics of that trade. It also refers to the lack of experience in options trading more broadly. A trader can complete and submit an options application and make any claims he or she wants. The primary concern for the broker is that the claims are made and signed for, ensuring that the broker does not accept liability for allowing inexperienced traders to adopt risks they do not understand. However, if a trader makes false claims concerning knowledge and experience levels, he or she may face the unrecognized risks involved with options trading.

Diversification risk refers to two distinct levels of risk. A trader may underdiversify by focusing too narrowly on a small number of underlying securities, as well as using too few types of options strategies. So if the trader only makes bullish spread trades but the market turns bearish, the underdiversification (or lack of flexibility) in the range of strategies presents greater risks in adverse markets.

The opposite, or overdiversification, presents a different range of problems. It is possible, for example, to employ options to set up control over shares of many different underlying securities. However, if the range of securities averages out to a mundane net return, what is accomplished through the leverage of options? Just as an ETF might underperform a leading issue within the basket of securities, an overdiversified options portfolio may experience a mix of profits and losses netting out to poor overall performance.

Asset allocation risk is a serious concern when options are involved. Options cannot be treated as a separate asset class. For example, if a specific percentage limitation is placed on options trading, how do you count a set of spreads in which long and short positions are offset? The net cost of such activity might be at or close to zero, while risk exposure is quite high. Asset allocation risk involves not only violating preset asset class levels, but also being able to violate the risk reduction standards by employing both long and short options. The only effective solution is to limit the dollar value by specifying the kinds of transactions allowed in an options asset class. For example, the allocation may be limited to insurance strategies with long puts only, a dollar limit on long calls, or to overall margin requirement dollar values. Allowing options activity at an investment manager's discretion and using net dollar or percentage limitations does not offset this risk.

Disruption of trading risk occurs in several situations. When a company is on the verge of making an important announcement (about a buyout, for example), trading can be halted for a period of time, usually less than a day. It may also be imposed when the exchange has questions about whether or not the company meets current listing standards, an ominous but legitimate concern. Trading may also be nonregulatory. For example, a large disparity between buy and sell orders can lead to a temporary halt.

In comparison, a trading suspension is imposed by the Securities and Exchange Commission (SEC) when serious financial information or uncertainty arises.

A trading curb (also called a collar, but not to be confused with an option collar) affects the whole exchange, and usually is put in place when the market at large suffers a large price drop. All of the halts and suspensions of markets and issues also apply to options trading, although exercise is still allowed.

The risk is a disruption of a timing strategy for the period that trading is halted or suspending. Equity options are exercisable because they are created under a contract. It specifies that an owner of an option can exercise an American-style option at any time before expiration. When a stock's book value falls to value, in other words when the underlying becomes worthless, what happens to an option? If a trader owns a long put, is it impossible to exercise it or to sell because the stock is worthless? No. In this situation, the option is sold at the strike, although the actual value of the stock is lower, even zero.

Discretionary account risks cannot be ignored, although a question has to be asked: Is it ever suitable to give someone else trading discretion in an options account? If it is a matter of skill and experience, a trader should not trade options without the requisite knowledge. Giving another person discretion over that account—while admittedly not knowing how the options market works—could be asking for trouble.

An exception applies when a large portfolio is managed professionally and the manager of the portfolio makes a case for the use of options as hedges against portfolio risk. However, it is questionable whether a discretionary account should allow a manager to speculate with options. This is a risk most traders are not willing to take, and the biggest risk in a discretionary account is in not knowing how specific strategies expose the owner to risks.

Lost opportunity risk comes in two varieties. First is the opportunity to take up positions that is lost when your entire equity and margin are at maximum. If your portfolio is full of paper loss holdings, you lose opportunities by being unable to move when those opportunities arise.

A second definition relates to covered call writing. A major argument against this strategy is that if the underlying price rises far above the strike, the short call is exercised, and the trader loses the opportunity that would have resulted by just owning the underlying. While this is a very real risk, covered call writers also recognize that it is a matter of percentages. For the relatively small percentage of times such a price rise occurs, covered call writing enables traders to earn consistent short-term profits. The occasional lost opportunity is worthwhile based on the reliability of short call premium income.

Discipline risk may be more accurately termed "self-discipline risk." All strategies, and especially options-based strategies, demand self-discipline. You set rules for when positions will be entered and exited, not only to achieve profit goals but also to accept small losses in order to avoid larger losses.

The primary reason that options trades fail among knowledgeable traders is the lack of their following rules. Setting rules is easy in comparison, and often is a matter of resisting the temptation to get greedy. For example, you purchase an option and set the goal that you will sell if the premium value doubles (a 100% profit) or loses half (a 50% loss). But then what happens to this simple but sensible rule? If the option premium does double, it is easy to pause, thinking it might continue to rise. But then time decay sets in, and the value begins to fall. Instead of quickly closing the position, an undisciplined trader decides that the high value is the new breakeven, and the position must be left open until the premium goes back to that level. This error most often ends up with a worthless expiration. In the opposite direction, gradual decline is watched anxiously, but the trader wants to hold on until the price gets back up to the original cost.

In this scenario, when can a trader ever sell? Without self-discipline, options traders might self-program never to take a profit or curtail a loss.

Tax risk is a hidden form of risk. So many legal oddities apply to options profitability that the risk often comes in the form of a surprise. For example, in some multipart strategies, you cannot claim a loss in the year in which one side is closed; you have to wait until the other side is closed as well, and then offset loss and profit in the same year.

Some traders have tried to use options to get around the wash sale rule. So they sell their stock at a loss on December 1 and then buy options within the 61-day window to protect against price movement (wash sales apply 30 days before and 30 days after the sale of stock). In some instances, offsetting an equity sale with an option replacement creates "substantially identical stock or securities." With calls, it does not even matter if the call is in the money; if you never exercise it; and if you never acquire the stock. The wash sell rule is automatically applied in this case.

If you sell puts, you face the same problem, although the wash sale is not automatic. It only applies when the short put is deep in the money, and the problem here is that there is not a specific definition of "deep in the money" to determine that the position constitutes a wash sale. The closest you can get is when there is a substantial likelihood of the put expiring without exercise, meaning the sale is similar enough to buying stock, thus creating a wash sale.

Options transactions also can create wash sales. If you close an option at a loss and then repurchase a replacement within the 30-day period, it could be a wash sale, but this is also poorly defined. It could mean buying the underlying, or buying an option with identical terms, or even buying an option with different terms that might offset the original loss.

The qualified covered call rule may convert what is assumed to be a long-term gain on the underlying, into a short-term gain. If you sell a covered call deep in the money at a time that you have not yet owned the underlying for a full year (making it unqualified), the time counting to the long-term kick-in is tolled. It will not begin again until the unqualified covered call is closed. However, if that call is exercised—even though the stock is held longer than one year by that time—it is treated as a short-term capital gain.

The options-based tax rules are complex and often seem illogical. The risk for traders is that tax outcomes might not be what they thought, especially if options are used intentionally or otherwise in a way that creates a wash sale. This could completely destroy an otherwise smart and thoughtful tax-avoidance and tax-planning strategy.

All of the risks associated with options are likely to affect how a dividend collar is structured and how profits accumulate. The collar generates monthly dividend income at double digits on an annualized basis. At the same time, the market risks of the underlying stock and other well-known options risks (exercise of short positions or lost value of long positions) are neutralized. The elegance of the dividend collar is its combination of attractive and reliable returns, with the conversion of risks into advantages. Exercise of properly selected short positions is acceptable and necessary for full implementation of the strategy. Time decay is not an issue on the long side, since those puts are held to eliminate underlying market risks. In the event of a price decline, you exercise the put to escape at the fixed strike. In either case of exercise (imposed on you on the short side or executed by you on the long side), the result is welcomed.

Even so, the range of options risks cannot be ignored. There are no 100% certainties in the markets, and so a trading halt or suspension may easily throw a strategy into disarray. When disposal of shares is tied to exercise of options, the many ways in which risk can affect the timing of a trade have to be kept in mind. The term "risk free" is used to describe the strategy, but to be more accurate, it refers to the best-known form, that of market risk. Additional risks are rarer or unlikely, but they continue to exist.

CHAPTER 3

THE ADVANTAGE OF THE COVERED CALL

> Human nature is the same everywhere; it deifies success, it has nothing but scorn for defeat.
> — Mark Twain, *Joan of Arc*, 1896

THE COVERED CALL. THIS IS A LONG-TIME FAVORITE AMONG options traders, and for many, the strategy of first choice. It also represents one of the important components of the risk-free portfolio.

A question has to be asked, however: Is the covered call truly a risk-free strategy or even a low-risk or manageable-risk strategy? For those relying on the known and consistent net returns from covered call writing, it seems that the strategy cannot go wrong. In fact, using a series of short-term strikes at the money (ATM) or slightly out of the money (OTM), annualized double-digit returns are inevitable. It appears that market risks are eliminated entirely while double-digit returns are assured. For the covered call writer who analyzes returns based on exercise or expiration only, the strategy looks flawless. But what if the price declines in the underlying below the net cost (stock purchase less call premium income)? In that case, you have a loss, at least on paper.

There are risks in this strategy. As a covered call writer in this situation, you face two choices: First, you can sell the depreciated stock and take the loss. This frees up capital and you are able to then move to the next position. Second, you do nothing, and wait out the market until the stock price rebounds. This might work, but how long will it take? Many covered call writers end up with a portfolio full of depreciated stocks, unable and unwilling to make a move and only waiting for stock prices to rebound. Based on the markets in recent years, this could take a long time. This is a serious risk involved with covered call writing, but it is actually less risky than just owning stock.

The second choice—waiting for prices to rebound—is the one most often used, but there is a problem with this. It keeps capital tied up. and other opportunities have to wait or be passed up. This lost-opportunity risk may be severe if the underlying price takes many months to return to profitable levels, and it might never get back up to that breakeven price at all. There is a troubling aspect to covered call writing. You might generate double-digit returns month after month, only to have all of those impressive profits wiped out in a single bear market.

In *theory,* the well-selected underlying security should rebound as long as the initial purchase price was reasonable or at a bargain level. But as most traders discovered, the "should" factor is not always in play, and perceptions about a company's value often have little to do with how a stock price "should" act. Even so, selection of the underlying security should be the first step in developing a covered call strategy. Remember, though, that stock prices can and do fall and that the exposure of a portfolio to a covered call writing strategy is not a sure thing. Selecting stocks wisely minimizes your risk of depreciating prices. This does not mean it cannot occur, but it does mean the likelihood is lower than average if you pick high-quality companies. For these, the duration of a decline also tends to be lower than average.

Even if you pick stocks wisely, are you still at risk? Traders who hold stock and who think about covered call writing might analyze the risk from another perspective: As a stockholder, you face a continual market risk without even thinking about covered call writing. As a stockholder, you have to decide what to do if the price falls below your basis. Do you sell and take a loss, or wait out the market? Many covered call writers are more concerned about exercise risk on the upside, even to the extent of rolling out of a position to avoid exercise when, upon study, exercise might be the most profitable alternative.

Covered call writing does not increase market risks associated with owning stock. Rather, it reduces the market risk because covered call writing generates net income, lowering your net basis in stock. For example, if you buy 100 shares at $50 per share and the price falls to $47, your paper loss is $300. However, if you buy 100 shares at $50 and sell a 50 call for 2 ($200), that same decline to $47 per share represents a net loss of only $100 ($50–47–2). Even in this situation, it is possible to offset the $100 loss with subsequent call writing or with rolling. For example, the still-open 50 call can be rolled forward to a later expiration. If that roll generates an additional 1.25 points of premium income, the net position is now $25 profitable. Options can be used skillfully in this manner not only to generate income but also to create recovery strategies when prices fall.

If a stock's price falls off the cliff, a short-term, modest recovery strategy will not do much good. But for situations in which the underlying price falls a few points, recovery is not difficult and may even speed up the recovery period. The simple act of rolling one short position forward generates additional income, reducing the paper loss.

The problem with the rolling strategy is that even with losses offset, the exposure period is extended. Covered call writing easily traps you into keeping the stock position open, even if the price subsequently continues to decline. This is the worst-case scenario. In other words, you buy stock at $50, and it falls to $46. You use covered calls to offset these losses and create a small net profit. However, the stock price falls even more. There comes a point at which recovery with options will no longer be possible. Smart traders will create a small profit or breakeven and then get out of the position before the price falls further.

This alternative—rolling forward to a minimally profitable position and then selling the stock and taking the profit—has problems even beyond the paper loss. This leaves the call open as an uncovered position. At this point, it is OTM, meaning that exercise is not imminent. However, for a majority of covered call writing, the purpose to the activity is to maintain a conservative stance (covered) and not to become exposed to a high-risk stance (uncovered). Actual risks are going to rely on probability and volatility, not to mention moneyness (in this case, OTM represents a low risk at the moment) and time to expiration.

Covered call writers need to be concerned with three major issues: selection of the underlying, calculating returns, and risk management.

SELECTION OF THE UNDERLYING SECURITY

Picking the right underlying security based on fundamental analysis is a logical first step in building a covered call writing program. Some options traders are surprised when this idea is put forth. Their emphasis is on the net profit from the call, and the underlying is viewed only as the vehicle for reducing risk exposure. This is a mistake. The inherent risk levels of the long security position define the related implied volatility in options contracts, both long and short. The degree of historical risk, expressed as market risk and price volatility, is at the core of whether a covered call strategy may yield consistent but modest returns, versus exceptionally large profits *and* losses. An evaluation of potential losses due to depreciating prices of underlying securities may easily outpace the returns possible through covered call writing.

Higher call premiums are going to be possible with higher-volatility underlying securities without any doubt. However, the higher premium levels do not justify the attendant higher risks for a majority of traders. Historical volatility represents market risk in the most directly related manner, and is the most direct and specific method for distinguishing risks between one underlying security and another. This risk, expressed as "fundamental volatility" or higher-than-average breadth of trading, is simply high risk, although traders may believe they are avoiding that risk through a covered call program. It is not always the case. A trader who self-defines as "conservative" but who is not concerned with the underlying security's market risk, violates the most important tenet of conservative trading: placing capital at exceptionally high risk in the interest of augmenting short-term profits. This might be the most common error made by covered call writers. You are less likely to experience exercise *and* to suffer a decline in the stock's price by selecting underlying securities that are low volatility and well priced (meaning selecting a value investment whose current price is reasonable, based on trading trade, PE ratio, and earnings history, for example).

Covered call writers are likely to generate consistent profits if their fundamental analysis is employed for the wise selection of companies whose stock will be included in the portfolio. It makes the most sense to compromise for lower volatility and more modest option premium than to emphasize rich premium along with higher fundamental risk. Although covered call writers are likely to consider the stock as unimportant or secondary, the fundamental attributes will determine the ultimate success or failure of the covered call writing strategy. The market risk of high-volatility stock is a serious risk in comparison to the potential profits to be gained from writing rich-premium covered calls.

The most important program of fundamental analysis has to include tests that makes sense to you individually. However, four trends should be included at a minimum in every fundamental analysis program. In addition, a test of market risk should be based not on the latest indicator, but on the consistency and reliability of indicators over the long term. Testing for ten years is smart. For example, performing fundamental analysis using the *S&P Stock Reports* is convenient, easy to use, and involves a ten-year record. These reports are provided free of charge by many of the best-known online brokerage services (including Schwab, Scott Trade, TD Waterhouse, Vanguard, Wells Fargo, Ameritrade, Bank of America, e*trade, Fidelity, and Firstrade, as well as many other brokerage services).

A ten-year record reveals a lot. It demonstrates the consistency of each indicator as well as the trend itself. For example, are revenues rising or falling, and are they moving in a predictable manner, or are they erratic? How do earnings compare? Is net return (earnings divided by revenues) keeping pace, rising, or falling?

You can judge volatility by viewing the ten-year history of fundamental indicators, as well as for related technical ratios.

The four most important fundamental indicators include the Price-Earnings (PE) ratio and dividend yield, as well as revenues/earnings and the debt ratio. These are well-understood tests, as they distinguish true growth and improvement versus decline over time. A declining company will exhibit falling revenues (or rising revenues with falling earnings), a rising debt ratio, rising or erratic PE ratio, and skipped or reduced dividends.

The PE ratio is merely a reflection of market judgment about the value of a company's stock. The multiple represents the number of years of earnings per share reflected in the current price. The higher the PE, the more expensive the stock. A counterargument is that a high PE reflects market anticipation of higher future profits, and is justified for that reason. The multiple itself is only part of the value in analyzing PE over several years. Rather than locating only the current PE (which is outdated by publication, because earnings are already at least one to two months behind), it makes more sense to review the ten-year range of PE, seeking two important points for comparison:

1. The *range* reported each year, keeping in mind that the broader the range, the more volatile the earnings and price. A relatively small range of PE should be reassuring to the trader seeking less volatile issues for covered call writing.
2. The overall direction of the PE range. Is the annual range growing or shrinking? If the development is extreme, meaning the PE range has increased substantially, it could be seen as an indicator of instability during periods of growth, perhaps pointing to the market's exaggerated reliance on growth in the company's future earnings. If the range is unpredictable, it might also point to unpredictable outcomes of both earnings and price. This indicates uncertainty within the market about future growth and profits.

The dividend yield is one way to narrow down a list of potential investments, whether for covered call writing or simply to locate high-quality companies. Dividend Achievers (companies that have increased their dividend every year for at least ten years) tend to report lower volatility and more consistent profits than average, and by the nature of this test, manage cash effectively enough to grow dividends every year.

The Dividend Achiever group is one of many ways to select stocks for covered call writing. Most covered call writers do not realize that dividend yield often represents a substantial portion of overall income. Many companies yield 4–6% annual dividend while also offering competitively priced options. However, some high yields are the result of falling price levels in the underlying, and that may occur for a number of reasons. Before you select a company for covered call writing, you should conduct a thorough review of fundamentals, price history, and recent news.

Most investors expect revenues to rise, but forget to also check earnings trends. If revenues are flat or falling, it signals that the market share is losing out to other companies in the same industry. If revenues are rising, earnings should be rising as well. However, if the net return is declining each year, that can signal a declining quality of management. A basic test of good management is maintenance of net return in periods of steadily growing revenue.

The debt ratio is the most important test of working capital. It is the percentage that long-term debt represents to total capitalization (long-term debt plus shareholders' equity). This percentage should be steady or falling each year. If a company's debt ratio is rising, it is a serious danger signal, demonstrating the increased reliance on borrowed money and less on equity. This means future dividends will have to decline as more and more profits will have to go toward debt service. Over many years, a rising debt ratio is a signal that the company is no longer a competitive leader in its industry.

When fundamentals are combined with selective technical indicators, stock selection is made easier and more rational. For example, among the more reliable technical indicators is a test of breadth of trading and the strength of resistance and support. Breadth of trading is the point span between resistance and support, and the lower the range, the less price volatility is in effect. A comparison among three companies in the same industry makes this point. Casino stocks were especially volatile in 2012, and a view of three of these demonstrates how volatility plays out in different ways.

Figure 3.1 lists the volatility of Las Vegas Sands (LVS) for three months.

This company had a volatile and uncertain trading range for the three months shown on the chart. As resistance level declined, the newly established support was tested immediately. This chart provides very little assurance of stability due to the weak resistance and support levels. For the entire period, the price ranged between $40 and $62, a 22-point breadth of trading. This represents 55% change from the low of $40.

Figure 3.2 is for Wynn Resorts (WYNN), showing a varied trading-range history.

In this case, the company's trading range changed entirely during the three months. With this in mind, it would be inaccurate to define volatility over the entire period. Instead, it is more realistic to describe Wynn's history as having two separate trading ranges, the first from $120 to $135 (a change of 12.5% from the low point to the high), and the second from $100 to $108 (a breadth of eight points or 8%). Analyzed in this manner, the volatility of each range was quite low. The low breadth of trading is a sign of low volatility, but like most of the casino stocks, Wynn's price history is not reassuring, and for investors concerned with long-term stability, it would be a questionable choice, not only for covered call writing but also for inclusion in the portfolio.

Figure 3.3 charts the volatility of Boyd Gaming (BYD). This chart exhibits an often observed phenomenon in charting, a "support/resistance flip," in which old support becomes new resistance. To judge breadth of trading, only the last segment is valid, due to the shift in these levels. It ranged from 7.7 down to 6.9, or 0.8 points, or 11.6% from the low.

The breadth of trading at 11.6% is not large; however, the reliability of both support and resistance are not firmly set.

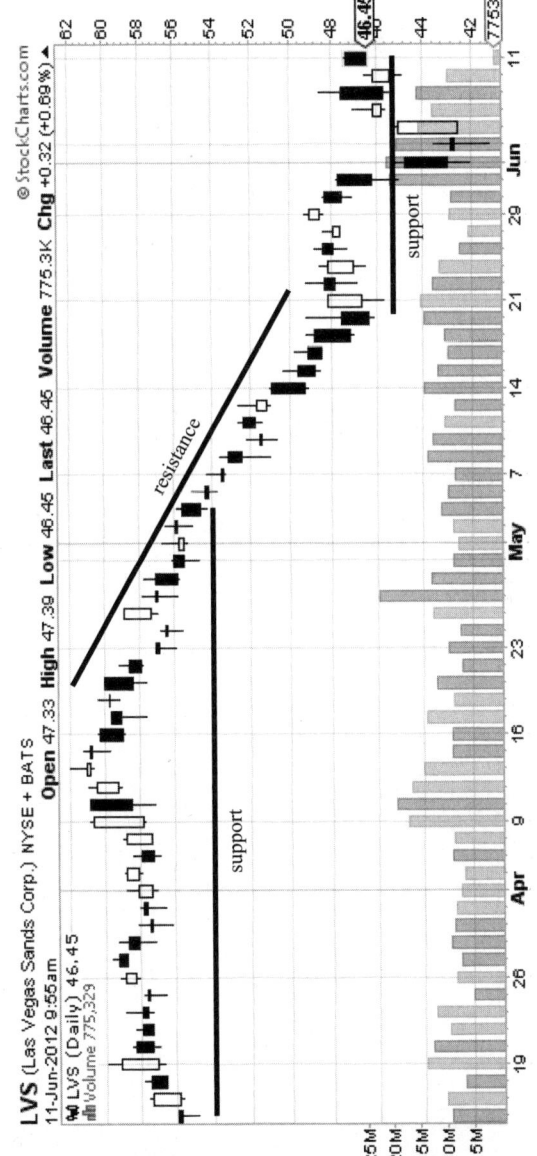

Figure 3.1 Volatile and uncertain trading range
Source: StockCharts.com.

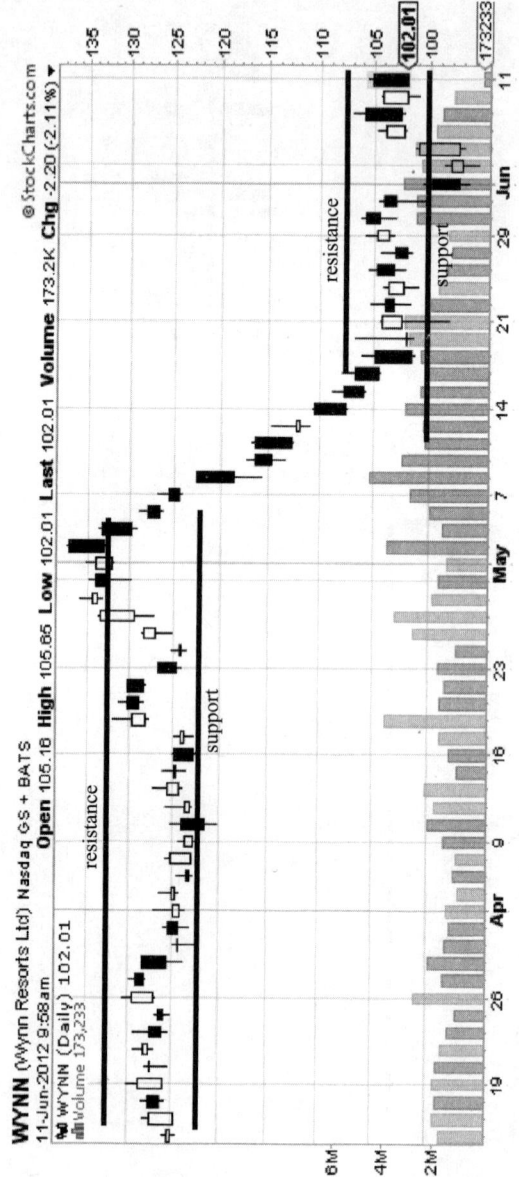

Figure 3.2 Changed trading range
Source: StockCharts.com.

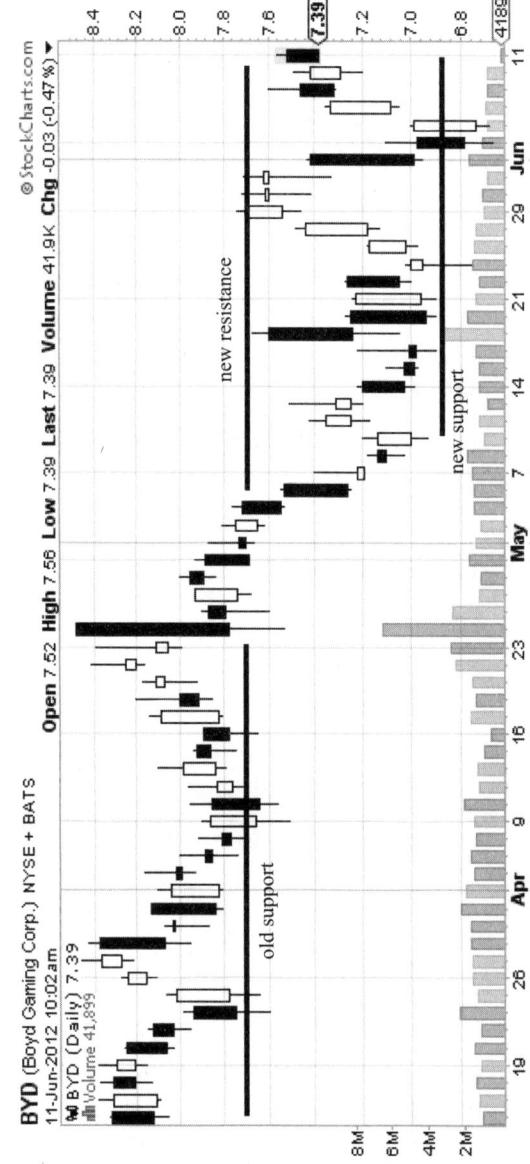

Figure 3.3 Support/resistance flip
Source: StockCharts.com.

The comparison among these three charts points out an important qualification in all charting: Volatility has to be judged in terms of (1) how well resistance and support hold up and (2) the percentage of change in the breadth itself. These cannot be judged visually between different charts, because smaller scaling makes the price history appear more volatile than it is in comparison to larger scaling. The LVS chart is scaled in 2-point increments; WYNN is scaled in 5-point increments; and BYD's scaling is only 0.2 points. The scaling range is considerable among these three companies, so visual comparisons are not dependable.

These brief technical analyses of three companies in the same industry show that judgments about sector volatility as well as the specific volatility of each company are worthwhile tools accompanying fundamental analysis. In picking stocks for covered call writing, the first test has to be the value or market risk of the company itself.

Calculating Returns

After qualifying and comparing different underlying securities, the next step is determining which covered calls to write (in terms of moneyness and expiration). Methods of calculation are complex, since many questions arise: Which version of the underlying "basis" should be used, original cost of the underlying, current value, or strike? Second, should stock capital gains be included in the overall return on an "if-exercised" basis? The selection of strike certainly affects income levels, and the greater the distance between original purchase price and the strike, the higher this dollar value is going to be. Yet, it is unreliable to include capital gains when comparing various scenarios of option strike and expiration outcomes; thus, it makes more sense to separate option returns and capital gains.

A related question is whether or not dividend yield should be included with option returns. This "total return" assumption makes sense based on how specific covered calls are picked. If all else is equal between two or more underlying securities, traders are likely to pick the one that (1) has an ex-dividend date occurring prior to option expiration and (2) offers the highest dividend yield. Dividends affect option profits as well as selection.

The most basic version of calculation is called the "static" rate of return. This is one of two benchmarks in measuring covered call outcomes. It is the annualized percentage of profit based on the assumption that the stock price remains unchanged between purchase price and option expiration, when the call is not exercised. Although these assumptions are not realistic, it forms the basis for accurate comparisons between two or more option choices. The calculation requires adding premium income to dividends earned during the holding period, minus the cost of transaction. This is divided by the net investment, which is the cost of the underlying (including the transaction cost), minus the premium received when the call is sold.

This net is then annualized. However, including dividends makes this more complex. There are two methods to annualize. First, make the initial calculation and then annualize. This is accomplished by determining the percentage return; dividing that by the holding period; and then multiplying by the full year. (Example: Premium income on a 37.50 covered call was $250, and the single dividend earned was $45. This equals 1.3% quarterly dividend yield ($45 ÷ $3,500). Total income is $295. The original cost of stock was $35 per share, or $3,500. Net income is cost of stock minus option premium ($3,500–$250 = $3,250). Time to expiration is 75 days, or about 2.5 months. The calculation is

$295 ÷ $3,250 = 9.1%.

Annualize (based on 2.5 months to expiration):

(9.1% ÷ 2.5) x 12 = 43.7%.

The second method is to isolate dividend income and add it to the annualized option premium income. In this method, the initial return is[1]

$250 ÷ $3,250 = 7.7%.

Annualize:

(7.7% ÷ 2.5) x 12 = 37.0%.

Add quarterly dividend:

37.0 + 1.3 = 38.3%.

The rationale for not annualizing dividends is based on the fact that dividends are earned at fixed periods. If the sample position, which would be open 2.5 months, were opened a few days before the ex-dividend date, the dividend yield would still be 1.3%. It should not be annualized based on the time between selling a covered call and the expiration date. The annualized 38.3% calculation is a more accurate one.

The second benchmark is the "if-called" rate of return. This is the annualized profit, assuming the underlying price rose to the strike and the stock was sold at that price on the last trading day. Three steps are involved:

1. Add income to gain.
2. Divide the result by net investment.
3. Annualize the result.

Returning to the previous example, the trader bought stock for $35 per share and sold a 37.50 call for 2.50. Dividend was $45, 1.3% per quarter; and only one quarter's ex-dividend date was in play in this case. The calculation is

1. Gain was $250 ($37.50 minus $35 per share, on 100 shares); call premium was an additional $2.50, so total gain and income was $500.

2. Net investment was $3,250 ($3,500 less call income of $250). Dividing income and gain by net investment yielded 15.4% ($500 ÷ $3,250).
3. Annualized for 2.5 months and then adding dividend income,

(15.4% ÷ 2.5) x 12 = 73.9% and 73.9 + 1.3% = 75.1%.

The static and if-called rates of return provide useful comparative methods for judging one underlying and its calls against another.[2]

However, inclusion of the gain on stock distorts the calculation as well. Consider the substantial difference made if the original basis of the stock were 20 points lower than strike, and the stock had been held for three years—versus stock purchased the same day that the covered call was written, with only 2.5 months to expiration. The if-called and static benchmarks are both distorted when attempting to compare situations with a dissimilar stock basis and holding period. For this reason, isolating returns among options and stock makes greater sense and adds more reliability to the comparison.

With this in mind, calculation of covered call profit potential is broken down into two distinct parts, *return if unchanged* and *return if exercised*. These are somewhat equivalent to the static and if-called methods, but capital gains are excluded. The capital gains certainly are a part of overall outcomes, but a comparison of covered call activity is clearer when performed in isolation. In both return methods of calculation, dividends are left in for consistency.

Another complexity in this calculation is the selection of the basis in the underlying to be used to calculate the option return. There are three possible prices: original cost of stock, current value at the time the call is sold, or the strike price of the call. You may use any of these, but it comes down to a question of reliability and consistency. The original basis in stock might be unrealistic to use for calculation of covered call returns, since that basis might be fairly recent or quite seasoned. If you have owned stock for years and it has doubled in value, the selection of original cost distorts covered call income. This assumes that the strike was selected based on the then-current price of stock and not on its original cost.

Should you use the cost of stock at the time the call was sold? This is more reliable, but it also distorts the outcome to a degree. This is because the underlying price is likely to change often, and the price on the day the call was sold is not a consistent indicator of the call's initial value. Depending on how far to expiration, proximity of strike to value, and the level of implied volatility at that moment, the price per share is not an accurate base either.

The strike of the call is the most reliable price to use in figuring all covered call returns. If the call is exercised, the stock will be called away at the strike. Thus, the premium received for selling that particular call is directly tied to the price, and comparisons among two or more different call selections is at its most consistent when the strike is used.

The entire calculation is distorted if and when the short call is closed and rolled forward. For the sake of consistency, when this occurs, the roll should be treated as two separate transactions. These are the return on the close of the first short call (return if closed), and the second is an entirely new position, with the outcomes calculated all over again based on the new strike and the new premium received for selling the call (not the net between the two calls, but the premium value itself).

Return if unchanged is similar to static return, and return if exercised tracks the if-called calculation. But both exclude capital gains on the underlying. The calculations assume that the covered call expires worthless because it remains OTM or in the money (ITM) (return if unchanged) or ceases to exist upon exercise (return if exercised). In both cases, the call is gone, due to expiration or exercise.

For example, you purchase stock for $35 per share and sell a 36.50 call and receive 2.50 in premium income. The calculation of return if unchanged or if exercised is

$2.50 \div 37.50 = 6.7\%$.

Annualized:

(6.7% ÷ 2.5) x 12 = 32.2%.

Add dividend:

32.2% + 1.3 = 33.5%.

By excluding the capital gain on stock, this presents a realistic annualized return. The outcome is modified if the call is closed before expiration, as often occurs. In this case, the calculation involves only the option premium and nothing else. For example, if the option costing 2.50 was closed exactly 1.5 months after it had been opened, at a value of 1.00, the income would be 1.50 points, or $150. The return, if closed, would be

1.50 ÷ 2.50 = 60.0%.

Annualized:

(60.0% ÷ 1.5) x 12 = 480.0%.

This calculation demonstrates that all calculations of option net returns are useful for comparisons and estimates—but they should not be used to assume the annualized return will be an accurate display of what you should expect to earn from covered call activity. Even the relatively modest 33.5% annualized return if unchanged, while attractive, should never be assumed as typical. It ignores the potential for losses or for alternative outcomes. The 480% annualized return if closed is not a "typical" outcome either, but poses a baseline for comparisons among strike selection, expiration, and underlying security.

These outcomes have to be based on a key assumption: The underlying stock was purchased at a price below the covered call's strike. If you pick strikes above the basis in stock, even an impressive option return will be offset by larger capital losses on the stock. Based on this assumption, exercise becomes a desirable outcome because it results in a net capital gain. But to compare return if exercised (both to other outcomes and to potential outcomes in other underlying securities), capital gains are excluded.

Risk Management

The most obvious form of risk management requires awareness of the basis in stock. A covered call's strike should always be higher than the price per share of the underlying, or exercise would produce a net capital loss.

A second, equally obvious form of risk is that the underlying price per share might fall. This market risk exists for anyone holding stock, whether covered calls are written or not. Covered calls mitigate this risk, but they do not eliminate it. Traders have to live with the market risk involved in stock ownership in both instances.

Lost opportunity risk has two forms, committed capital and the potential for lost profits due to the exercise of a covered call. However, in quantifying lost opportunity risk, you need to be keenly aware of the potential use of capital if covered calls are *not* written, versus the premium income you earn from this activity. This involves rates of return as well as time to expiration. Longer option expirations are also equal to "exposure risk" in the sense that the longer the option remains open, the greater the chance it will move ITM. Writing a series of shorter-term (one month, for example) options will yield much greater annualized returns than those from longer-term options.

For example, in June 2012, Caterpillar (CAT) had options available on five separate expiration dates, spanning 1, 2, 5, 7, and 19 months. The farther out the expiration, the higher the dollar value of calls. Ignoring annualization, it appeared that the more desirable expirations were those providing higher premium income. However, you would earn more money and a better yield by writing a series of one-month options each month. The available calls are shown in figure 3.4.

In this example, the one-month premium of 3.65 annualized to over 50%. Another way to look at this is that one-month

Caterpillar (CAT)

Price on June 11, 2012: $86.83

Expiration	Strike	Premium	Annualized calculation	Annualized
July 21, 2012	87.50	3.65	(3.65 ÷ 87.50) ÷ 1) x 12 =	50.1%
August 18, 2012	87.50	4.95	(4.95 ÷ 87.50) ÷ 2) x 12 =	17.0%
November 17, 2012	87.50	7.55	(7.55 ÷ 87.50) ÷ 5) x 12 =	20.7%
January 19, 2013	87.50	9.00	(9.00 ÷ 87.50) ÷ 7) x 12 =	17.6%
January 18, 2014	87.50	14.25	(14.25 ÷ 87.50) ÷19) x 12 =	10.3%

Figure 3.4   Annualized returns based on expiration
Source: Charles Schwab & Co., options listings November 6, 2012.

premium income yields much more than later-expiring options. Earning $365 per month is more profitable than earning $495 over two months:

$365 x 2 = $730
$495 x 1 = $495.

A trader writing a $365 covered call two months in a row would earn $730 (based on today's price) versus gaining only $495 for writing one two-month covered call. By writing options expiring sooner rather than later, exercise is also less likely to occur. For example, were the price to rise to $89, it would make greater sense to write the next covered call at a 90 strike.

A disadvantage to maximizing annualized returns is the loss of some downside protection. A one-month option in this example provides 3.65 points of downside protection, while the two-month option provides 4.95 points. In the event of a price decline, time decay for the richer two-month option has more time to go, and thus provides potentially greater price recovery as well as net profit from the covered call itself. For example, if the underlying fell 4.5 points, the one-month trade at 3.65 would net out at a loss of 0.85, or $85 on the combined stock and option trade—assuming the position were left open until expiration.

But the two-month 4.95 premium nets out at a combined stock/option profit of 0.45, or $45. In this case, you would remain at a net profitable position, although the option would take an additional month to expire.

A holder of 200 shares could open one call at each strike, with an average income of 4.30 points for the two (an average between 3.65 and 4.95). Given the same scenario of a 4.5 point drop in the underlying, you would be at a position of a 0.20 loss, or $20. This is not bad considering that the underlying had dropped 4.5 points from the basis.

At this point, you can take several steps. The entire position can be closed at a minimal loss. You can hold and wait out the price dip, given the stock's tendency to swing back and forth in relatively quick moves, as shown in figure 3.5.

This risk management example demonstrates the issue with covered calls. The shorter the term, the higher the yield in most instances. At the same time, the longer the term to expiration, the greater the risk exposure *and* the higher the downside protection. Risk management is a balancing act between these offsetting considerations.

Risk management relating to downside protection often is an argument used critically of the covered call strategy. This risk should be viewed in comparison to owning stock without any covered call writing. The market risk is identical, but receiving premium for writing the covered call reduces that risk. The premium itself can also be used to create cost-neutral strategies such as collars or synthetic stock. This is a major aspect of the risk-free dividend collar.

The risk associated with exercise is often exaggerated. Although exercise can occur at any time before expiration, it is only going to occur when the short call is ITM. Even then, exercise only makes sense in most instances at two points in the call's cycle. First is on or right before the ex-dividend date. An ITM call will be exercised in two instances: first, the call must be ITM or exercise makes no sense. Second, time value premium has to be lower than the dividend dollar value, or

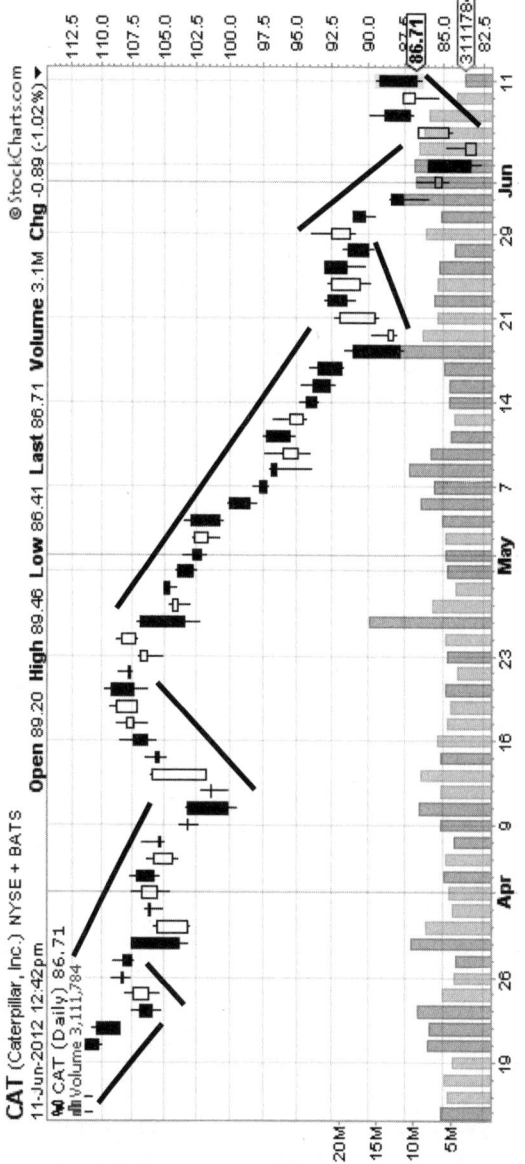

Figure 3.5 Short-term price volatility
Source: StockCharts.com.

exercise makes no sense. If either of these requirements is not in place, an owner of a long call will not exercise. This explains why not all ITM calls are exercised immediately before the ex-dividend date. A long call holder can exercise at any time prior to expiration, so unless the exercise is profitable in terms of dividend income versus time value premium, it makes more sense to hold until the last trading day. If the underlying does not include a dividend, there is no logical reason to exercise a call before the last trading day. Whether exercised early or on the last day, the buyer pays the same value for the underlying. It would make more sense to wait until the last possible moment. The risk management caveat in this is that you should monitor the ex-dividend dates when you have open covered call positions. If your short call is ITM and has little or no time-value premium remaining, you will want to close or roll to avoid exercise.[3]

Risk management ultimately is perceived as a subset of selecting strikes and expiration dates for covered calls. What is the "ideal" strike or expiration?

Because time decay accelerates during the final weeks of an option's life, call writers benefit from this and may want to focus on shorter-term expirations. Even though the dollar value is lower for these than for later-expiring contracts, the annualized yield is significantly higher.

The "ideal" strike is one that maximizes premium income while keeping the exercise risk as low as possible. Most traders will agree that this is a strike close to the money but slightly OTM. As a writer of the call, this is the most advantageous position for you to be in. Time decay will be rapid during the last 30 days of the option's life, meaning its premium value will decline. Even if the call moves ITM, it is more than likely that time decay will outpace the intrinsic value. Thus, the short position ITM can be closed at a small profit to avoid exercise, and then replaced with a higher-strike short call. Whether this is considered a roll or a separate position, it is maximum use of the strike and expiration combination, enabling you to manage risk while continuing the covered call program.

Perhaps the most crucial of covered call risk management rules is that exercise has to be viewed as one of many possible outcomes, and as an acceptable conclusion to a trade. Strike selection to ensure a net capital gain (and not a loss) is essential; but if you are not willing to have shares called away, the covered call should be avoided. It is an appropriate and profitable strategy, but only if you will be happy if and when exercised.

VARIATIONS OF COVERED CALL WRITING

Covered call writers tend to think of one-to-one match-up, in other words one short call per 100 shares. Of course, much greater flexibility and lower costs are benefits of trading in higher counts. For example, if you own 300 shares and write three covered calls, you can close out some of the positions without closing all of them, or roll into variations of strikes and expirations. The use of multiple groupings of short calls and numbers of shares reduces some forms of risk while also reducing downside market risk.

A good example of this is the ratio write. This is an expansion of the covered call in which more calls are written than can be covered with stock. For example, if you own 300 shares and write four calls, you create a 4:3 ratio write. This can be viewed as four calls that are each 75% covered, or as a combination of three covered calls and one uncovered call. Risk levels vary with the ratio as well. A 2:1 (two calls versus 100 shares) is much greater than a 3:2, and a 4:3 ratio write is even less risky.

You manage downside risk with a ratio write because premium income is increased. Returning to the Caterpillar (CAT) example, recall that the one-month (July) 87.50 call was worth 3.65 when the stock price was $86.83. These were 0.67 points OTM with only one month to expiration. If you own 300 shares of CAT, you create a 4:3 ratio write by selling four July 87.50 calls, each at 3.65. This creates premium income of 14.60 ($1,460), or downside protection of 4.87 points ($1,460 ÷ 300 shares). This 4.87-point downside protection is more desirable than the one-to-one 3.65-point level. However, this also exposes you to higher risks.

This risk might be acceptable considering two factors:

1. These options are 0.67 points OTM and expire in one month. This means time decay will occur rapidly, and the current premium contains zero intrinsic value.
2. These positions can be rolled or partially closed if and when the underlying moves upward. In order to avoid exercise, you can take one of these steps, or cover the position with the purchase of a later-expiring long call, or even an additional 100 shares of stock. Buying more shares converts the ratio write into a straightforward covered call position.

The exercise risk can be even further diminished by creating a *variable* ratio write. In this expanded strategy, you write the ratio, but you use two strikes instead of one. For example, CAT was worth $86.83 per share. A 4:3 variable ratio write may be a combination of two 87.50 calls and two 90 calls. The July 90 contracts were worth 2.54, so total income from the two calls at each strike was $1,238. Although this is lower than the $1,460 from the one-strike ratio write, the risk is significantly lower. Both strikes were OTM, but the 90 strikes were 3.17 points OTM. Given the short time to expiration of only one month, it is very unlikely that the increase in the underlying market value would be able to move in the money *and* that intrinsic value would outpace the decline in time value.

You certainly would have enough time to see a gradual move toward the money in the event that CAT did move upward. The higher 90 strikes could be closed, probably at a profit, as long as they remained OTM as time decay continued. Or they (or the lower strikes) could be rolled forward to avoid exercise on all four exposed contracts.

Flexibility is increased even more by opening a 4:3 ratio write using two-month contracts. The August 87.50 calls were at 4.95, and the 90 calls at 3.85. Selling two of each would yield $1,160. The same benefits apply: Time decay is likely to outpace the growth of intrinsic value even if CAT does move higher than 90. Any of the four contacts can be closed at a profit or rolled forward (or later covered) at any time before expiration. And as long as they remain OTM, they are not going to be exercised.

The variable ratio write does involve some uncovered portion, but is much lower risk than the ratio write and adds very little risk to the traditional covered call. It is a worthwhile strategy for any covered call writer.

Both the ratio write and the variable ratio write are prominent in variations of the dividend collar that will be examined in coming chapters.

Chapter 4

Downside Protection, the Insurance Put

> Security is when everything is settled, when nothing
> can happen to you; security is the denial of life.
> —Germaine Greer, *The Female Eunuch*, 1970

STOCK SELECTION IS A STARTING POINT FOR EVERY PORTFOLIO. Even when you pick stocks expertly, however, market risk is never eliminated. A long portfolio is never completely safe, and this points to the value of puts to insure against downside risk.

The dividend collar is designed in such a way that the options protect against price decline, but this is not always going to be the entire portfolio. Investors may apply the idea to several holdings, while other long positions remain "at risk" in a volatile market. In addition, the dividend collar will not work for those stocks in your portfolio that pay no dividend. In this situation, the insurance put enables you to insure your portfolio for the life of the put, and limits potential losses if and when the underlying price does fall. This is one of many ways that you can mitigate risks.

The Insurance Put and How It Works

The insurance put is a long put purchased to protect 100 shares of long stock in the event the market price declines. The protection fixes the maximum loss in your portfolio at:

PUT STRIKE—PREMIUM

For example, in April you bought 100 shares of Dominion Resources (D) at $49 per share. Over the next two months, the stock was in an uptrend, and as of June 12, had a market price of $52.62. At this point, you bought a July 52.50 insurance put and paid 2.05. This is summarized in figure 4.1.

The breakeven on the insurance put is

$$52.62 - 2.05 = 50.57$$

The basis was $49 per share, so the value in this insurance put is that it protects slightly more value than the original basis. This is a very conservative strategy, since almost all of the gains in the position are spent on the put. It is advantageous, however, if (1) you do not want to sell shares at the current price; (2) you are worried about the possibility of a price decline; and (3) in the event of the price decline, you intend to hold onto shares and sell the put to offset losses in the stock.

The insurance put can also be exercised so that stock is sold at the strike. In this case, if the stock price fell many points, you could exercise the put and dispose of 100 shares at $52.50 per share, no matter how far the stock price had fallen.

The insurance put provides protection against price decline, which is worth more than preserving the paper profits. However, it is not only a bearish trend that these puts protect against. They also provide safety and opportunity in volatile markets. The put serves both as a protective device to offset temporary paper losses, and also as a swing-trading device for additional profits. The alternative to the insurance put—selling the shares and taking profits—presents a dilemma for every investor. Where should you invest funds next? If you do sell and the stock price resumes its upward move, it means you lose out on future profits. So the insurance put is advantageous no matter which direction the price goes:

- If the price falls, the insurance put protects the original basis and enables you to sell at $52.50 per share by exercising the put, or to sell the put to offset stock losses.

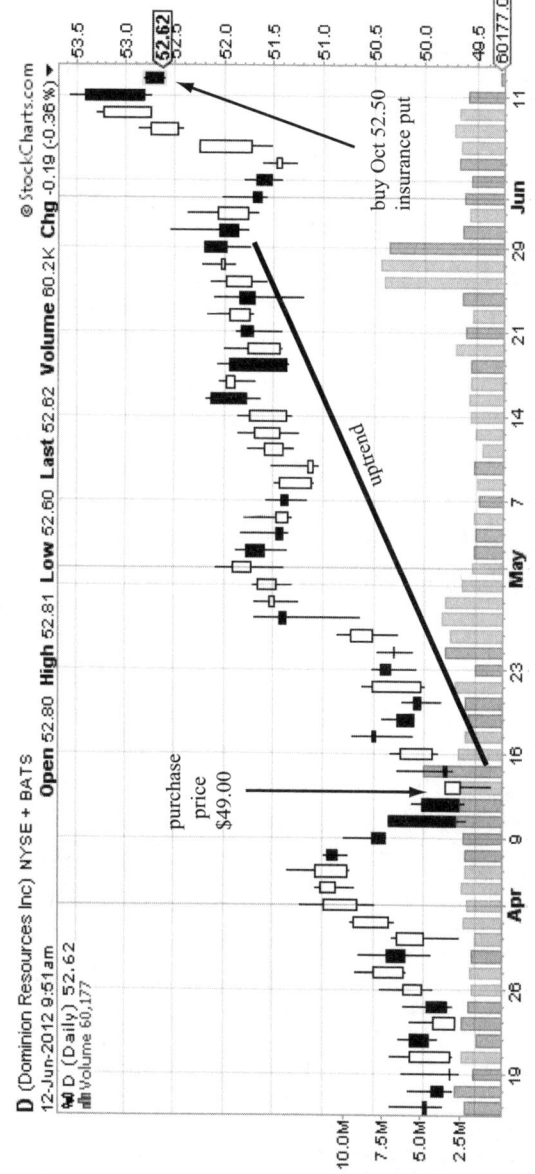

Figure 4.1 Insurance put example
Source: StockCharts.com.

- If the price rises, you benefit from the higher price per share, and the cost of the insurance put was worthwhile protection, the cost of which is more than offset by further price gains in the underlying.

For example, you purchase shares of stock at $35 per share, and over a period of time, the price rises to $42. You now have a seven-point gain. Do you sell and create a short-term capital gain? Or do you hold on in the hopes that the price does not retreat? There is a third alternative: buy an insurance put. The put will cost a portion of the seven-point paper profit. For example, if a 40 put requires payment of 2 ($200), it protects three points of gain. The fixed strike of 40 gives you the ability to sell a put or exercise it anywhere below $40 per share. However, the real protection level resides at $38 per share. The strike of 40 is reduced by two points for the cost of the insurance put.

This is a strategy with many names. The term "insurance put" makes the most sense because it describes the purpose and outcome of the position. It is also called a "married put" when the strike is approximately identical to the current price of the underlying. It is also called a "synthetic long call" because the position (combining long stock with a long call) changes in value in the same manner as a long call by itself. If the stock price declines, the loss in stock is capped by the put (strike minus premium). If the stock price rises, the long put becomes worthless but the stock gains value, just like a long call. By whatever name it is called, the insurance put solves the dilemma of appreciated stock. It avoids the need to sell and take profits when you would rather keep the stock since you are bullish on its longer-term prospects. However, if you are fearful of a possible decline in price, the insurance put is one way to plan for either eventuality—offsetting potential losses while keeping stock to profit from potential gains.

The long put is an essential part of the dividend collar. However, whether used as insurance or for other reasons, such as an offset to other spread or straddle positions, puts provide many strategic possibilities.

Long Puts as Alternatives to Shorting Stock

The insurance put offsets the market risk of holding stock, and the main problem with this strategy is the cost. The premium you pay for the put takes part of your profit away, so it makes sense only under two circumstances. First, the profit is substantially higher than the premium cost. Or second, the insurance put is a segment of a more complex strategy, preferably one in which an offsetting short position pays for most or all of the long put's premium.

Another use of long puts is to provide an alternative to shorting stock. Borrowing and then selling stock is expensive and high risk, and most traders and investors prefer to pass up opportunities rather than take the risk involved. However, when you anticipate a short-term bear market, buying puts is a sensible alternative. Unlike short selling stock, which requires the payment of interest on borrowed stock, the market risk of a long put is limited to the relatively small premium you pay. As long as the put remains open, you face the potential for profits when the underlying price declines

Selecting strikes close to the money but slightly out of the money (OTM) is the maximum advantage. The cost of OTM strikes will be much lower than in the money (ITM) puts, and being close to the money offers the potential for rapid accumulation of intrinsic value if the underlying price declines. Long options are not easily turned profitable, however. Time decay is rapid for soon-to-expire contracts, and longer-term puts have two distinct disadvantages: They are expensive, and intrinsic price movement may be offset by changes in extrinsic value (volatility premium or implied volatility [IV]).

However, if you believe that a short-term bear condition prevails (e.g., when the underlying price has jumped strongly and moved through resistance in a gapping price movement), then chances are good that a correction will occur. This is the time to swing trade with the long put. Swing traders traditionally short stock in this condition, especially if they find strong reversal signals as well as confirmation. However, using the long put is safer, provides better leverage, and may produce profits more rapidly. Swing traders expect short-term trends to last between three and five sessions, so the anticipated profits are likely to develop very quickly.

One criticism of long puts is that profits are limited, since the price of the underlying can move down only so far. This criticism is the opposite of the short put advantage. A short call is high risk because the price can rise indefinitely, in theory. A short put is safer because the price can only fall so far. Now look at the opposite: the long put. The maximum the price can fall is zero, but realistically the true likely maximum is the tangible book value per share.

Although this is a criticism of the profit potential, it is the same flaw in shorting stock, but with much less risk. A short seller of stock lives with the same limitation. The price can only fall so far, and so likely profits are "limited." But why do investors short stock? The usual reason is to take advantage of an expected bearish move in the stock. Most short selling is short term, so investors expect to exit with a "buy to close" move fairly quickly. At the same time, they are exposed to the very real risk of unlimited upward price potential. In comparison, the long put is cheaper and provides the same limited downside potential. However, the upside risk does not exist, and the maximum loss is equal to the premium paid for the long put.

Another way to look at and compare shorting stock and using long puts is the potential return on the investment. For example, you may think a $26 stock is likely to retreat in price down to $22. If you short stock and you are right, you walk away with a $4 profit per share (before transaction and interest costs). As an alternative, if you buy an at the money (ATM) put and pay 6 ($600), that four-point price decline may create a three-dollar profit (assuming some time decay). The short stock profit is 15% (based on the original sale at $26 per share). Profit on the put of three dollars per share versus a six-dollar initial premium, is 50%.

Puts as Part of Collars

The collar is the core of the risk-free portfolio strategy based on creating dividend income. Even without this approach, collars are created to accomplish several goals: (1) remove downside risk, (2) create protection without cost or for very little cost, and (3) trade limited profit for the elimination of risk.

The collar, however, is not an aggressive strategy, but a defensive one. So as a means for generating income, it will not provide very much help. Collars are appealing because they lock in existing paper profits. If you own appreciated stock and you do not want to sell at the moment to take profits, the collar is one possible solution. For example, if the tax year-end is approaching, you want to shift profits to the following year, but at the same time, you are exposed to the risk of downside movement. Another situation is when an ex-dividend date is approaching, and you want to earn the quarterly dividend. The collar eliminates or caps downside risk, while allowing you to hold onto your shares.

Construction of the collar involves two OTM options opened against 100 shares of stock. These are a short call with a strike above current value, and a long call with a strike below. If your basis in the stock is in the middle of the two strikes, an upward move resulting in exercise of the covered call creates a profit on the stock; a downward move creates a loss equal to the difference between the basis and the put's strike (adjusted by the net debit or credit on the collar). For example, on June 14, 2012, Eli Lilly (LLY) was worth $41.65 per share. Your basis is much lower; you purchased 100 shares the previous August for $36 per share. You believe the stock is going to continue upward, but you are concerned about possible corrections. The stock was yielding an impressive 4.71% dividend, so you want to hold onto shares at least until after the coming August ex-dividend date. A collar is a solution to this situation.

You can create a collar by selling an August 42 call for 0.75, and buying an August 41 put for 0.60. This creates a net credit of 0.15, which should cover the transaction fee, or most of it. By doing this in June, you create a downside safety put at the 41 put level. Since the basis was $36 per share, this protects five points of paper gains for the next two months. On the upside, you would be quite happy to sell at $42 per share, or a profit of six points. You would also like to earn the next quarterly dividend, but you are willing to have shares called away if and when the underlying price rises above $42.

In the dividend collar developed later in this book, the collar itself is the structure for creating a series of dividends. However, the collars are set up with the *intention* of exercise. You either want the short call exercised within a short time (after the ex-dividend date), or you will exercise your long call and dispose of shares at the strike (also after the ex-dividend date). This eliminates all market risk below the put's strike, while providing you the quarterly dividend. The following month you repeat the strategy with a different underlying whose ex-dividend date occurs in that month. In this manner, the quarter dividends for a series of underlying stocks are converted to monthly dividends, while market risks are eliminated. If you use a series of companies, each yielding 4% per year (1% per quarter), the annual result is a dividend yield of 12%. The collar is only one method for accomplishing this, however. As long as the higher call strike and the lower put strike are at par, the only issue is that of minimal loss on the put in the event of exercise. If a price decline below strike creates even a small loss, the strategy might not work. For example, a one-dollar loss between the basis and the put's strike, versus a 0.75 quarterly dividend, creates a scenario of net loss. Ideally, you want to be able to keep most or all of the dividend. For this reason, the ideal collar should involve the put's strike extremely close to the stock's basis. It also helps if the basis in the stock is at or below the put's strike. This means that upon exercise of the put, you will earn a net profit.

For example, you purchased 100 shares of AT%T (T) at $32 per share in April. By June 14, the price had risen to $35.21. You want to hold on until after the July 5 ex-dividend date and earn the quarterly dividend (annual yield = 50.3%). You are also concerned about a possible price decline, so you open a July collar. This consists of selling a July 36 call for 0.23 and buying a July

35 put for 0.80. The net cost is 0.57, but upon exercise you make a profit of $3.21 per share (if you exercise the put) or $4.21 per share (if your call gets assigned). Although the dividend is only 0.44 (versus the cost of the collar at 0.57), the purpose here is to set up a profitable outcome whether the stock rises or falls. If its price remains in-between the two strikes, you can allow the short call to expire or buy to close, and then replace the position with another collar or with a covered call.

Puts in Synthetic Short Stock Positions

An alternative to the collar is the synthetic short stock. This is very similar to a collar in the sense that you combine a long put and a short call. However, the strike and expiration of both options are identical. This is a form of straddle.

To avoid the market risk associated with the short call, when you also own 100 shares, the synthetic short stock position is a combination of an insurance put and a covered call. This position acts exactly like stock and gains one net point of value for each point the underlying stock drops. For example, Verizon (VZ) pays a dividend of 0.50 cents per quarter, coming out to 4.65% yield. As of June 14, stock price was $43.30 per share, and the next ex-dividend date was July 6. A synthetic short stock position would protect against downside loss. Such a position could be created by selling a July 43 call at 0.94 and buying a July 43 put for 1.00. The net debit is 0.06. If either side is exercised, the net loss on stock would be 0.30. (However, if you bought stock below the strike level, then the exercise of either option would produce a net profit equal to the difference between basis and strike.)

This position allows you to earn the dividend unless the price rises and the call is assigned so shares are called away. In that case, the dividend is lost but a capital gain replaces it if the basis was lower than the strike. The purpose in this example of opening the collar was to earn the dividend whose ex-dividend date was July 6. If the stock price were to fall below the strike, the call would not be exercised. To avoid exercise if the price remained above, the call could be rolled forward or closed.

Synthetic positions can be used in place of collars as part of the dividend collar strategy. In many instances, a synthetic short stock position or a synthetic long stock position may provide breakeven or better, and enable you to accomplish the desired result found in the collar, and perhaps even a better outcome.

The issue of covered or uncovered calls is a critical risk element in the synthetic short position. Because the emphasis is on earning dividends, you are most likely to prefer the covered synthetic short stock position (100 shares, one short call, one long put).

If you employ a synthetic long stock position, the reverse applies. It consists of a long call and a short put. In this situation, you need to ensure that the short put risk is acceptable, as it cannot be covered in the same manner as a call. This requires that you monitor the position to avoid its moving ITM. If this does occur or the price trend approaches the money, the short put can be closed or rolled, or exercise can be accepted. If you open a synthetic long stock position, exercise is a distinct possibility. So you need to be willing to acquire shares at the put strike. This is desirable for value investments whose put strike is a desirable entry price. If you focus on stocks paying exceptionally high dividends, it tends to reduce the risk of early exercise, since owners of the stock also will find high dividends desirable, and are going to be likely to hold onto shares rather than put them to you just before an ex-dividend date. Focus on short puts whose expiration precedes the ex-dividend date. If the price declines below strike and you are required to buy shares, the paper loss will be offset to a degree by earning the quarterly dividend on those shares.

THE PUT-BASED REVERSE HEDGE

Another way that long puts can be employed to manage and augment portfolio income is through the reverse hedge. This is a combination of 100 shares of long stock plus two puts. If and when the underlying price rises, the position is profitable (however, the price has to rise higher than the combined cost of the long puts). If the stock price falls below the strike of the puts, the puts gain two points in value for every point lost in the underlying stock.

The worst outcome for the reverse hedge occurs when the stock price does not appreciate enough to offset the put cost, and as a result, the puts expire worthless or are closed at a loss. The intention of the reverse hedge is to gain the best of both possible outcomes, but price movement must occur. For example, the three-month chart for the SPDR Gold Trust GLD (figure 4.2) demonstrates how a reverse hedge works in both uptrends and downtrends.

GLD is a volatile exchange-traded fund (ETF) that tracks gold, and the chart demonstrates this volatility. Three points are highlighted on the chart and marked A, B, and C. The first of these, "A," marks a point within the established trading range, where it appears that upward momentum has faded. Entering a reverse hedge at this point could make sense if a trader did not want to close out the position. For example, you could buy two June 158 puts. By the end of May, GLD has fallen to 149, representing the intrinsic value of nine points in each put, or $1,800 of intrinsic value. The puts could be closed at this point and profits taken.

The second point, marked as "B," marks a strong downside price gap that also falls below support. In that moment, a chart reader does not know whether this identifies the beginning as a downtrend, or a point that will reverse and return to the previously set range. If you opened a reverse hedge here by buying two puts, a downward movement would be profitable in the options, and a significant upward movement would be profitable in the underlying. For example, if you had bought two June 155 puts, within three weeks the GLD price was $149, so each put would have gained six points in intrinsic value, or $1,200.

The third point, "C," marks a strong upward price gap. As with the previous gap, you cannot know whether the price will continue upward or reverse. At this point, opening a reverse hedge would be a good defensive move, leaving the profit potential in place. For example, buying two 153 or 154 puts would

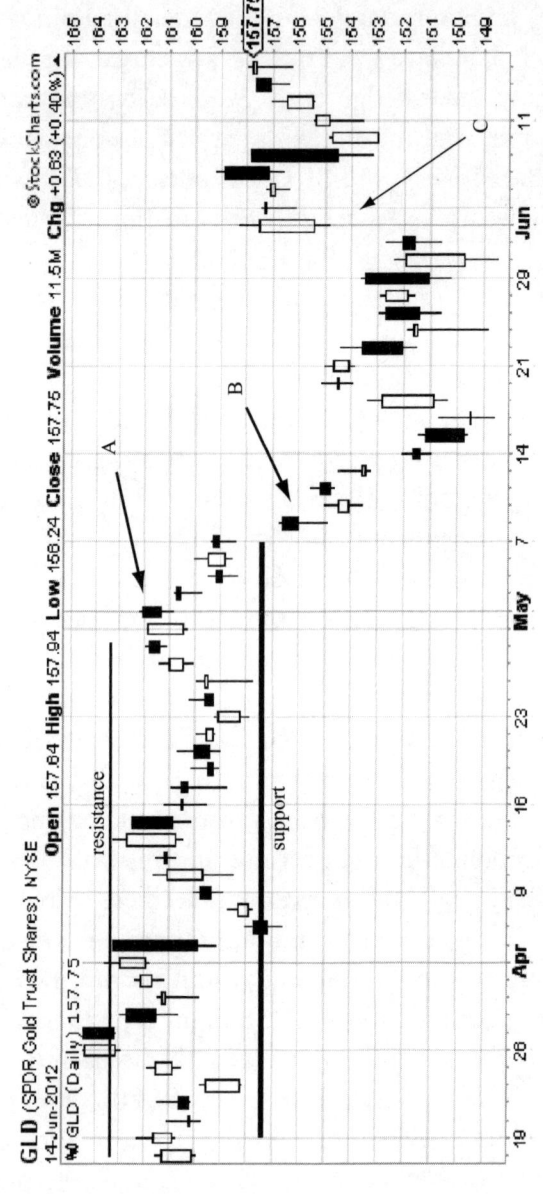

Figure 4.2 Reverse hedge
Source: StockCharts.com.

provide that downside protection without your needing to sell shares.

The reverse hedge allows you to benefit from strong price movement in either direction. It is most likely to yield profits in exceptionally volatile underlying securities like GLD. For less volatile securities, the trend works against the reverse hedge.

Another variation on this is the *variable* reverse hedge. In this type, you employ two different strikes. It lowers the price because both strikes are OTM. The GLD puts are very expensive, so a variable reverse hedge makes sense. For example, as of June 15, the last day shown on the chart, GLD was at $157.53. If you owned 200 shares, you could open a variable reverse hedge, buying one June 22, 2012, 156 put at 1.45 and one June 22, 2012, 155 put for 1.12. Total cost would be 2.57 ($257) before transaction costs. In comparison, you could open a regular reverse hedge using the June 22, 2012, 157 puts at 2.35 each, in which case the cost would be 4.70, or $213 more.

Puts in Straddle Strategies

Long puts represent one side of either a long or a short straddle. In this approach, the two sides are opened at the same strike and expiration. On the long side, profits accrue only if the underlying moves farther than the total points of the position; on the short side, a middle-profit zone equal to the points received is offset by growing loss zones both above and below.

So the straddle may be long or short, and risks are determined by the level of price volatility in the underlying. In the synthetic short stock position, the call was short and the put was long. In straddles, in comparison, both the call and the put are long (or both are short). This is the distinction, and it also defines a higher level of market risk. Even so, traders find straddles attractive when conditions warrant those risks.

For example, taking another look at GLD: on June 15, the July 158 call was at 4.30, and the July 158 put was at 4.45. You can study either a long or short straddle based on these price levels, as shown in figure 4.3.

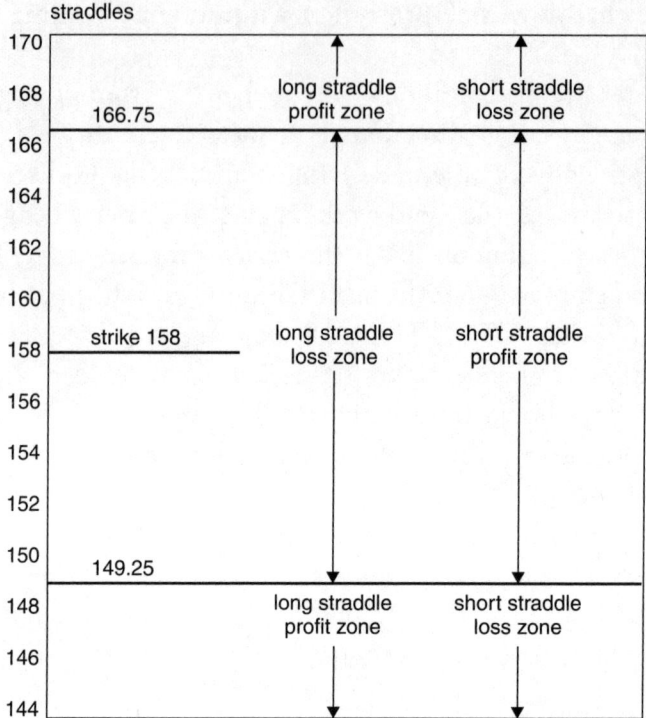

Figure 4.3 Straddles
Source: Figure created by author from raw numerical data.

The total debit of a long straddle or credit of a short straddle equals 8.75 points (4.30 plus 4.45). So in the long position, you need the underlying price to move this far just to break even, and to move beyond to create a profit. This profit zone is found both above and below the strike.

For a short straddle based on the same 158 strike, the same middle zone of 8.75 points goes in both directions, above and below the 158 strike. This 17.5-point range is the profit zone for the short straddle. However, if the price were to move above or below these markets, the short straddle would lose money.

One expansion of the straddle is the *strangle*. This is a straddle with one change. The strike prices are different. For example, instead of buying a call and a put at the 158, you could have set up a GLD strangle, buying or selling a 159 call at 3.85 and a 157

Downside Protection, the Insurance Put

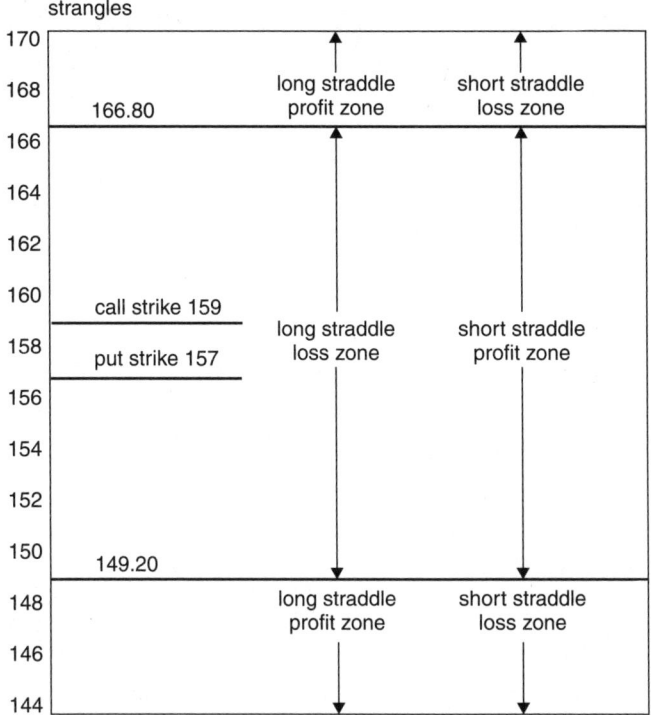

Figure 4.4 Strangles
Source: Figure created by author from raw numerical data.

put at 3.95. The total cost would be 7.80, a savings of $95 over the straddle at 8.75. This is shown in figure 4.4.

The profit and loss zones are only 0.05 different from those of the straddle, and there are now two strike prices. The profit and loss zones extend above and below these levels, but the net outcome is similar. Given this very small difference, the strangle is most advantageous for long positions, because the cost will be lower. In this example, that difference represents a savings of $95 on the entire position.

LONG PUTS TO COVER SHORT PUTS

Options traders know that short puts cannot be "covered" in the same manner as short calls. However, a credit put can be covered, completely or partially, with the use of long puts. Such combined positions often are not opened at the same time, but instead after price movement in the originally opened short puts requires additional steps.

Rolling puts is one way to avoid exercise and even to move from ITM to ATM or OTM status. For example, McDonalds reported a price of $90.25 on June 15, 2012. At that time, the July 90 puts were at 1.81 and the September 90 puts were at 3.60; the 87.50 puts were at 2.56; and the 85 puts were at 1.81.

If you had two short July 90 puts open, exercise would become a distinct possibility. The credit puts had moved in the money. You could close and replace them with two September 90s and earn an additional 1.79 per contract, coming out to additional income on these two contracts of $358. This defers likely exercise by two months. You could also roll forward and down. You could move OTM with two 87.50 puts at 2.56 each, earning an additional 0.75 per contract at the same time. This is a sensible roll because you move 2.5 points lower and still make more profit. Or you could roll forward and down a full five points, replacing the current 90 puts with September 85 puts at the same price. This moves the put five full points out, and costs you only transaction fees. A roll can also consist of two strikes. For example, you could roll one put to an 87.50 and the other to an 85, for a total net income of 0.33 (1.81 − 1.48). Both outs would then be OTM, but at two different strikes.

Another alternative is to cover a short put with a long put. For example, your July 90 puts were slightly in the money and each was worth 1.81. You could offset these with one September 87.50 long put at 2.56. This long position protects half your short put position below 87.50, which mitigates the market risk. You are still able to roll forward and away from potential exercise before the July expiration, but with the long put you give up a portion of your original premium for selling the two puts. If the price continues lower, you can roll the short puts forward while gaining profits in the September 87.50 long position. The offset between long and short puts also forms part of the put backspread.

The Put Backspread

The use of long and short puts in a single strategy is typical in the put backspread, also called the reverse put ratio spread. This is a combination of short puts and a higher number of long puts. The long puts have a lower strike. This sets up a bearish strategy with unlimited potential profits and limited risk of loss.

For example, you want to open a put backspread on Conoco-Phillips (COP). On June 15, 2012, the stock was at $54.83. You sell three July 52.50 puts, each at 0.88, and you buy five July 50 puts, each at 0.43:

Sell three July 52.50 @ 0.88 =	$264
Buy five July 50 puts @ 0.43 =	215
Net credit =	**$49**

Because the long puts outnumber the short puts, any strong downward movement below the long strike of 50 produces increasing profits. For each point you lose in the three short 52.50 puts, you gain five points in the 50 puts. Between the two strikes, with a point range of 2.5, the three higher puts set up a potential loss capped at $701 (2.50 x 3, minus the net credit of $49). If the stock price remains at or above $52.50 per share, all of the puts expire and the $49 net credit converts to a profit.

Breakeven on the downside is the number of points of difference between the two strikes. For example, this situation has 2.5 points, or $750 of potential loss on the three 52.50 puts. However, once the price falls below the 50 strike level, you gain five points of intrinsic value for each point the stock falls. So the break even is found 1 point below $50, or at $48.01 (1.5 points x 5 = $750, minus the net credit of $9, or $48.01). So the middle zone (of only 3.5 points in this example—2.5 between the strikes plus 1 point below) is the loss zone, accompanied by a fixed profit zone on the top and a growing profit zone on the bottom.

The next chapter expands on the discussions in this and the previous chapter, to introduce the collar and its variations. The collar is the options portion of the dividend-based risk-free strategy. Along with the long shares of the underlying and selection for the ex-dividend date and attractive dividends, the collar represents the foundation of the strategy. It eliminates market risk, while enabling the positioning of stock to gain monthly dividends.

CHAPTER 5

THE COLLAR: REMOVING ALL OF THE RISK

> In the stress of modern life, how little room is left for that most comfortable vanity that whispers in our ears that failures are not faults!
>
> Agnes Repplier, *Books and Men*, 1888

DO YOU NEED TO DIVERSIFY YOUR PORTFOLIO? TRADITIONAL wisdom tells you that diversification is essential in order to manage risk. However, the *collar* could contradict this traditional "rule" of investing. If you focus on ownership of shares in a company yielding exceptionally high dividends, would you place all of your capital in shares of that company? You might, except for the need for diversification. This chapter challenges this rule and demonstrates why you might not need to spread money around at all, and that it could be more profitable to put all of your eggs in one basket and then set up an ironclad protective strategy so that market risk is eliminated completely.

Options traders are always looking for that "perfect" strategy; they seek a balance between potential income and limited loss. Some strategies are designed to accomplish this, but unfortunately, they tend to be complex and demand high maintenance. The butterfly and the condor, for example, are so-called "neutral strategies" (also called "nondirectional strategies"), because they combine bullish spreads with bearish spreads, limiting both profit and risk.

The collar does the same, but has much easier features and positions. A comparison between butterflies and condors on one hand, and collars on the other, is instructive. Both limit the two sides of outcome (profit and loss), and both are designed to protect positions whether markets rise or fall. However, there are also notable differences.

All of these offsetting risk/reward strategies share similar goals, but are used to achieve different outcomes. For example, the collar by itself provides safety but limits upside movement of an underlying security; butterflies and condors are not tied to an underlying security, but rather are designed to operate without any stock positions.

The complexity of butterflies and condors (especially in comparison to the collar) also leads to another observation: the range of long and short positions opened together leads to the tendency to close portions of the overall strategy as they become profitable. This is sensible in one respect: taking profits as they develop is understandable. However, it also might lead to unintended short-side exposure. If long positions are closed because profits develop rapidly, there is always a short-side offset that is then left exposed. As long as the butterfly or condor exposed short is out of the money (OTM), it can be managed, as time decay erodes any value, leading to profitable closure of those positions as well. Traders get into trouble when they forget to track the uncovered short positions and end up being assigned because they did not take preventive steps (closing, covering, or rolling). In comparison, a collar opened *specifically* to generate exercise within a few days effectively avoids risk no matter which direction the underlying moves.

FEATURES OF THE BUTTERFLY

In developing a no-risk portfolio, the collar works where the butterfly does not. The collar is perfectly suited for this strategy, because it sets up the ability to exercise out of the position whether the underlying prices rises or falls. Either your shares are called away when your short call is exercised, or you exercise the long put and dispose of shares at the strike.

The butterfly is not as closely associated with the ownership of stock. In fact, it is designed for traders interested in profiting on options without the involvement of equity positions. The frustrating aspect of butterfly trading is in the limitations it provides. For many traders, the relatively small profits are not worth the equally limited risks. Although the butterfly provides positions that help manage, avoid, and offset exercise, it does not tie in to the potentially profitable annualized income you earn by extremely short-term stock ownership and dividend income. For that, the collar makes good sense.

The butterfly is an options-only neutral strategy that combines a bull spread and a bear spread on the same underlying and expiration, and using three separate strikes. It can be built using either calls or puts. The *long call butterfly* consists of the following positions:

- One long in the money (ITM) call
- Two short at the money (ATM) calls
- One long OTM call

The ITM call and one of the short ATM calls is a bull spread; the other short ATM call and the long OTM call are the bear spread. You would create a long call butterfly when you believed the underlying was not likely to move very many points by expiration (or that exceptionally high time value in the short positions will enable you to close them profitably). For example, you could create a long call butterfly spread on Walt Disney (DIS) with the following options:

Long call butterfly	
One long ITM Oct 48 call	−2.24
Two short ATM Oct 47 calls @2.79	5.58
One long OTM Oct 46 call	−3.40
Net debit	**−0.06**

This is practically a zero-credit/debit initial outlay before transaction costs. The outcome by expiration at various price levels of the underlying is shown in table 5.1.

Table 5.1 Outcome by expiration

Price	Long October 48	2 Short October 47	Long 46	Net
43	−2.24	5.58	−3.40	−0.06
44	−2.24	5.58	−3.40	−0.06
45	−2.24	5.58	−3.40	−0.06
46	−2.24	5.58	−3.40	−0.06
47	−2.24	5.58	−2.40	.94
48	−2.24	3.58	−1.40	.94
49	−1.24	1.58	−.40	−0.06
50	−.24	−.42	.60	−0.06
51	.76	−2.42	1.60	−0.06
52	1.76	−4.42	2.60	−0.06

Source: Generated by author.

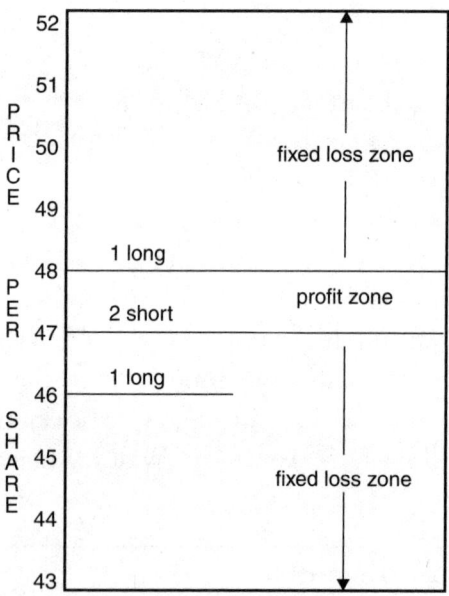

Figure 5.1 Long call butterfly, Disney (DIS)
Source: Figure created by author from raw numerical data.

The very limited profit zone spans only two points, and the loss zones above and below are both fixed. This outcome is summarized in figure 5.1.

The profit potential of this butterfly is extremely limited, and given the recent trend in price for Disney, the value of entering the position is questionable, as shown in figure 5.2.

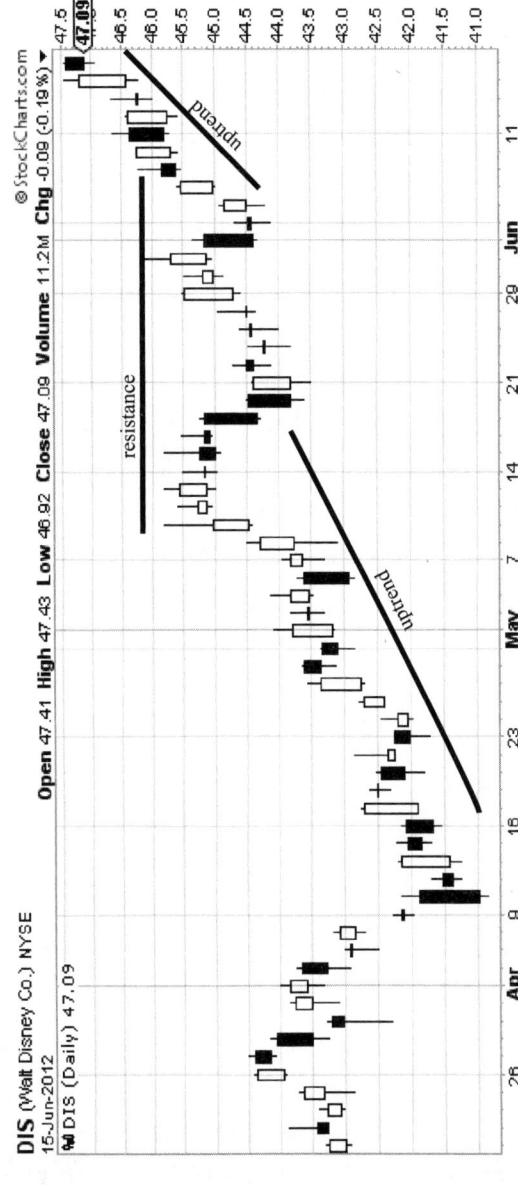

Figure 5.2 Long call butterfly
Source: StockCharts.com.

The uptrend was strong on this chart and even broke through the resistance level. While this might correct and retreat, it could also keep moving in the established uptrend. So in this case, the long call butterfly might not be advantageous.

Three additional strategies are also possible: the short call, long put, and short put. All contain similar limitations, with fixed profit and loss zones. An example of the short call butterfly would be a reversal of the previous example, and creation of a middle-loss zone with fixed profit zones above and below:

Short call butterfly	
One short ITM Oct 48 call	2.24
Two long ATM Oct 47 calls @2.79	−5.58
One short OTM Oct 46 call	3.40
Net credit	**0.06**

Puts also can be used to create butterflies:

Long put butterfly	
One long ITM Oct 48 put	−3.15
Two short ATM Oct 47 puts @2.66	5.32
One long OTM Oct 46 put	−2.27
Net debit	**−0.10**
Short put call butterfly	
One short ITM Oct 48 put	3.15
Two long ATM Oct 47 put @2.66	−5.32
One short OTM Oct 46 put	2.27
Net debit	**−0.10**

In each of these examples, the close proximity of the strikes limits the middle zones. If these were stretched out to more distance in-between, the middle zones would also expand. The larger the gap, the bigger the middle zone. So traders can alter the butterfly to create differing levels of potential profit or risk based on the selection of strikes above and below the ATM strike. They can even offset unevenly, for example, picking a one-strike difference below but a five-point strike difference above. This tends to favor price movement in one direction over the other (the direction depending on whether the butterfly consists of calls or puts, and is set up as long or short).

To a degree, the butterfly is a perfect hedging instrument because it is adjustable and can be set based on perceptions about the market and price direction. However, no matter how it is built, risk is limited but so is potential profit. This can be stretched as well by picking strikes many more points above and/or below the ATM level. But compared to the collar as a hedge, the butterfly is complex to a flaw. For the risk-free strategies introduced in coming chapters, the collar is preferred over the butterfly due to its simplicity and singular position in short calls and long puts.

A Related Strategy: The Condor

Another neutral (or, nondirectional) strategy is the condor. Like the butterfly in its various configurations, the condor is complex and provides a very limited potential profit and risk. It works best in situations where the underlying security has little volatility.

It is made up of four strikes: a long condor contains one short ITM call, one long lower-strike ITM call, one short OTM call, and one long higher-strike OTM call. For example, Juniper Networks (JNPR) closed on June 18, 2012, at $16.35 per share. A

One short August 18 call	0.54
One long August 17 call	− 0.89
One short August 14 call	2.78
One long August 15 call	−2.02
Net credit	**0.41**

long call condor could consist of the following:

This combination of long and short ITM and OTM positions will create middle-zone offsets to a higher strikes and lower strikes (see table 5.2).

Table 5.2 Profit and loss zones

Price	Short 18 call	Long 17 call	Short 14 Call	Long 15 call	net
12	0.54	−0.89	2.78	−2.02	0.41
13	0.54	−0.89	2.78	−2.02	0.41
14	0.54	−0.89	2.78	−2.02	0.41
15	0.54	−0.89	1.78	−2.02	−0.59
16	0.54	−0.89	0.78	−1.02	−0.59
17	0.54	−0.89	−0.22	−0.02	−0.59
18	0.54	0.11	−1.22	0.98	0.41
19	−0.46	1.11	−2.22	1.98	0.41
20	−1.46	2.11	−3.22	2.98	0.41
21	−2.46	3.11	−4.22	3.98	0.41

Source: Generated by author.

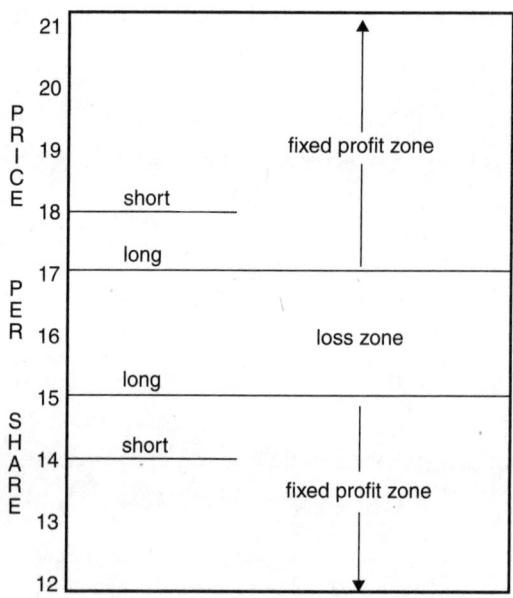

Figure 5.3 Long call condor, Juniper Networks (JNPR)
Source: Figure created by author from raw numerical data.

These profit and loss zones are summarized in figure 5.3.

This demonstrates the drawback to the condor. In this example, a very narrow three-point loss range is offset by fixed minimal profit zones above and below. Considering the very small profit, the strategy is of very limited value. Employing wider strike increments increases the middle zone, and in some cases will also increase both maximum losses and profits.

This is converted to a short condor by reversing the long and short positions. In that case, the three-point middle zone would represent the fixed profit, and the upper and lower zones would represent maximum losses. Condors can also be constructed using puts with the same variation and combined long and short positions.

The iron condor has become a popular strategy among options traders. It is a combination of two other positions, a bull put spread and a bear call spread. This offset limits the potential profit as well as risk, but it varies from the long or short condor because it involves both calls and puts on the same underlying and at the same strike.

For example, an iron condor on JNPR could consist of:

One short August 15 put	0.65
One long August 14 put	−0.41
One short August 18 call	0.54
One long August 17 call	−0.89
Net debit	**0.11**

This strategy, like other condors and also like butterflies, restricts both profit and loss, but involves several different calls and puts. It is likely that a similar or even better outcome would be possible with a simple spread or, if the underlying were also held, with a basic collar. And the fewer contracts involved, the lower transaction costs will be as well.

THE SIMPLICITY OF THE COLLAR, A DEFENSIVE STRATEGY

The many variations of spreads may be overly complex and potentially expensive to enter and exit. In comparison, the collar (also called a hedge wrapper) is a defensive strategy with three parts: 100 shares of the underlying, one OTM short call, and one OTM long put.

The cost of the long put is mostly or completely offset by the premium received from selling the call. The purpose of the collar is to cap downside risks for no cost or for very little cost. At the same time, you have to be willing to give up potential profits above the strike of the short call. So it makes sense when you hold appreciated stock and you would be willing to sell at the call's strike, but you would prefer not to sell shares. Your concern for losing paper profits is addressed by the long put.

For example, you bought 100 shares of Microsoft (MSFT) two years ago in the low 20s. Today, the stock is priced above $30 per share. As of June 19, 2012, it was valued at $30.70. You are able to create a collar using either the August or September contracts. Ideally, both contracts should OTM, and the pricing of MSFT is well situated for this:

August
  31 call = 0.93,
  30 put = 0.91,
  Net debit before transaction fees: 0.02.
September
  31 call = 1.16,
  30 put = 1.18,
  Net debit before transaction fees: 0.02.

In both of these cases, the upside yield is fixed at $31. If the price moves above this price, the short call will be exercised. This can be avoided by closing the call or rolling forward. The downside is also fixed at $30 per share. If the underlying price moves below that level, the long put gains intrinsic value. It can be closed at a profit or exercised, and 100 shares of stock disposed of at $30 per share.

Another example: Altria (MO) was valued at $33.92 on June 19. A collar could be established using the August or September contracts:

August
  34 call = 0.69,

33 put = 0.42,
Net credit before transaction fees: 0.27.
September
34 call = 0.84,
33 put = 0.76,
Net credit before transaction fees: 0.08.

The question concerning collars is logical: If you are worried about the possibility of a downward turn, why not just sell appreciated stock? In the case of MO, dividend yield at the time these trades were available was 4.84%. So the no-cost collar addresses the concern about downside risk, while maintaining stock ownership in order to earn the dividend. At a threat of exercise, the position can be closed or rolled, and a trader has to be willing to get assigned, especially if ITM immediately before the ex-dividend date (at the time of the MO analysis, the next ex-dividend was July 10). If nothing else, a trader would prefer to maintain ownership at least until the ex-dividend date.

The timing of dividend yield versus management of market risk is central to the no-risk portfolio. This uses collars to move in and out of equity positions timed to earn the dividend. However, without the collar, traders face the same market risks as those faced by all stock investors: the stock value may decline, in which case the intended short-term profits would be offset by paper losses. The great danger in a stock-only timing strategy is ending up with a portfolio full of depreciated stocks. The collar is a powerful management tool in situations where you want to protect against market risk while being willing to accept exercise, and if you are able to maintain that balance, you will also earn the dividend without having shares called away.

A collar is especially worth considering in cases where you have little or no diversification in your portfolio. Although the traditional wisdom tells you to always diversify, collars might make this unnecessary. Consider once again the case of Altria (MO). With a dividend yield of 4.84%, why not invest all of your equity in that one stock?

The traditional answer is: The lack of diversification is reckless, and the market risk for any one stock is too high.

The use of collars dispels this entirely, because market risk below the put's strike is entirely eliminated. If the stock price falls below the put's strike, you can exercise the put and dispose of shares at the fixed price, or you can keep shares and offset the loss in stock by selling the put. One collar per 100 shares sets the market risk firmly. If you are interested in the 4.84% yield on your capital and you do not care as much about potential capital gains, the collar makes perfect sense. There is no need for diversification if you focus strictly on dividend yield. Without market risk, this is possible with the simplicity of the collar. Because it costs nothing when properly selected, even a long-term collar makes sense.

For example, an Altria (MO) January 2013 collar could consist of:

January, 2013
   34 call = 1.36,
   33 put = 1.68,
   Net debit before transaction fees: 0.32.

In this case, dividends would be earned in July, October, and January. Throughout this entire period, the downside risk is managed with the long put, and the upside profit is capped with the short call (and exercise can be avoided by rolling forward). The net cost of this long-term collar is only $32 plus fees, coming out to an estimated total cost under $50 for the collar.

This is an example of how options can be used to cap portfolio risks while ensuring maximum income. Most investors will be very happy with a portfolio yield of 4.84% given the elimination of what is otherwise an unknown level of market risk. In this example, that risk exists anywhere below $30 per share. With the collar, the downside risk is about 1.4 point (92 cents between the price of the option and the put's strike, plus the net cost of the collar after transaction costs). Given the high yield and the ability to roll to avoid exercise on the upside, this very small risk is acceptable for most situations. For example, MO's dividend was 41 cents per quarter, so the three periods that earn dividends are approximately equal to this worst-case outcome.

Because collars present an example of why diversification is not always necessary within a portfolio, they offer an interesting and powerful alternative to how portfolio management actually works. The old-style diversification required spreading capital among equities with dissimilar risk attributes, market cycles, and competitive scenarios, and beyond this, also required allocation among different markets (equities, debt, real estate). The collar may be viewed as a demonstrable way to create high yield in an undiversified portfolio with little or no market risk. In the example above, MO's dividend yield offset the maximum loss in the event of a downward slide. Even this does not have to be realized. For example, instead of selling shares at a net 1.4-point loss, the put itself can be sold and profits applied to offset the loss of stock value. The short call then expires as worthless, and you can create a new collar based on the revised net basis in stock. This can be continued indefinitely, with any price decline or mostly or completely offset by increased value in the put, and with the expiration and replacement of collars with new strikes and new expirations.

Even when you hold a diversified portfolio, a collar protects your position in times of high volatility in the market. Rather than needing to sell stock to avoid market risk, the collar allows you to create a position that combines a "contingent sale" with little or no cost. The contingency occurs if the price moves too far in either direction. On the upside, your stock is called away when the call is assigned; on the downside, you exercise your put to sell stock at the fixed strike.

The contingent sale is a wise move when the market is volatile, but you would prefer to hold stock for the long term. The market volatility might be cyclical, but your concern is a valid one: If the stock price declines, how long will it take to recover? The collar does away with this concern, because price decline is offset when you exercise your long put. With a strike of 33, even if the price declines 50% or 75%, your sales price will always be $33 per share as long as the put is open, no matter how much volatility or price decline the stock experiences.

If market volatility takes the underlying price down, holding a long-term put as part of a collar provides stability to your portfolio. The put can be exercised or closed at any time prior to expiration. Meanwhile, the underlying price might rebound and move into the original range or even higher. In this case, the collar, which costs little or nothing, provides a form of cost-free insurance to your position—again demonstrating that you do not need diversification if risks are managed and eliminated with no-cost or low-cost options strategies. The collar is such a strategy, and it is the structure for the dividend-based strategy developed throughout this book.

The Collar as a "Passive" Form of Risk Management

The premise behind using options to eliminate risk and protect your portfolio is by no means revolutionary or unique. However, conventional wisdom tells you to diversify, pick value investments, hold for the long term, and know when to cut losses. There is another way, based on the skilled use of options strategies that avoids losses rather than accepting them.

Why would any investor plan for loss mitigation, when it is possible to eliminate all or most of the inherent market risks that come with the territory? The reason is that so many investors hold unrealistic views of the market. These include three widely held beliefs, all of which are false:

1. *The entry point is the zero price.* Many investors buy shares of stock and other equities and fall into the mistaken belief that their price represents a starting point, or the "zero price." For example, if you buy 100 shares at $35 per share, the price of $35 is the floor, and the price is expected to rise above that level. So if and when prices fall below this assumed "zero price," it is an unexpected surprise. The truth is, the price of any security is part of an ongoing

struggle between buyers and sellers to find the current and ever-changing fair price. That is the price where buyers and sellers can meet, or the highest price that buyers are willing to pay, versus the lowest price that sellers are willing to accept. These change constantly, and where they intersect, trades take place. There are an unknown number of causes and effects that change these prices, but the entry price an investor pays is not a factor in determining whether a stock's price rises or falls.

2. *Timing price and trend cycles are easy with the right indicators.* The belief holds that with the right indicators, you can effectively time the market and enter at the lower, hold, and then exit at the high. It all sounds simple, but it is not that easy. You need to make a distinction between intermediate and long-term trend cycles, which can be studied and understood. What is more mysterious is how long trends last. However, price movement in the short term is likely to be very chaotic and unpredictable. The chaos of short-term price changes troubles investors and traders who want to make a fast profit and get out quickly. That fast profit could end up being a fast loss, and the chances of loss are at least as good as the chances of gain.

3. *Moving in and out of positions harms the market and other investors.* Moving in and out of positions does absolutely no damage to the markets or to other investors. You will recall from the first chapter that over time, the average holding period of stocks has been declining from what once was years to more recent averages in months, even mere weeks. The implication is that this somehow harms the markets, but how? The number of shares available to trade is going to be held or traded at a price both sides agree upon. If shares trade every few weeks, it does not make any real difference in how markets operate, except that brokerage commissions increase on the higher volume of trading. The Internet and discount brokerage services have made it possible and economically feasible to trade actively. But there is no evidence that a higher volume of trading adversely

affects the markets or prices of stocks. This is a myth without foundation.

Options, however, can and do have a significant effect not on how stocks are priced, but on how you can control your exposure to market risks. The myths about investing and trading prevent people from recognizing the realities of the market:

1. *Reality # 1: Taking up equity positions is risky.* The entry price of equities is not a zero price but a part of an ever-evolving price level, dictated by supply and demand, and also by perceptions in the market. It is risky when done alone, because even value investments go through volatile periods of time, and these may be jarring and uncertain.
2. *Reality # 2: Cycles are recognizable, but their duration is never certain.* No one can tell how long a primary trend or intermediate trend is going to last. The closely related economic cycle is equally unpredictable. In spite of what you hear from financial journalists, economists, politicians, and other market "experts," the simple truth is that no one knows or can predict how the markets move, or why.
3. *Reality # 3: High-frequency trading by individuals has no adverse affect on markets or on prices.* The modern reality is that people hold onto securities for a shorter period of time than in the past. The causes are many, but the Internet, fast access to free information, discount brokerage, and many other changes have brought this about. Whether it is viewed as a good or a bad trend, it is the reality. Holding securities for a very short period of time does no damage to others. As long as you can find a buyer to sell your shares to and you agree on the price, no harm results.

Working with strategies like collars does reduce downside risk (while limiting upside profit at the same time). In this respect, collars turn an active portfolio with great market risk into a passive portfolio with little or no risk. This is why with the proper construction and control of a portfolio that protects long stock with collars, you do not need diversification, asset allocation, or some secret formula for beating the market. You beat the market by creating no-cost or low-cost strategies that eliminate risk.

Why is this approach considered passive? Think about a very volatile stock. You buy shares expecting prices to rise. But they fall, so you cut your losses and get out. Then the price rebounds, and you see that you need to get back in. You buy shares, but again, the price falls. And again, you become fearful and you sell. In other words, you follow the advice: Buy *high*, sell *low*. This is a very poor investment strategy.

Why does it happen to so many investors? The answer is clear: They are trying to actively manage their portfolio in an environment that is not manageable. That is a stark reality, but anyone who has been in and out of the market knows how difficult it is to earn profits consistently, without offsetting them with equal or bigger losses. The process of active management is truly a gamble, and most individuals cannot consistently beat the markets.

The stocks-only timing strategy of market investing is a very poor model because it is chaotic and random in the short term. This is why the common response to short-term trading is to advise a buy-and-hold strategy. But even this is poor as a model. What if you had put a buy-and-hold strategy into place many years ago and bought several of the most highly esteemed companies, such as General Motors, Eastman Kodak, Polaroid, Sears, or Citibank? All of these "blue chip" investments would have been disastrous in a buy-and-hold portfolio.

In comparison, setting up stocks and protecting them with collars eliminates downside risk after the put's strike has passed. The limits on upside profit potential trouble many investors, but there are mitigating reasons why this is not a big concern:

1. You can roll out of the current strike/expiration and into a later one.
2. You can close calls at a profit to avoid exercise, and then replace it later with another, higher-strike call.

3. If you focus on exceptional high-dividend stocks, the majority of profits in your portfolio will come not from option premiums or capital gains, but from dividends. And there are hundreds of listed companies yielding 4% or more—not a bad yield in any portfolio. So if you focus on dividends and stop trying to actively manage your portfolio, the collar begins to look more and more attractive.

The Collar Ladder

For many investors who open a collar, the stock price rises and presents a dilemma. The original purpose of the collar is to protect against downside risk, and in exchange to be willing to accept the exposure to possible exercise. By doing so, the collar is made into a no-cost or low-cost strategy. Risk is eliminated beyond those downside strikes. This is a beneficial situation, especially when dividend yield is also high on the underlying. But what if the underlying price rises?

In this situation, you can use the rolling collar ladder to move both options forward.

The put's strike is fixed, and of course, it would be desirable to roll that long option into a later-expiring, higher-strike option. That has the effect of fixing the strike at a higher level, so that in the event that the underlying price declines, if you exercise the put, you receive a higher payment for the 100 shares. However, to move the put requires incurring an expense. This is where the rolling collar ladder comes into play.

The goal of this is to roll the call forward in order to move the strike upward, and at the same time, use the additional income from the call strike to also move the put forward to a higher strike. This improves both sides of the collar. The increased strike of the short call represents potential exercise at a higher price. The increased strike of the long put does the same. If you end up exercising the put, your capital gain will also be higher. This delays the time the collar is left open, but that is desirable as long as the purpose of the collar is to continue earning better than average dividends while managing and eliminating market risk.

For example, Con Agra (CAG) yielded 3.80% dividend as of June 2012. You bought 100 shares last August and paid approximately $10 per share. The stock closed on June 21 at $25.26. You had originally created a collar based on a short August 25 call and a long August 24 put. Today, those contracts are valued at 0.70 (call) and 0.30 (put). You want to roll these forward to higher strikes, extending your ownership of CAG and continuing the dividend.

The first step in the roll is to close the current positions:

August 25 call, buy to close	−0.70
August 25 put, sell to close	0.30
Net cost	**−0.40**

Next, replace this with later-expiring, higher-strike positions:

January 2014 27 call, sell to open	1.10
December 25 put, buy to open	−1.25
Net cost	**−0.15**

Both the short call and the long put were rolled into higher strikes. The call moved up two points and the put moved up one point. The overall net cost is 0.55 (debit on closing the current positions, added to debit for opening the new positions). Offsetting this is the gain in potential strikes, representing $200 if the short call is assigned, and $100 additional if you exercise your long put. In either outcome, you accomplish two benefits: First, the risk protection is extended on both sides, and second, in the event of exercise, the net outcome is improved even after the debit is paid. All of these outcomes are prior to transaction costs, so the overall cost has to be weighed against the benefit of receiving a higher-than-average dividend in the future.

The other point about this roll to keep in mind is the disparity between the two sides of the collar. This roll converts the position into a calendar spread, with the put expiring in December 2012 (6 months from execution date), and the short call expiring in January 2014 (19 months from execution). There is a potential problem in this disparity, especially if the long put expires as worthless, meaning the position continues without the downside protection unless additional steps are taken. At the point of the put's expiration (meaning the price of the underlying would be above $25 per share, the put's strike), the overall position is profitable based on the original price paid of $18 per share.

The choices at this point are to roll the put once again; let it expire and accept the market risk; close both positions and replace with a new collar; or close both positions and sell the underlying. All of these outcomes end up at a net profit, either realized or on paper. If the underlying is retained, those paper profits can be protected indefinitely by replacing one or both sides of the collar.

If the roll opens up a possible outcome that is not considered desirable, the August call and put can just be left in place and (1) allowed to expire) or (2) closed closer to expiration and then replaced with a new collar. The consideration of rolling or waiting out expiration should be based on paper profits, volatility, and the differences between the values of calls and puts at the most desirable strikes (based on current price). The point of the collar ladder roll is to extend ownership and downside protection, in order to continue receiving dividends, and at the same time, to increase the exercise price of both the call and the put with little or no net cost.

THE OTM STRUCTURE OF THE COLLAR

Why are collars best structured OTM? The desirability of this is found in the relatively low premium and the likelihood that the net cost will be small, or even result in a net credit. However, it would be more desirable, when possible, to create a collar with an OTM call and an ATM or ITM put. The desirability of this is found in the potential exercise level of the put at a strike above the current market value of the underlying. This is likely to require a calendar-spread version of the collar.

For example, Eli Lilly (LLY) was worth $41.89 on June 22, 2012. At that moment, a collar could be created, combining an August 42 call at 1.77 and an August put at 1.65. The net credit before transaction costs was 0.12.

This consists of an OTM call (by 1.11 points) and an ATM put (actually 0.11 OTM). However, the net cost is close to zero even with transaction fees. This position provides complete market-risk elimination below the $43 per share level (if you calculate the cost of opening the collar at about $50 round trip, the actual level is about $42.60 on the downside). On the upside, exercise produces a $111 net profit.

This calendar-spread variety of the collar leaves an expired put (August) with a continuing covered call until October. At this point, the put can be replaced at a net cost, or you can live with the market risk for two months and then close the short call or let it expire, and then set up a new collar. Why go through this when an original collar might have worked to protect against downside risk without the roll? It would be desirable, because LLY yielded 4.69% dividend. The premise here is that it is worth holding onto shares as long as possible to continue earning an exceptional level of dividend.

When this strategy is compared to the same-expiration collar, the disparity of expirations clearly presents a problem. Market risk returns as soon as the put is closed or expires. This is why extending with different strikes works, but only if exercise occurs at a level ensuring net profits, whether the short call is assigned after a price increase, or you decide to exercise or close your long put after a price decline.

Alternatives to Achieve the Same Risk Management

The collar is a desirable strategy when the right elements are present. These are higher-than-average dividend yield, the original basis in the underlying below both the call and put strikes, and net low-cost or no-cost options positions. Exercise in these cases can be accepted at a profit, or rolled forward to extend the period of no-risk ownership.

A very similar benefit is accomplished with another strategy: the synthetic stock position. This is the use of options to set up a no-cost or low-cost strategy that duplicates price movement in the underlying. It is most often described without stock ownership; however, it can also be opened while shares of the underlying security are owned.

The synthetic long-stock position consists of a long call and a short put, opened with the same strike and the same expiration. The combined price change will duplicate movement of the underlying, with the best results occurring when the underlying value increases. If the price decreases, the synthetic position loses money on the put side, but market risk is not actually protected. Because the net cost of the synthetic long-stock position is designed to mirror upward price movement, it is valuable only if you do not own shares of stock. In that case, the low-cost or no-cost strategy is the epitome of leverage. If the stock price does rise, the value of the call climbs as well, while the short put expires worthless. If the stock price falls, the risk associated with the short put is identical to the market risk of buying 100 shares. Exercise would occur at a loss. However, an important distinction demonstrates why the risk of the synthetic long stock position is less than the risk of owning shares: If the price declines and the put is at risk of exercise, it can be rolled forward to defer exercise, or it can be rolled forward and down to reduce the potential exercise price.

For example, ConocoPhillips (COP) yields 5.00%, an exceptional annual return by just about anyone's standards. However, risk-sensitive investors are fearful of the risks of long stock, so they might not be willing to buy 100 shares. An alternative is to create a synthetic long stock position. The combined options will increase in value if the stock price also rises. The synthetic position consists of a long call and a short put such as:

July 52.50 long call	−1.34
July 52.50 short put	1.36
Net credit	**0.02**

This outcome is before transaction costs. With the stock price at $52.78, the synthetic is 28 cents away from the two strikes. The benefit here is found if and when the stock price rises. Based on estimated transaction costs of $20, where does this position become profitable?

$52.78 current price minus 52.50 strike	–28
Estimated transaction costs	–20
Total cost/loss	**–48**
Current price	$52.78
Plus: combined cost/loss	0.48
Breakeven on the upside	**$53.26**

If the underlying rises above this price before the July expiration, the position begins to become profitable. If the underlying declines below $52.50 per share, the short put will be at risk of exercise. If this position is opened without also stock being owned, it presents the equivalent profit or loss potential above $52.26 or below $52.98 (strike of $52.50 plus 48 cents cost/loss). However, the synthetic long-stock strategy does not eliminate market risk; it only duplicates market risk for stock in a highly leveraged version that controls 100 shares.

The synthetic short stock position is more interesting as a device for eliminating downside risk while maintaining a high-dividend stance. This is a reversal of positions, involving a short call and a long put. If the synthetic short-stock position is entered while shares of the underlying are also held, then the market risk of the short call is covered.

For example, using the same options on ConocoPhillips (COP), a synthetic short-stock position would consist of

July 52.50 short call	1.34
July 52.50 long put	–1.36
Net debit	**–0.02**

Now the synthetic is set up to gain the greatest value if the underlying price declines. This is a low-cost strategy similar to the collar. It eliminates downside market risk beneath the net of 52.50 per share (adjusted for the estimated 48 cents of cost/loss, or a net of $52.02). The put is paid for by the short call, also at a $52.50 strike.

This strategy makes sense when (1) the dividend is exceptional, such as in the case of COP with a 5.00% yield; (2) the basis in stock is well below the breakeven near $52 per share; and (3) the net cost of the synthetic short stock is at or close to zero.

The synthetic short stock can be rolled forward to defer exercise and even to increase the potential strikes, in the same way as that of the call. The strikes and expirations can also be varied to create the combined higher strikes with desirable cost levels.

Collar Modification for Extra Price Weighting

The collar (or synthetic short stock with covered call on the short side) can be modified to increase the net credit or to reduce the net debit. This is accomplished with the acceptance of either higher market risks or higher costs, but potential outcome might justify these modifications.

The first adjustment strategy is the ratio write or variable ratio write, described in chapter 3. When the ratio approach is used in conjunction with a collar, it presents an interesting variation. The variable ratio write reduces call-exercise risk because two strikes are used. So on the upside, the short-call income is expanded with the variable strategy, and on the opposite side of the collar, the long put limits the market risk of long stock.

For example, Merck (MRK) would be a viable candidate for a dividend-based strategy. As of June 2012, the dividend yield was 4.236%, and on June 23 the stock price was $40.21. At that time a straightforward collar could have been opened with:

August short 41 call	0.63
August long 40 put	−0.91
Net debit	**−0.28**

If the intention of this collar is to reduce and cap downside risk while earning a quarterly dividend, it is marginally effective. If $40.21 was the basis in stock, exercise of the short call would produce a profit of 0.79, netted against the collar's cost of 0.28, for an overall net of 0.50. If the stock priced declined before the August expiration, the breakeven would be $39.51 (40 strike minus 0.28 cost of the collar and 0.21 loss on the stock).

The picture changes when a variable ratio write is employed as a modification of the collar. For example,

August short 41 call	0.63
August short 42 call	0.31
August long 40 put	−0.91
Net credit	**0.03**

This improves the collar by reducing the breakeven somewhat (0.21 loss on stock, minus 0.03 credit on the collar, or 0.18 before transaction costs). The higher-strike calls can be closed or rolled to avoid exercise before the calls go in the money, and this provides improved downside breakeven, with risks capped at $39.82 (40 strike, minus loss on stock of 0.21, and plus credit on the collar of 0.03). A similar collar could be set up for October, with the advantage of providing longer-term protection for about the same net cost:

October short 41 call	1.45
October short 42 call	1.04
October long 40 put	−2.39
Net credit	**0.10**

The net credit is only slightly improved, so the transaction is quite similar, with the only difference being that this provides downside protection for an additional two months.

Another example involving a variable ratio write with multiple strikes and an exceptionally high put strike can be set up on Google (GOOG). The stock value on June 23 was $569.17. Google does not pay a dividend, so this demonstrates only how a long position can get accelerated short call income with exceptional downside protection. If you owned 200 shares of Google, you could open a complex collar with the put strike *above* current market value and a full 16 points ITM, but with a net credit on the overall position. Normally a collar consists of OTM strikes, but in this case the volatility is high enough, and the premium also quite attractive for the short calls, so that the collar can be flipped. In this example, you open a variable ratio write using four short calls, but offset the downside risk on the 200 shares with two ITM strikes. The collar could consist of:

July short 570 call	1,940
July short 575 call	1,690
July short 580 call	1,470
July short 585 call	1,270
July long two 585 puts @ 28.40	–5,680
Net credit	**690**

The advantage to this variable write collar is that there is only one month to go until expiration. The four short calls are all OTM, meaning time value is quite high and will decline rapidly. If the underlying price moves up, any or all of these positions can be closed or rolled forward to avoid exercise. Only two of the four are at risk, give the 2:1 ratio write position, and with variable strikes, the net risk is far less than it would be with a single strike.

If the price declines below the put's strike of 585, the stock can be sold at a profit. The basis is $569.17, a difference of $1,583 per 100 shares, or potential profit on 200 shares of $3,166 (plus $690 for the collar net credit, a total of $3,856). You can exercise the two puts at any market price desired, and the sales price will always be $585 per share. If you want to keep the shares but the price has declined, the puts can be sold, which recognizes that the put intrinsic values will grow by one point for each point the underlying price declines.

A lot can change in one month, especially on a stock whose price moves in either direction and often by many points. However, the fact that only one month remains to expiration is a significant advantage for a variable write, because even with movement toward or into the money, rapidly declining time value provides an offset and potential net profits.

Collar Strategic Analysis—Entry and Exit

There can be several reasons for opening a collar, either on a one-to-one basis or employing a ratio write or variable ratio write to augment net credit. The premise in this book is that the collar sets up a cap on market risk while allowing you to gain from higher-than-average dividend yield.

As the Google example demonstrates, though, collars can also be used to eliminate market risk while creating exceptionally high current income from option premium. The margin requirements for that trade would be substantial, but the same strategy works on lower-priced issues as well.

You can use collars not only to create risk-free dividend income, but also to defer selling of the underlying at a profit, which would be taxed in the current year. With a collar, you set up a covered call while also preventing downside risk from eroding profits. However, this raises an entirely different risk: tax risk associated with hedging strategies. The tax rules are complex, and you could end up with an unintended short-term gain (when you expected a long-term gain) on the stock; a constructive wash sale; or the inability to deduct current-year losses until the other side of a hedge is closed in the following year. The tax rules are set up to prevent traders from taking advantage of how options can be used to control and time both profits and losses, so you need to be familiar with these rules before setting up collars with a tax motive.

A collar may be *protective*, meaning it guards against downside risk—the examples in the preceding pages have been of this type. Another kind of collar is termed *appreciating*. The protective collar is best used when you have a short-term bearish outlook, or you do not know the likely direction, but you are concerned about possible price decline and yet you would like to keep your shares. An appreciating collar is one in which the options will appreciate beyond the original net values enough to create profits in the underlying. For example, the combination of a long ATM put and a short OTM call creates a low-cost or no-cost scenario. However, if the stock price declines, you accumulate profits from the long put as long as intrinsic value offsets time decay, or if you decide to exercise the put and sell shares at the higher strike.

The appreciating collar provides downside protection, but has a distinction. It is set up not only to cap potential losses, but to also create a growing profit in the event of a price decline in the underlying. In either case, but especially so with the appreciating collar, selling a rich long-term call versus a series of short-term ATM puts can also provide protection and potential appreciation on the downside, with an overall net credit.

Analysis of net profit and loss for all types of collars is a crucial step in determining whether or not such a strategy makes sense. Given the commitment time, margin requirements, and transaction costs for strategies like the collar, a marginal profit might not be enough if it only provides downside protection but little or no profit potential.

The next chapter explores how using several different stocks based on ex-dividend cycles can help you to convert an attractive quarterly dividend into an even more attractive, double-digit annual return, with no market risk.

CHAPTER 6

ROLLING THE STOCK POSITIONS: TURNING 4% INTO 12%

> Dissatisfaction with the world in which we live and determination to realize one that shall be better, are the prevailing characteristics of the modern spirit.
> G. Lowes Dickinson, *The Greek View of Life*, 1898

THE OLD-STYLE BUY-AND-HOLD APPROACH TO INVESTING WAS based on one assumption: buying high-quality companies and holding stock for many years led to slowly evolving but consistent profits. The blue chips of the past were believed to give investors an ironclad assurance of wealth building that could not be matched elsewhere.

The modern investing environment has unraveled the markets of the past. Now, with Internet access to virtually everything about the market, you can download annual reports, analysts' opinions, and live-feed market data. This has changed the stock market and the options market in dramatic ways:

1. *Costs are much lower today than ever before.* Past transaction costs were prohibitively high, for two reasons at least. First, you had no choice but to pay someone to execute your trade manually from a hand-completed order form. Second, the process truly was expensive because executing an order was labor

intensive for everyone, including a stockbroker as well as floor personnel who were needed to execute, control, and follow up.

This lower cost has revolutionized both stock and options trading. For stocks, you can buy or sell for around $10 per trade, a small fraction of what it used to cost. So in the old days, you had to build in profits adequate to cover the round-trip transaction costs and still produce a profit. Today, you can close a position with smaller profit margins and still net out profitably. For the options market, the change in costs is even more dramatic. It is possible now to trade very actively, and a round-trip fee is usually less than one-quarter point. This makes high-activity options trading practical, and profits appear much sooner than in the past.

2. *You no longer need to rely on a broker to execute trades.* Before the advent of online brokerage services and Internet automated execution, you had to rely on a stockbroker to execute your trades. Before discount brokerage, even knowledgeable options traders had to struggle with stockbrokers who wanted discretion over a trading account and often knew too little to offer any real help. So costs were high, and by its nature, options trading should be self-directed. If you need guidance from a stockbroker to decide which trades you should execute, you probably should not be trading anyhow.

The stockbroker was necessary for another reason: access to the trading floor. Today, every trader goes through the automated system, and trades are generated with no direct contact, unless you want to pay more to speak with someone. (And if you want to exercise a long option, for example, you probably have to phone your broker and talk to someone to place the order.) In the pre-Internet days, the process was more complicated and time consuming, which of course killed the viability of many trades in fast-moving sessions. The process was:

a. A trader had to telephone or visit the broker. This meant he or she needed to make an appointment or hope the broker was available. In a high-volume trading day, with all trades entered manually, this could be difficult or impossible.

b. The trader placed the trade, and the broker confirmed its terms.

c. The broker phoned the exchange or, in the more "advanced" version, placed a trade on a Quotron machine. [1]
  d. The person who executed the trade advised the broker, electronically or by telephone, about execution and price.
  e. The broker phoned the customer, often well after execution and often after the close of the day's session.
3. *You can perform your own analysis with a mouse click.* Traders used to rely on brokers in an additional way: for research and recommendations. A stockbroker, whose main function was to execute trades, relied on the other side of the brokerage firm, the research department. Their recommendations often were tied to the underwriting activity for which the firm was responsible, institutionalizing a permanent conflict of interest. Today, you can discover your own opportunities online for little or no cost. Setting criteria and finding candidates is so "mainstream" today that relying on a brokerage firm for guidance and trading ideas is obsolete for many traders, and especially for those employing options.

Today, finding appropriate stocks for your portfolio is a matter of risk analysis, application of basic principles (fundamental analysis, diversification, sector selection, cyclical timing, and an individual company's competitive position, for example). Aside from this, investors check historical volatility in stock selection.

Dividend collars come in two forms. First is the very short-term one in which the collar is opened before the ex-dividend date and closed afterward, to then be replaced with another whose ex-dividend date occurs the following month. This version creates consistent double-digit returns, but requires a great deal of research and analysis.

The second version is useful when positions in your portfolio have increased in value. You face the dilemma of either seeing how to take profits, or holding on to high-quality companies. If you sell, you have to figure out where to reinvest; furthermore, selling is a problem because it creates a taxable event, and why sell a high-quality investment? If you hold on to shares, you face the risk of a price reversal. The dividend collar in this case allows you to eliminate all market risks while capping maximum capital gains, in exchange for being able to keep shares and continue earning dividends.

Both methods are practical and work well. The first approach earns double-digit returns without market risk; the second ensures continued better-than-average dividend yield and also eliminates market risk. The decision to use one or the other is personal, and requires making a decision between a profitable but high-maintenance strategy and a consistent, risk-free method of managing your portfolio as part of a long-term investment program.

IDENTIFYING APPROPRIATE HISTORICAL VOLATILITY LEVELS

Historical volatility refers to the price volatility of the underlying security. If the price trend is small (meaning the breadth of trading or the distance between resistance and support), the stock exhibits low historical volatility. However, scaling may affect how you judge this. The breadth of trading should be reviewed in consideration of the average stock price during the same period.

For example, Google's trading range over a three-month period covered a breadth of 40 points. The stock price closed at $571.48, as shown in figure 6.1.

The volatility can be measured by dividing the price by the point range:

$571.48 ÷ 40 = 14.3.

In comparison, Yahoo's trading range covered only 1.2 points, and the price on the three-month chart ended up at $15.61. Applying the same volatility measurement:

$15.61 ÷ 1.2 = 13.0.

The first impression of this is that Google's historical volatility is much great than Yahoo's, because it covers a range of 40 points. However, while Yahoo's breadth was only 1.2 points, it was nearly as volatile as Google.

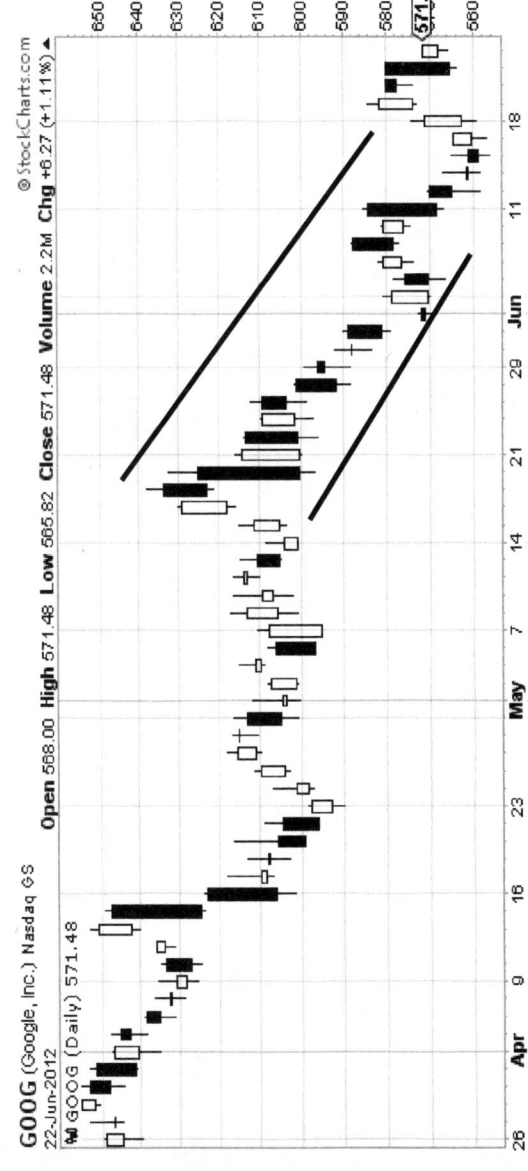

Figure 6.1 Historical volatility—40-point trading range
Source: StockCharts.com.

This "volatility factor" is useful only in making comparisons between different issues. The actual statistical calculation of historical volatility is far more complex and is focused on individual stocks and how their volatility level evolves over time. The purpose of this exercise is only to demonstrate how the breadth of trading cannot be universally applied; it has to be based on a comparison between the price breadth and the price level. So a stock selling at $595 per share compared to one selling at $15 should expect to have much different volatility levels. Google's price level is 40 times greater than Yahoo's, so a much wider trading range makes sense.

What is "appropriate" in the selection of a company and its stock? Historical volatility does not include a set universal standard of market risk, nor a limitation on how much price breadth equals "safe" or "risky." To identify historical volatility, one method is to rely on the strength of resistance and support within the current trading range. However, while this will provide a realistic look back at trading trends, it provides no assurance of future price action. Some of today's low-volatility stocks might become very high volatility (high risk) in the future, due to a variety of causes.

For example, Wal-Mart (WMT) exhibited an evolving trading range over six months, as figures 6.2 and 6.3 reveal.

In this example, the historically low-breadth trading in Wal-Mart moved from a 2-point average breadth, to a 2–5 point, and then to an 8-point range. Given the historical breadth of trading, which had been consistently set at a 2-point range for the past three years, the price was likely to settle down into a smaller trading range, but this makes the point that very little remains unchanged forever.

Just because price levels are rising or falling, that does not signal that volatility is changing. The breadth of trading can remain the same over time even as price ranges rise or fall. One symptom of this is the flip between resistance and support, or between support and resistance.

For example, Deere (DE) demonstrated over three months how a 5-point trading range remained intact even while the range price levels declined (figure 6.4). Previous support became new resistance.

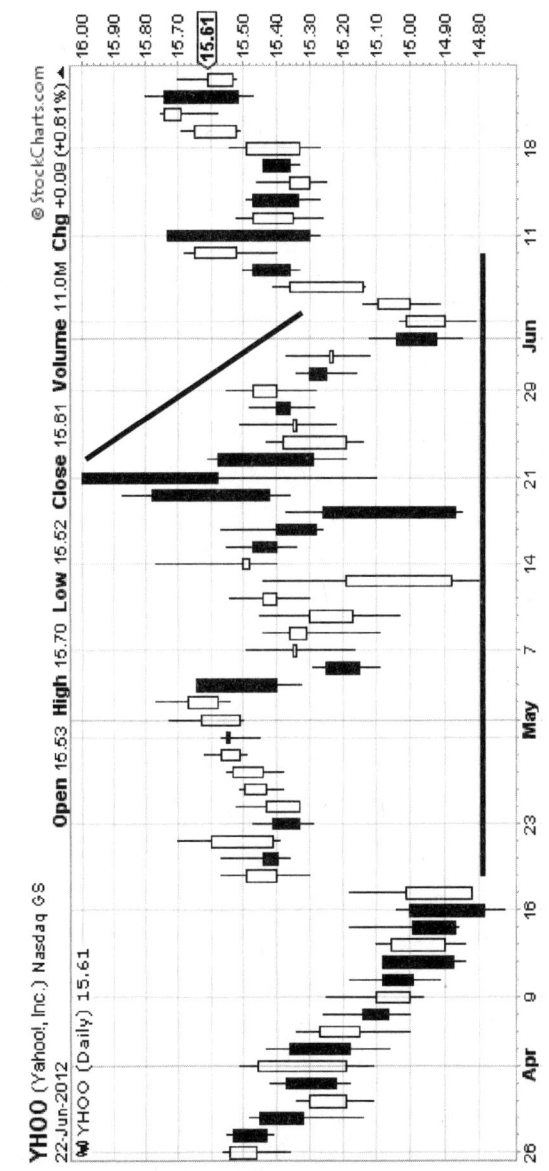

Figure 6.2 Historical volatility—1.2-point trading range
Source: StockCharts.com.

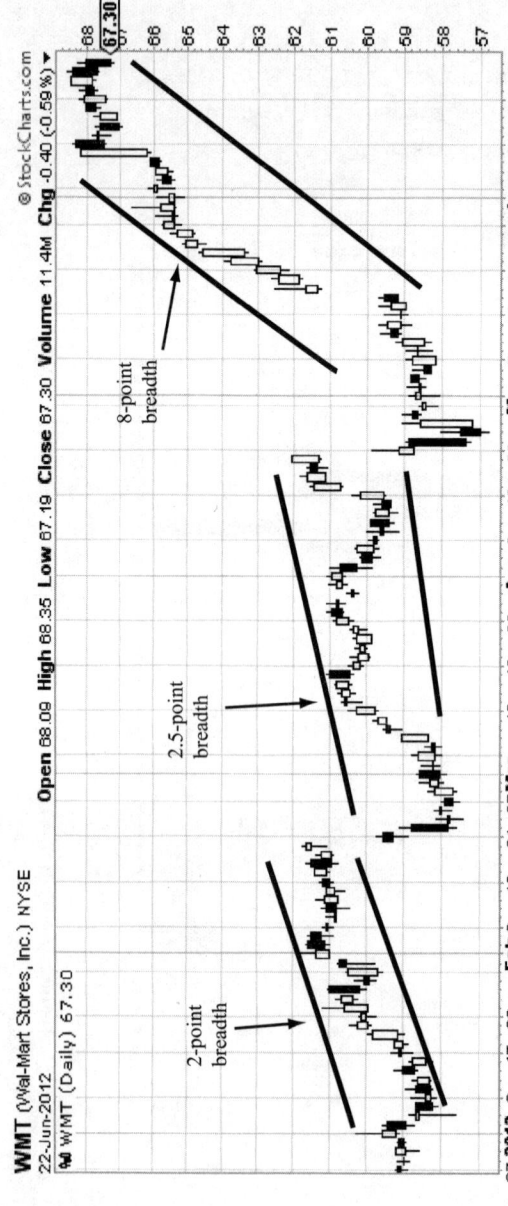

Figure 6.3 Evolving price volatility
Source: StockCharts.com.

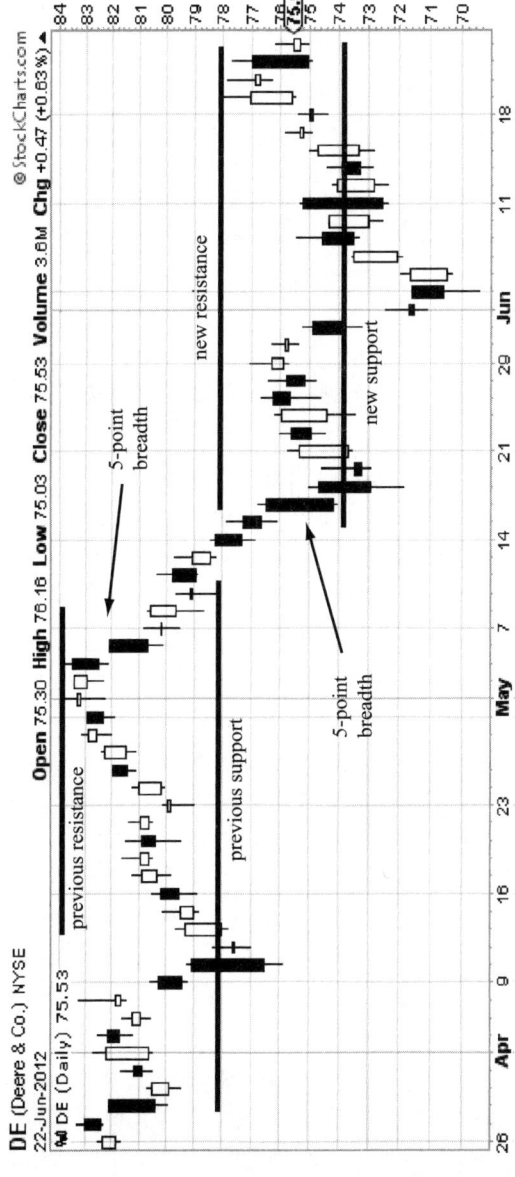

Figure 6.4 Trading range flip
Source: StockCharts.com.

Although the price levels are unpredictable in a volatile market, it is reasonable to assume that the historical breadth of trading (one version of price volatility) has remained at about five points, and as a result, estimates of future breadth are likely to be within the same range.

More Volatility Tests: Long-Term Fundamental Volatility

Historical volatility, whether revealed through a statistical formula or through breadth of trading analysis, relates specifically to price. This is important to options traders, of course, who will want to compare historical volatility to options' implied volatility. The study of historical volatility is a technical method for picking stocks based on varying levels of risk found in price trends. However, the same risk level can be measured with a different method, that of testing fundamental volatility.

This refers to the reliability of fundamental trends, notably revenues; earnings, net return and earnings per share; and dividend per share. If your ability to reasonably estimate the direction of a trend, then it is equally reasonable to assume you can rely on that trend as part of your fundamental analysis. However, if these criteria are erratic and cannot be forecast forward, then the high fundamental volatility makes it impossible to estimate future growth potential for that company.

Revenue analysis involves tracking a long-term trend. You expect revenues to rise in a thriving company. If the revenue record is falling or erratic, it indicates declining growth and falling competitive edge, and it is also a sign of weak economic times.

For example, a comparison of a ten-year record between 3M (MMM) and J.C. Penney demonstrates how different track records of revenue reveal a company's strength or weakness (figure 6.5).

MMM's ten-year record was steady and consistent. On the basis of revenue growth, revenues were low-volatility. In comparison, J.C. Penney's revenue history appeared to be falling lower on average, even without the huge downward spike in the first year

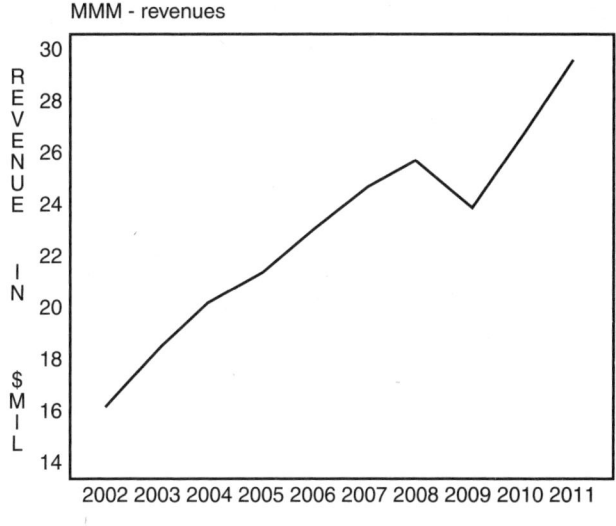

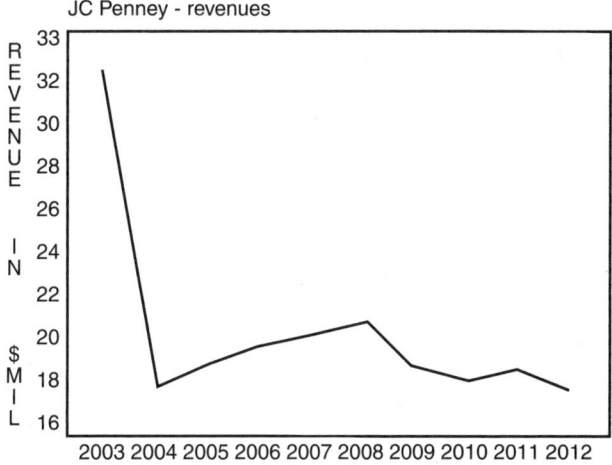

Figure 6.5   MMM—revenues
Source: S&P Stock Reports.

of the ten-year trend. This is a weaker and a more volatile fundamental record.

The graphs for these two companies are vastly different. Although they are not in the same market sector, the point is valid: If you are looking solely at the revenue history of a company—in spite of a specific weakness throughout one industry—then analysis and comparison of revenues makes perfect sense.

Earnings, Net Return and *Earnings per share* analysis is not quite the same as tracking revenue. While revenue can be expected to continue rising year after year, earnings might track on a dollar basis but net return might not. It is not realistic to expect net return to grow without limits, and in most industries, accomplishing a level net return in all kinds of markets is considered successful.

Two trends to look out for in stock selection: First, if revenue and earnings are rising but net return is declining, it is a negative indicator. It means that management is not exercising adequate internal controls, or is allowing certain types of costs or expenses to rise in relation to revenue, or that management is paying itself bonuses based on growing revenues (but in excess of the rate of growth). In some situations, rising revenues could indicate movement into a new market where the expected net return is not as high; acquisitions could have the same effect. So you need to study the underlying causes of declining net return. If there have been no expansions into new markets or acquisition of new companies, then declining net return is troubling.

Second, the net return should be expected to remain consistent whether revenues are rising, falling, or flat. Revenues do not have to rise every year, but as a test of fundamental volatility, a steady record of growth (meaning rising earnings dollars and at the very least, a consistent net return) is a reasonable expectation.

A comparison of earnings between MMM and J.C. Penney makes this point. Figure 6.6 compares the dollar value of earnings.

While the differences in these two charts are obvious, one factor worth study is the earnings for J.C. Penney relative to their revenues. The previous chart showed that other than the first year in the ten-year trend, JCP's revenues were flat. However, their earnings were erratic and declined steeply in the most recent years. This is a signal that management is not managing costs and expenses at all well, and that the relationship is on the decline.

Another method for comparison is based on net return and earnings-per share (EPS). Figure 6.7 shows the comparison between MMM and J.C. Penney for both of these trends.

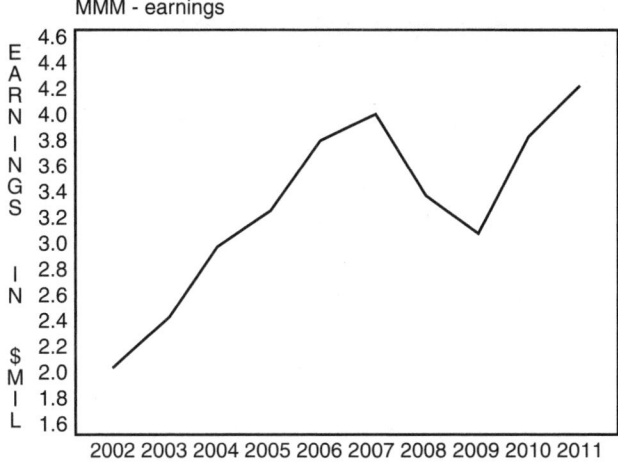

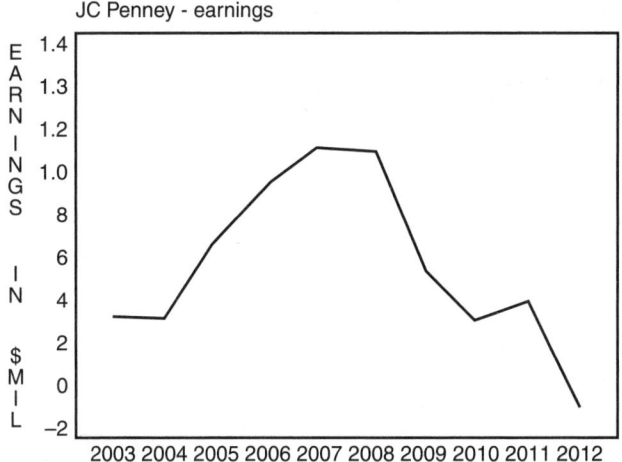

Figure 6.6 Earnings trends
Source: S&P Stock Reports.

Net return and EPS track fairly closely for both companies. In fact, this is expected in all situations except when additional shares of common stock are issued (or retired). That distorts the historical outcome, of course. This similar curve in both organizations confirms the accuracy of the net return analysis. The most important disparity is found in the J.C. Penny earnings, net return, and EPS, all of which were highly volatile—versus the flat revenues during the same ten-year period.

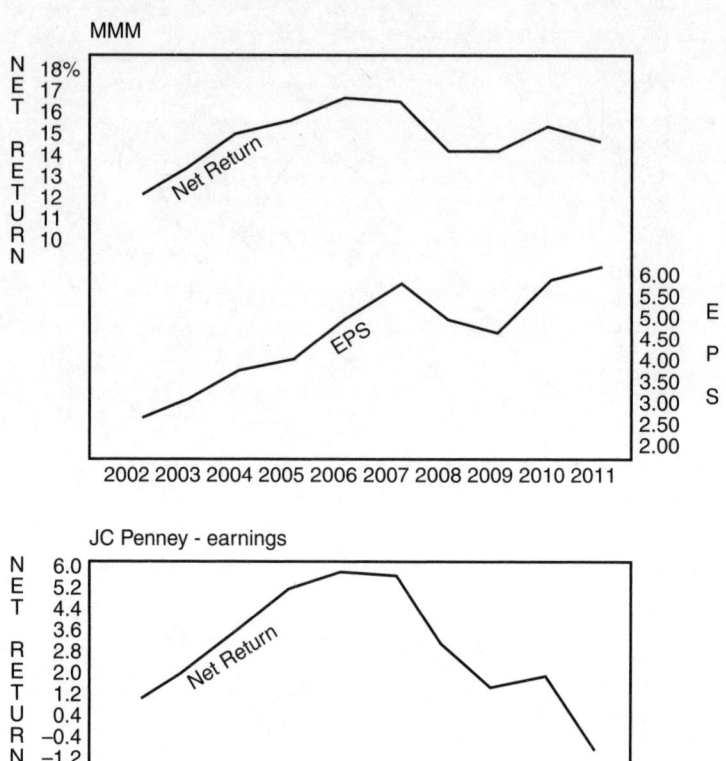

Figure 6.7 Net return and earnings-per-share trends
Source: S&P Stock Reports.

THE "IDEAL" DIVIDEND COLLAR

Testing historical volatility *and* fundamental volatility is one way to narrow down the selection of stock. This applies whether you want to invest long term or move in and out of positions in a matter of months or even weeks. These tests reveal the strength or weakness of management's control over both net earnings and the historical trend.

Ironically, options trading at times works contrary to the buy-and-hold strategy. Investors who want to buy exceptionally well-managed companies at bargain prices (value investors) seek low volatility with a lot of growth potential. This often is a contradictory aspect to the fundamentals, however. But it can be found. In such companies—with very low historical and fundamental volatility—the options-implied volatility also tends to be very low. As a consequence, these are often not suitable for options-based strategies, where so many strategies are based on entry and exit tied to rapidly changing levels of implied volatility (IV).

The dividend collar is an unusual strategy in the sense that it does not rely on either of the usual volatility tests. Historical and fundamental volatility do not truly matter, since the strategy is based on the selection of issues with two attributes: First is a better-than-average dividend yield. The examples in this book are based on dividends at or above 4% per year. Second is the net zero cost or small credit between a short call and a long put, at an advantageous strike (meaning a strike above basis or at basis; or at a strike below but with a large enough credit in the options to offset the small capital loss upon exercise).

These tests are not met easily or by most stocks. In fact, out of the more than 700 stocks with dividends above 4% (and approximately 370 with dividends between 4% and 6%), you might discover approximately 60 (divided among the three dividend cycles).

This does not mean that the 60 or so stocks are always appropriate. They may be so on the day the numbers are checked. However, next week or even tomorrow, the mix will be different and, depending on size of underlying price movement and reaction among options, the whole picture can change very quickly. Volatility is not a deciding factor in limiting the list of possibilities; the strategy is designed to eliminate market risk no matter how much or how little volatility is involved. However, while not a deciding factor, volatility certainly affects the premium value of both calls and puts. Because you are likely to seek strikes as close as possible to the current price of the underlying, the IV levels are likely to be less sensitive to implied volatility than other options farther in the money (ITM) or out of the money (OTM).

Another factor in this sensitivity analysis is time to expiration. The dividend collar is designed to focus on options expiring soon after the ex-dividend date. For example, if the ex-dividend occurs during the first ten days, the most likely contracts to use will expire later the same month. If the ex-dividend date occurs after the current month options expiration date, the most likely options contracts will be those in the following month. The closer to expiration, the less sensitive the option premium is likely to be to implied volatility.

These distinctions (short term and near the money means less sensitivity, and long term or farther away from the money means more sensitivity) make sense. If you think of implied volatility as "expectation value," the variations of time and proximity are all about future expectations. When a lot of time remains until expiration, options traders recognize that there are greater possibilities of an option gaining in value. This has nothing to do with time value, and everything to do with the uncertainty (and higher expectation) of how value changes over time.

The same argument applies to moneyness. When an option is at the money (ATM) or very close to it, traders recognize that the chances of the option moving far ITM or OTM are small (especially near expiration). This lower expectation is thus translated to lower implied volatility.

This does not mean that time and proximity are the only factors affecting implied volatility. However, these two certainly are major contributors, along with market-wide historical volatility and underlying-specific historical and fundamental volatility.

The advantage you have in pursuing the dividend collar is that you are less concerned with levels of the various types of volatility, and more concerned with locating the strikes and dividend yields that work. This is not easy, because there tends to be an offset between calls and puts that creates a debit situation. Ideally, if you can find options at or slightly ITM, in which the premium for both is equal or slightly to the credit side, you have a "perfect" dividend collar.

This is so because the exercise of either option produces a net capital gain. If your short call is exercised (meaning the underlying will have moved above its strike), you gain the difference between the call's strike and your lower basis. If the underlying price remains below the strike, you are able to dispose of shares by exercising your put and selling shares at the fixed strike. Your capital gain will be the difference between the strike and your basis—the same gain upon exercise of the call.

Because this ideal scenario is set up with a net zero outcome between the call and put, the option positions cost nothing (except transaction costs); you will earn the dividend; and either outcome produces a net capital gain in the underlying. The only outcome that causes this not to occur is the early exercise of your short call. This might take place immediately before the ex-dividend date because the long-option owner wants the dividend just as you do, but it will occur only when three conditions are present:

1. *The call is in the money.* The call is only exercised if the current price is higher than the strike. If this occurs, you can avoid exercise by rolling forward or up. However, as part of the dividend collar, if it is properly structured, exercise of the short call is one of the possibilities, and it produces a net profit.
2. *The long-option owner can exercise at a net gain.* Just because a call is in the money does not mean that the long-position owner can realize a true net gain. For example, if the call is one point in the money, and the dividend yield is only 50 cents (equal to 1/2 point), the call is going to be exercised only if the option was bought *below* 1.50. The combined gain on stock and income from the dividend has to exceed the original cost, and when transaction costs are taken into the equation, this is often quote marginal. Exercise is much more likely when the current price is significantly higher than the strike.
3. *The assignment hits you and not someone else.* Unlike the automatic exercise that takes place for ITM options on the last trading day, only a portion of long-option traders are going to exercise to get the dividend. So you are one in a field of

people with short calls open, and the assignment of a short option is going to be randomly determined by the Options Clearing Corporation (OCC). [2]

A Short List of High-Yield Candidates for Each Cycle

The following is a list of companies with dividends between 4% and 6%, divided by the ex-dividend dates occurring in one of the three annual cycles (Jan–Apr–Jul–Oct; Feb–May–Aug–Nov; and Mar–Jun–Sep–Dec).

The first step in picking a candidate for the dividend collar is to isolate the issues expiring within the next 30 days, and then to decide whether any of them work. If not, you need to go to those with ex-dividend dates in the 60-day period (table 6.1).

Among these, it makes sense to focus on the most immediate choices, those expiring the soonest and with ex-dividend dates within the first month. The valuation of options will change over the next two to three months. Based on closing prices as of June 25, 2012, analysis of the four companies with July ex-dividend dates is shown in table 6.2:

AT & T

In this collar, both the short call and the long put are out of the money. The net credit is 0.02, which after trading costs will be approximately a 0.20 debit (this is based on an estimated average transaction fee of $10 per contract. As long as this position is held through the ex-dividend date, you get the 44 cents per share, or $44 per 100 shares.

Possible outcomes: the price moves above $35 per share, and the call is exercised. In this case, you are close to breakeven on a net basis. If the price moves below $34 per share, the 34 put can be exercised. Based on the price at the moment, this creates a net loss of $95 on the stock, but if the actual purchase price was at or below $34 per share, exercise creates a profit.

This is a workable dividend collar based on the assumptions; however, it is not ideal because a loss is possible.

Table 6.1 Companies yielding between 4% and 6% dividend

	Dividend yield		
Company name	JAJO	FMAN	MJSD
Altria (MO)			4.8%
AT&T (T)	5.0%		
Atmos Energy (ATO)		4.1%	
Avon (AVP)		5.9	
Conoco Phillips (COP)		4.9	
Duke Energy (DUK)		4.4	
GlaxoSmithKline (GSK)		5.0	
Hasbro (HAS)	4.3		
Kinder Morgan (KMI)	4.0		
Leggett & Platt (LEG)			5.6
Eli Lilly (LLY)		4.7	
Lockheed Martin (LMT)		4.7	
Merck (MRK)			4.2
NYSE Euronet (NYX)			4.8
Pepco Holding (POM)			5.7
PetMed Express (PETS)		5.0	
PG & E (PCG)			4.2
Potlatch (PCH)			4.1
Reynolds America (RAI)			5.4
Safeway (SWY)			4.0
Southern Co. (SO)		4.2	
Thompson Reuters (TRI)		4.6	
Verizon (VZ)	4.6		
Waste Management (WM)			4.4

Source: S&P Stock Reports.

Table 6.2 Companies with July ex-dividend dates

| Company | Symbol | Ex-Div | Dividend | | Closing | Call | Put |
			per share	Yield	Price		
AT&T	T	July 5	0.44	5.00%	$34.95	Jul 35 0.35	Jul 34 0.33
Hasbro	HAS	July 30	0.36	4.25	33.16	Aug 32.50 1.75	Aug 32.50 1.40
Kinder Morgan	KMI	July 26	0.32	4.04	30.83	Aug 32.50 0.45	Aug 30 1.00
Verizon	VZ	July 6	0.50	4.55	43.65	Aug 43 0.97	Aug 43 0.68

Source: S&P Stock Reports.

Hasbro

The short call at 1.75 and the long put at 1.40 produce a net credit of 0.35. The distance between the current underlying price and the strike is 66 cents, or a potential net loss of 31 cents per share if exercise occurs for either side. However, if the basis in the underlying was at or below $32.50 per share, this position works out profitably, since exercise of either side will produce a small net capital gain.

This is not ideal since its success relies on a lower basis in the underlying. The dividend collar works only if that is the case.

Kinder Morgan

This is a more attractive situation, since the call strike is higher than the current price of the underlying, at $30.83. So if the call were exercised at $32.50, it would produce a net capital gain of $167. If the put were exercised, the net loss would be only 17 cents (both before transaction costs).

The net debit is 55 cents, versus the dividend of 32 cents, or net loss of 23 cents. Thus, exercise of the put is not desirable; this serves as a loss limitation position rather than as risk-free. This is not ideal either, but it has more profit scenarios than the two previous examples. Exercise of the long put would make sense only if the underlying price had fallen far below the put's strike.

Verizon

This sets up a short call at 97 cents and a long put at 68, or a net credit of 0.29. The strikes of both are 65 cents in the red, totaling an overall debit of 0.94. The dividend is 0.50, so potential net loss was 0.44.

These four situations present no ideal dividend collars, demonstrating that it often requires a holding period beyond the immediate ex-dividend strike. Analysis of the positions one month away shows how this works (table 6.3).

This set of potential dividend collars offers much greater potential for positive outcomes and with zero market risk. For example,

Table 6.3 Companies with August ex-dividend dates

Company	Symbol	Ex-Div	Dividend Per share	Yield	Closing Price	Call	Put
Atmos Energy	(ATO)	August 23	0.35	4.06%	$33.70	Oct35 5.00	Oct 35 5.00
Avon	(AVP)	August 15	0.23	5.94	15.10	Aug 15 1.05	Aug 15 1.05
Conoco Phillips	(COP)	August 17	0.66	4.94	52.96	Aug 52.50 1.98	Aug 52.50 2.12
Duke Energy	(DUK)	August 16	0.25	4.37	22.93	Aug 22 1.20	Aug 23 0.65
GlaxoSmithKline	(GSK)	August 9	0.55	4.96	45.86	Aug 45.84 1.10	Aug 45.84 1.50
Eli Lilly	(LLY)	August 13	0.49	4.66	41.47	Aug 42 1.09	Aug 41 1.34
Lockheed Martin	(LMT)	August 30	1.00	4.69	84.25	Sep 80 5.80	Sep 80 2.00
PetMed Express	(PETS)	August 10	0.15	4.99	11.97	Aug 12.50 0.45	Aug 10 0.25
Southern Co.	(SO)	August 3	0.49	4.21	46.25	Aug 46 0.95	Aug 46 1.03
Thompson Reuters	(TRI)	August 22	0.32	4.62	27.36	Oct 25 3.50	Oct 30 3.90

Source: S&P Stock Reports.

Atmos Energy was at $33.70 per share. Setting up a short call and a long put, both at 35 strikes for October, was two months away from the ex-dividend month, but it provides profitable outcomes no matter what outcome occurs. The net cost would be limited to approximately $20 transaction costs, but the capital gain upon either exercise would be $130. So estimating the net profit of $110 after fees, added to the dividend of $35, produces profits of $145 over the period. This is a successful dividend collar since both strikes are higher than the current value.

Out of this entire group, Atmos was the most promising of all, since a net profit results in any outcome. This shows that out of all the issues selected, you will find only a minority for which the dividend collar will work. This analysis included only 24 companies out of a total of about 740 with dividends above 4%, and the 24 companies were further limited to those yielding between 4% and 6%. And yet, only *one* of the 24 worked out profitably.

That is enough, however. You only need one company. And the share price does not matter either. For example, if you have approximately $10,000 to invest, you can purchase 300 shares of Atmos and transaction three calls and three puts. This is approximately the same capital outlay as 100 shares of a $100 stock or 1,000 shares of a $10 stock.

Focusing on only one issue is not a problem, either. If you are able to completely eliminate market risk with a dividend collar, you do not need to diversify. In any outcome you will earn a net profit. (The one exception would be exercise right before the ex-dividend date if the short call went in the money. In that case, you still get the capital gain.)

Is finding one company out of 24 a large enough outcome to justify the strategy? Yes, it is, considering how the result annualizes. In this case, if you were to enter the position on July 25, and if you held everything open until the last trading day of October 19, the net outcome would be a capital gain (whether your call is exercised or you exercise the put) of $130, plus $35 dividend, minus $20 estimated transaction fees: net $145. This would occur over 116 days.

This return is annualized based on the strike of 35:

$145 ÷ $3,500 = 4.14%.

The holding period is 116 days. To annualize, divide the return by 116 and then multiply by the full year:

(4.14% ÷ 116) x 365 = 13.03%.

An alternate method for annualizing is to base it on months. The period of 116 days is approximately 3.9 months, so this is rounded to four months and annualized to a full year:

(4.14% ÷ 4) x 12 = 12.42%.

This is somewhat less precise, but it is often easier to calculate. Annualizing is not intended as a representation of what you should expect to earn on average from your trades, but enables you to make valid comparisons between two or more transactions.

While the dividend collar requires a lot of legwork, generating double-digit annual returns with the complete elimination of market risk makes it worthwhile. The idea is to execute one transaction per month with available capital, close out the position, and then enter another position using the next month's list of stocks with ex-dividend dates within the next 30 to 60 days. It often is necessary (as the previous example demonstrated) to go out farther than the next 30 days just to find a situation that completely eliminates market risk. But you only need one per cycle.

Does the Underlying Matter?

The question has to be addressed, based on the fact that market risk is eliminated completely in the ideal dividend collar. Does the underlying matter? Do you care about its volatility and market risk, given the fact that the dividend collar eliminates market risk? It would seem that the fundamental analysis and the study of historical and fundamental volatility are not important as long as you earn the double-digit annualized return.

There are two ways to look at the dividend collar, and these affect the selection of the underlying and how often you roll it. First is the strategy in which you transact all three segments at the same time: purchase shares of the underlying purchase puts and sell calls.

The second involves using the dividend collar to manage an existing portfolio that includes appreciated positions. Even if your portfolio is full of excellent companies whose stock has performed above average, you face the endless dilemma: Do you sell and take profits now, or continue holding these exceptional issues? Selling now means you have to invest funds elsewhere, and sooner or later you are going to suffer a loss, thus converting today's paper profits into paper (or realized) losses. You would prefer to keep these in your portfolio, but you are concerned about the possibility of price decline. This is where the dividend collar makes a lot more sense and can be effective at eliminating market risk while ensuring high dividend yield indefinitely. When your original basis is lower than current value, the dividend collar will work in many situations. Consider once again the original list of July ex-dividend stocks (table 6.4).

If your original basis in each of these was four points below current value, all would work out profitably. An AT & T dividend

Table 6.4 Companies with July ex-dividend dates

Company	Symbol	Ex-Div	Dividend Per share	Yield	Closing Price	Call	Put
AT&T	T	July 5	0.44	5.00%	$34.95	Jul 35 0.35	Jul 34 0.33
Hasbro	HAS	July 30	0.36	4.25	33.16	Aug 32.50 1.75	Aug 32.50 1.40
Kinder Morgan	KMI	July 26	0.32	4.04	30.83	Aug 32.50 0.45	Aug 30 1.00
Verizon	VZ	July 6	0.50	4.55	43.65	Aug 43 0.97	Aug 43 0.68

Source: S&P Stock Reports.

collar on a basis of $30 per share would produce a net capital gain of $500 on an exercised call, or $300 on an exercised put, even if the stock price declined below your basis. The same profitability works for Hasbro, Kinder Martin, and Verizon. With a lower basis in the underlying, the dividend collar provides the elimination of all market risk along with exceptionally high dividend yield.

For anyone interested in investing in stocks for the long term, volatility does matter. It is reasonable to assume the possibility that you will want to divide your portfolio among several companies with higher-than-average dividend yield, and still eliminate market risk over a longer term. This is achieved by opening LEAPS-based dividend collars instead of short-term ones. This allows you to achieve a 4–6% annual yield with no market risk. The advantage to this strategy is that the yield is quite attractive and you still get rid of all market risk, but you do not need to continuously evaluate dozens of stocks to find the perfect dividend collar.

You might, in fact, encounter some months in which no dividend collar works. This means you will have to either accept some market risk or wait out the market until volatility levels make the put/call premium relationship more attractive. For many traders and investors, eliminating market risk for a full year or more, while enjoying a 4% or 5% net yield, is good enough to justify the strategy.

In these cases, the underlying does matter because it represents part of a longer-term strategy combining high dividend yield, elimination of market risk, and selection of companies whose long-term growth prospects are very attractive. If the stock price does rise, a LEAPS call can be rolled forward indefinitely, and as long puts expire, they can be replaced. The net premium received for a roll provides a budget for the purchase of new puts to maintain the risk-free status of the investment, and the annual dividend yield can then continue without interruption.

For example, if you own shares of Verizon that you purchased at $39.65 per share, the current price is four points of profit. You want to protect all or most of that and you do not want to sell;

you would like to continue earning the 4.55% dividend. The dividend collar can eliminate market risk for little cost. You can open a January 2013 position consisting of a 43 call (2.14) and a 42 put (2.22). The debit before transaction costs is 0.08. So for an overall net cost of about $30, you gain six months of ownership with market risk eliminated below $42 per share. This is 2.35 points above your basis, so if the stock's value fell below $42, you could exercise your put and sell shares at that fixed net profit. If the stock price rose above the call's strike of 43, you would have a choice. You could accept exercise and earn a capital gain of 3.35 points, or you could roll the short call forward to defer exercise, extending the period over which you will continue earning the dividend. The long put can be replaced upon expiration using the additional premium earned with the roll of the call. Employing this technique enables you to eliminate market risk indefinitely while continuing to earn better-than-average dividends. And if you also roll forward and up with the short call, you can gain a higher strike if and when the short call is exercised.

THE DIVIDEND COLLAR AS A PORTFOLIO MANAGEMENT STRATEGY

The dividend collar works in virtually all situations when the basis in the underlying is well below the strikes used to set up the collar. As a result, it eliminates market risk without your needing to sell shares before you want to. This assumes several points, however:

1. You are willing to have the call exercised and dispose of shares at the call strike. (Alternatively, you intend to close at a profit or roll forward to a later expiration and/or a higher strike.)
2. You recognize the value of the long put in the event of a price decline in the underlying. Your right to exercise at the put's strike ensures that you will not have any losses in the position as long as the put exists. Unlike the plain insurance put

requiring decline below the net basis (purchase price less put premium), the dividend collar is a cost-free or no-cost event, so exercise of the long put makes sense anywhere below the strike.
3. You might further consider a series of rolls and replacements to keep shares indefinitely without market risk. This makes the most sense when dividend yield is exceptionally high or when you believe the future growth potential for the underlying is promising.

The dividend collar as a portfolio management device is unique for two reasons. First, it entirely eliminates market risk below the put's strike, so as long as your basis is lower than this strike, even a catastrophic price decline can be managed profitably. Second, it is no-cost or low-cost (perhaps even producing a small net credit), making it more practical than other risk management strategies, such as the insurance put alone.

In a volatile market, and notably when portfolios include stocks that have themselves become quite volatile, many investors—including long-term investors—sell out of fear of a potential decline. The dividend collar expands the possibilities. A covered call strategy produces income and discounts basis, but only to the extent of the premium for the short call. A legitimate criticism of the covered call is that it does not protect against price decline in the underlying. When a covered call strategy is compared to simply owning shares, the covered call mitigates the risk but does not eliminate it.

The dividend collar solves this problem. If the put strike is higher than the basis in the underlying, you cannot lose even if the stock declines. The disadvantage to the dividend collar is that profits are also limited. This is not necessarily a negative, however. Consider the alternative: Your stock has appreciated in value, and you are considering taking profits now to avoid the possibility of a decline in the future. This might be prudent, but it presents a new dilemma: Where do you invest funds next? If your stock yields an attractive dividend, you would prefer to keep earning it. The covered call caps profits at the strike.

However, there are two offsetting advantages here as well. First, the strike is higher than your basis, so exercise will be profitable. Second, you continue earnings dividends as long as the call is not exercised.

If and when the short call moves toward or in the money, you can defer or avoid exercise with a forward roll. However, once the sooner-expiring put expires, are you not then exposed to market risk all over again? Yes. However, by purchasing a new call, you also renew the protection afforded with the insurance put. The amount you receive when you roll the call to a later-expiring contract provides a budget for the purchase of another put without your having to spend additional funds.

The ideal dividend collar is based on opening a position every month prior to the ex-dividend date; earning the dividend; and then closing and replacing the position through exercise of either the call or the put. This has the effect of converting quarterly dividends into *monthly* dividends. Thus, stocks yielding 4% per year collectively yield 12% due to the monthly rolling of long stock positions.

So there actually are two distinct versions of the dividend collar. First is the very short-term version designed to move in and out of stock positions in as short a time as possible and earn the right to dividends by being a stockholder of record and for as close to zero as possible in the net cost of options and capital gains. Second is the portfolio management strategy in which the covered call and the insurance-put sides of the collar eliminate downside risk while capping upside profit, all designed to ensure a safe environment for earning better-than-average dividends.

Both versions can work within your portfolio, and both are designed to create dividend yield in a risk-free environment. The short-term version provides double-digit returns from dividends, but requires a lot of work every month. The portfolio management approach also eliminates market risk and focuses on long-term earnings of higher-than-average dividends. Both varieties are practical, and you might find yourself entering into a short-term income-producing strategy and then deciding to hold shares for the long term, thus converting from the first version to the longer-term second version.

The next chapter expands on this discussion by examining several versions of the basic strategy, using a longer list of stocks yielding 4% or more.

Chapter 7

Examples of the Basic Strategy

> There is the greatest practical benefit in making a few failures early in life.
> T. H. Huxley, *On Medical Education*, 1870

THE DIVIDEND COLLAR DEMANDS A LOT OF RESEARCH; however, the risk-free, double-digit returns that are possible through this strategy justify the effort. For conservative investors who want to avoid risk while increasing net returns, the basic strategy works consistently to accomplish these portfolio goals.

The "basic" strategy consists of one long put and one short call per 100 shares in the portfolio. There are two ways to set up a dividend collar: control risk on appreciated, high-dividend stock already in your portfolio, or enter all three components (long stock, long put, short call) at the same time.

Dividend Collar on Appreciated Stock with Attractive Dividend Yield

The dividend collar can be applied to equity positions you own already. Once these positions have appreciated, you face a dilemma: Do you sell now and take the profits (and give up attractive dividends)? Or do you hold on, hoping the price does not fall? Many traders in this position buy insurance puts to cap potential losses, but as wise as this is, the insurance put costs money, so it reduces the capped loss by the amount of premium paid. For example, your original cost of 100 shares of Universal Corp. (UVV) was $43.60, and the stock was worth $46.33 at the June 29, 2012, close. Dividend yield was 4.22%. You decide to buy an insurance put with a 45 strike; if that put costs 0.50, you are protecting only 0.90 points:

Put strike	45
Less: put premium	−0.5
Net capped loss	**44.5**
Basis in stock	−43.60
Protected profit	**0.90**

Once the put expires, it will have to be replaced, meaning all of the profit will be absorbed. The solution is the dividend collar.

Given the same facts as above, you buy the 45 put and also sell a 45 call, which brings you 2.15; your net credit for this collar is 1.65 (2.15–0.50). Now the situation is different. You have acquired a cost-free insurance put and additional profits of net 0.32:

Call premium	2.15
Less put premium	−0.50
	1.65
Current stock value	46.33
Les: strike price:	−45
	−1.33
Net credit	**0.32**

If the stock falls below the 40 strike, you can exercise the put and sell at the fixed strike, or you can sell the put and take profits to offset losses in the underlying.

If the stock price rises above the 45 strike, the call will be exercised, and a profit of 1.72 points results:

Strike price	45
Less: basis in stock	−43.60
Net	**1.40**
Plus: net option credit	0.32
Profit	**1.72**

Although this is a modest profit, the dividend collar capped the potential loss at the strike of 45, and the dividend yield of 4.22%. If you want to avoid exercise, the short call can be rolled forward to a later expiration, or to a later expiration and a higher strike.

This is one example of how to create and use the dividend collar. It creates a net profit regardless of the outcome, because either your short call is assigned or you exercise or sell your long put. The position costs nothing, and in this example, it created a small credit. It also preserved the attractive 4.22% dividend. The market risk was eliminated below the strike for the time between the June 29 close and the July expiration.

This same situation can also be set up with a much longer time until expiration. This enables you to eliminate risk below the put's strike while preserving the dividend, and in exchange, you expose yourself to possible exercise of the short call at a profit.

For example, UVV reported closing premium for calls and puts as of June 29, 2012:

Feb 2013 45 call	4.10
Feb 2013 45 put	3.50

If you set up a collar using these options, you cap potential losses for the next 7.5 months for a net credit of 0.60 (4.10–3.50). Otherwise, the relationship between the current value and the strike is the same, at 1.33 points (closing price of 46.33 − strike 45). This allows you to continue earning dividends of 4.22% over the next 7.5 months with elimination of market risk below that strike. The short call can be managed to avoid exercise by rolling it forward to a later expiration, or forward and up to a higher strike.

The dividend collar is designed to serve as a short-term strategy to (1) earn the current dividend and (2) cap or eliminate market risk. So this longer-term solution is not so much a "dividend" collar as it is a risk-capping system. In fact, because the strike of both the call and the put are identical, it is not actually a collar at all, but a synthetic short-stock strategy.[1]

The advantage of the term expansion of the idea is that the two options are managed effectively in several ways. The short call (which in the example is rich due to the long time remaining until expiration) can be closed at a profit when expiration approaches and the call has not gone ITM. Second, it can be rolled forward to avoid exercise. Third, you can accept exercise and dispose of shares at the call's strike and take the capital gain.

The long put can be left open until right before expiration no matter what the underlying price does. You can exercise at the strike at any time, including the last trading day if the underlying price has moved far below that strike. For most holders of long puts, the declining time value is a problem. However, because you also sold a call, the net cost of the long put was zero, so you are not concerned about time value. In fact, as your long put loses time value, so does your short call. You are left with a "net advantage" because you do not need to exercise or sell the put until you are ready. A put held by itself has to be exercised only if the net difference between the strike and the current price is greater than the premium you paid for the contract. However, with a net zero cost, you can exercise the put at the fixed strike and create a capital gain regardless of how much time value has declined.

DIVIDEND YIELD WITH ALL COMPONENTS ENTERED AT THE SAME TIME

The second version of the dividend collar involves opening all three parts (long stock, long put, short call) at the same time.

This is a more difficult position to find because you need several elements to fall into place.

There are five criteria for this version of the basic dividend collar:

1. *Dividend yield, frequency, and consistency.* You need to determine the appropriate level of dividend yield to execute this strategy. Traders tend to shy away from stocks yielding too high a dividend, since yields grow as stock prices fall, so a very exceptional yield can be a symptom of a distressed company. However, with the dividend yield, your downside market risk is capped, so even if the company is heading for complete disintegration, the bigger question is whether or not the dividend will be paid. This is another of the criteria: If the company has missed dividend payouts in the past year, it places the next payout at risk as well. Avoid those issues whose dividend is not paid consistently.

In the underlyings in this book, only those yielding 4% or more have been studied. The rationale for this is that a 4% dividend paid quarterly, if earned every month, is 1% per month or 12% per year—more if the dividend yield is above 4%. This is accomplished by opening a dividend collar for the current month, earning the dividend, closing the position, and then repeating the process each month thereafter.

In addition to the limitation of a 4% or higher dividend yield, only those issues paying dividends quarterly have been used. Some stocks pay dividends monthly, semiannually, or annually. These can be used as well, but probably have to be mixed in with the quarterly dividend-yielding stocks in order to ensure that monthly ex-dividend dates are plentiful. None of the so-called "irregular" dividend yielding stocks are used in this book.

2. *Option net credit or debit.* The net difference in value between the short call and the long put have to be at zero, or a small credit. If the net is a debit (as it often is), the strategy will not work. If the dividend is greater than the net debit, it will work, but the annualized return will be reduced. This makes the strategy less

profitable, of course, but when you add in the cost of the overall transaction, you might discover that you cannot make a profit if the option positions are at a net debit.

This relationship is a difficult one to accomplish. You will discover that some option positions will work, but only within a small window of time. As part of this book, 740 stocks were tested, each yielding 4% or more per year. After eliminating those that paid dividends on an irregular basis and those that did not include options, the remainder fall into one of the three dividend cycles. Even so, only about 50 companies qualified as potentially viable for the dividend collar. The most common reason for eliminating a candidate was a debit between the long put and the short call.

The put often is much richer than a call at the same strike or close to it, so the "ideal" relationship may involve two strikes, both slightly out of the money (OTM) or at the money (ATM); this rule eliminates the majority of situations, but there remains a small number of viable candidates even after applying this stringent requirement.

3. *Strikes set so that exercise will create zero outcome or small capital gain.* Making the selection of viable candidates even more difficult, you need to ensure that the calls and puts you select will produce a profit or breakeven upon exercise. The most desirable and likely method for closing the dividend collar consists of your call being assigned, or of your exercise of the long put. In either case, a net capital loss diminishes the profitability of the dividend collar. A loss is acceptable only if and when the net premium from options was a high enough credit to match or exceed the net capital loss. This outcome is possible when volatility is exceptionally high, but in most cases you will not be able to set up a large enough net credit on the options to create this situation. A related problem is that this requires the short call to be in the money (ITM) when the position is created, and that increases the chances of exercise immediately before the ex-dividend date. To avoid exercise, you will need to roll the

short call forward, which defeats the purpose of the dividend collar—to move in and out of positions every month as a means for creating an attractive annual return. The alternative: accept exercise as an alternative form of profits in place of dividends. This also can be profitable as long as the net credit between the two options is attractive.

4. *Ex-dividend date within less than one month.* The timing requires that you enter into long stock ownership at least one day before the ex-dividend date. The settlement period for stock is three days, so executing the trade the day before the ex-dividend day or earlier ensures that you will be acknowledged as the owner on the record date.

You can select current-month positions at any time within the weeks prior to the ex-dividend date, which sets up your ownership. The only risk involved with an earlier opening of the dividend collar is the longer period during which the short call can be exercised. However, as long as the call's strike is higher than your purchase price, this produces a profit. Furthermore, not every ITM call is going to be exercised before the ex-dividend date. The call owner must be able to create a net profit through exercise. For example, if the call costs 4, and that same call is currently only 3 points ITM, the call will not be exercised, since it would create a net loss of 1 point. Because of this, *some* ITM calls will be exercised before the ex-dividend date, but not all.

5. *Options expiration in next cycle after the ex-dividend date.* Once the ex-dividend date has been identified, the options to be used in the dividend collar should be those expiring on the next expiration after the ex-dividend date. For stocks with the ex-dividend in the early part of the month, the same month's expirations should be applied. If the ex-dividend occurs after expiration, the following month's options have to be used. So the period in which the position remains open could expand anywhere from a few days to five weeks, all based on the time between the ex-dividend date and expiration, and on when exercise is viable.

Exercise after the ex-dividend date is likely to occur for the short call on the last trading day. You can exercise your long put at any time you want as long as it is ITM, meaning the current share price is lower than the strike. Because the options should have cost you zero (or created a small credit), you can exercise your put whenever the ITM condition exists, without regard for the degree of ITM profit. For example, if you were to buy an insurance put and you paid 3, you would not exercise the put until the stock had fallen more than 3 points below the strike. With the zero-cost dividend collar, your net basis in the options is zero.

One potential hidden risk: If you exercise your put to dispose of shares weeks prior to expiration, you are left with no stock and no put, but with an open uncovered call. If the stock price has declined far enough so that this exposure is not immediate, you can decide just to track prices. If your net profit from exercising the put exceeds the current value of the short call, you can buy to close and eliminate the risk. However, the most important point to keep in mind is that when you exercise the long put, it results in an uncovered call. For this reason, the most conservative course is to exercise on the last trading day when the put is ITM and the short call that is about to expire is worthless.

The criteria for the covered call you create with stock and options opened at the same time do limit your choices. The first version—creating the call when you own appreciated stock—is much easier to create because profits exist beforehand. However, this does not mean it is impossible to find a dividend collar based on the purchase price of stock at current value. The criteria limit the field, but they do not eliminate the possibilities.

A List of Candidates

Table 7.1 lists all stocks with 4% or higher annual dividends; with July, 2012 ex-dividend dates; which pay quarterly dividends; and which were analyzed as of their end of June (June 29) closing prices, for stock as well as options.

Table 7.1   Stocks with July ex-dividend dates

July NAME	TICKER	Ex-div	Per sh.	%	Price
Anworth Mortgage	ANH	7–5	0.21	11.97%	$ 7.05
Armour Residential REIT	ARR	7–12	0.10	17.02	7.11
AT & T	T	7–5	0.44	4.97	35.66
Banco Bilbao	BBVA	7–11	0.15	8.67	7.07
Banco Latino Americano	BLX	7–26	0.25	4.80	21.43
Banco Santander	SAN	7–10	0.29	13.24%	$ 6.56
BP Prodhoe Bay	BPT	7–12	2.64	8.48	116.57
Cellcom Israel	CEL	7–9	0.34	28.23	6.10
Cheniere Energy	CQP	7–27	0.43	7.59	22.61
City Holdings	CHCO	7–11	0.35	4.23	33.69
Commonwealth REIT	CWH	7–19	0.50	10.69%	$ 19.12
Compass Diversified	CODI	7–20	0.36	10.40	13.96
Consolidated Communications	CNSL	7–11	0.39	10.82	14.80
Copano Energy	CPNO	7–26	0.58	8.75	27.80
Costamare	CMRE	7–26	0.27	8.10	13.90
Crestwood Midstream	CMLP	7–27	0.50	7.84%	$ 25.86
Crosstex Energy	XTEX	7–30	0.33	8.13	16.40
Dorchester Minerals	DMLP	7–19	0.54	8.55	21.95
Dynex Capital	DX	7–3	0.29	11.26	10.38
El Paso Pipeline	EPB	7–27	0.51	6.10	33.80
Enerplus	ERF	7–0	0.09	8.35%	$ 12.87
Enterprise Products	EPD	7–26	0.63	5.01	51.24
Franklin Street	FSP	7–25	0.19	7.38	10.58
Genesis Energy	GEL	7–27	0.45	6.26	29.07
Government Properties	GOV	7–24	0.42	7.58	22.62
Hospitality Properties	HPT	7–24	0.45	7.52%	$ 24.77
Kinder Morgan	KMP	7–26	1.20	6.22	78.58
Kite Realty	KRG	7–3	0.06	4.81	4.99
Kohlberg Capital	KCAP	7–3	0.24	13.35	7.26
Legacy Reserves	LGCY	7–26	0.56	8.95	25.01
LRR Energy	LRE	7–25	0.48	12.91%	$ 14.90
Mack-Cali Realty	CLI	7–2	0.45	6.40	29.07
Memorial Production	MEMP	7–27	0.48	11.84	16.89
MFA Financial	MFA	7–26	0.23	11.72	7.89
National Retail Properties	NNN	7–26	0.39	5.49	28.29
Omega Healthcare	OHI	7–26	0.42	7.42%	$ 22.50
People's United Financial	PBCT	7–27	0.16	5.58	11.61
QR Energy	QRE	7–26	0.49	11.89	16.54
R R Donnelly	RRD	7–18	0.26	8.72	11.77
RAIT Financial Trust	RAS	7–9	0.08	6.84	4.62
Royal Bank of Canada	RY	7–12	0.55	4.45%	$ 51.22

Continued

Table 7.1 Continued

July NAME	TICKER	Dividends Ex-div	Per sh.	%	Closing Price
Senior Housing Properties	SNH	7–11	0.38	6.95	22.32
Suburban Propane	SPH	7–27	0.85	8.34	41.27
Targa Resources	NGLS	7–19	0.62	7.10	35.65
Teekay Corp.	TK	7–18	0.32	4.49	29.28
Teekay LNG	TGP	7–19	0.68	7.12%	$ 38.55
Teekay Offshore	TOO	7–19	0.51	7.40	27.95
Universal Corp.	UVV	7–5	0.49	4.22	46.33
Verizon	VZ	7–6	0.50	4.55	44.44
VOC Energy Trust	VOC	7–26	0.69	15.61	18.20

Source: Charles Schwab & Co., screener function for dividend yield.

This list is further broken down into several subcategories:

a) those that did not work—and why (this includes companies whose dividend collar could have worked if you had owned stock purchased at a lower price, but that would mean that all of the candidates would work).
b) a few companies put aside for now, to be studied in upcoming chapters and for use in expanded strategies (installment collars, ratio write collars, variable ratio write collars, and synthetic stock positions).
c) the few stocks for which the dividend collar does work.

THOSE THAT DID NOT WORK—AND WHY

Below is a summary for each of the stocks for which the dividend collar did not work, along with an explanation of the rationale. These represent a majority of the issues studied with a July expiration, a 4% or higher dividend, and available options trading. In fact, this list is 72% of the 50 issues in the study.

Even though the majority do not work, remember that you only need a few to make the strategy profitable, to eliminate all risk, and to produce double-digit annual returns. Those few issues on which the dividend collar did work as of the fixed closing date follow the list of those that did not work.

Anworth Mortgage (ANH)—The stock price was $7.05. The July 7 expiring call was priced at 0.10, and the 7 put was at 0.20. This is a debit of 0.10 before transaction costs. The total with the 0.05 capital loss would exceed the quarterly dividend of 0.21 per share.

Armour Residential REIT (ARR)—The stock closed at $7.11. The closest strike was 7.50, and the July call was worth only 0.05, compared to the put at 0.55. The dividend was only 0.10, so this would result in an overall loss even before transaction costs.

Banco Bilbao (BBVA)—The stock closed at $7.07. The July 7 call was worth 0.30, and the put was at 0.35, for a net pretransaction cost debit of 0.05. The dividend was only 0.15 per share, making this an unprofitable prospect.

Banco Latino Americano (BLX)—The stock closed at $21.43. The closest call was August 22.50 at 0.50. The 22.50 put was valued at 1.65. This would not have been a profitable dividend collar.

Banco Santander (SAN)—The stock price was $6.56 per share. The July 6 calls were at 0.70, and puts at 0.15 (net credit of 0.55). Exercise of either option would create a capital loss of 0.01 before transaction costs. Dividend was only 0.29 per share, so the net after transaction costs would be a loss.

Cellcon Israel (CEL)—The stock price was $6.10 per share. The July 5 call was 1.20, and the put was 0.15, or a net credit of 1.05. However, the capital loss would be 1.10 before transaction costs. The alternative was the 7.50 call at only 0.10, with the 7.50 put at 2.00. There was no alternative for creating a net profit, given the dividend of only 0.34 per share.

Cheniere Energy Partners (CQP)—The stock price was $22.61 at the close. The August 23 call was 1.30, and the put 2.00, for a net debit of 0.70. Exercise of either option would produce a profit of 0.39 before costs. The alternative was the July 22 call at 1.90 and the put at 1.55, for a net credit of 0.35. However, exercise would create a loss of 0.60, offsetting the credit, even before transaction costs.

Commonwealth REIT (CWH)—The stock price was $19.12 at the close. The July 20 call was worth only 0.15, and the put was at 1.55. This disparity of value makes the dividend collar impractical.

Compass Diversified (CODI)—The stock closed at $13.96. The closest call was the August 15, which was at 0.20, while the August 15 put was worth 1.75. This is not a viable candidate for the dividend collar.

Consolidated Communications (CNSL)—The stock price was $14.80. The July 15 call was worth 0.40, and the July 15 put was at 1.05. The net difference of 0.65 more than exceeds the dividend of 0.39. This cannot be entered profitably.

Copano Energy (CPNO)—The stock price was $27.80 per share, while the August 28 call was at 0.90, and the put at 1.60. The net debit of 0.70, versus exercise profit of 0.30, would be marginally profitable because the dividend was 0.58. However, transaction fees would exceed this small profit, creating an overall net loss.

Costamare (CMRE)—The stock closed at $13.90. The closest call was the August 15 at 0.25, with the August 15 put at 1.85. This net debit of 1.60 makes this issue unworkable at the current prices.

Crestwood Midstream (CMLP)—The stock closed at $25.86. The August 25 call was worth 2.05, and the put at 1.60. The net credit was 0.45, versus capital loss upon exercise of 0.86. Even with the 0.50 dividend, there was no way to enter a dividend collar profitably.

Crosstex Energy (XTEX)—The stock was at $16.40. The August 17.50 call was worth 0.25, and the put worth 2.00. The debit of 1.75 makes this impractical. The proximity between current price and the closest strike was also too great to have any value in the short call.

Dorchester Minerals (DMLP)—The stock closed at $21.95, and the closest strike was 22.50. The call was worth 0.40, and the put was at 1.25. This was another case of too large a net debit, even after exercise profit of only 0.55 and a dividend of 0.54. The transaction costs would offset the minimal profit and offset the dividend.

Dynex Capital (DX)—The stock was at $10.38. The July 10 call was at 0.45, and the put at 0.30, for a net credit of 0.15. However, transaction costs would exceed this level, meaning most of the 0.29 dividend would be consumed by those costs.

El Paso Pipeline (EPB)—The stock closed at $33.80. The August 35 call was 0.35, and the put was 2.55, making this strike impractical. The 32.50 call was at 1.90, and the put at 1.20, for a net credit of 0.70. However, the capital loss upon exercise would be 1.30. The dividend was 0.51 cents; however, transaction costs would take up all of the profit and produce a net loss.

Enerplus (ERF)—Stock price was $12.87. The July 13 call was at 0.30, and the put at 0.55. This 0.25 debit before fees (offset by a 0.13 capital gain upon exercise of either option) was not enough in light of the 0.09 dividend.

Genesis Energy (GEL)—The stock closed at $29.07. The August 30 call was at 0.50, and the 30 put at 2.30. This was far too much of a debit to allow this issue to work as a dividend collar.

Government Properties (GOV)—The stock closed at $22.62. The August 22.50 call was worth 0.50, and the put at 1.05. The debit of 0.55 added to the capital loss of 0.12 was greater than the dividend of 0.42, not to mention transaction costs.

Hospitality Properties (HPT)—With the stock at $24.77, the closest strike was 25. The August call was worth 0.50, and the put worth 1.30. The net debit was too rich to justify a dividend collar for HPT

Kinder Morgan (KMP)—This issue closed at $78.58. The August 77.50 call was worth 2.11, and the put worth 2.00. This large debit was inadequate, considering the 1.08 capital loss upon exercise. The dividend was 1.20; however, after transaction costs, this would result in a net loss. The 80 options did not fare better. The August 80 call was at 0.80, and the put was at 3.50.

Kohlberg Capital (KCAP)—The price of this stock was $7.26. The July 7.50 call was worth only 0.10, and the put was at 0.80. The 0.70 pretransaction cost debit compared unfavorably with the 0.24 dividend.

LRR Energy (LRE)—This issue closed at $14.90 per share. The August 15 call was worth 1.05, and the put at 1.80, a 0.75 debit compared to a 0.10 capital gain upon exercise. The net 0.65 pretransaction cost loss was greater than the 0.48 dividend.

Mack-Cali Realty (CLI)—At $29.07, the July 30 calls were worth 0.65, but the puts were at 2.70, creating a large debit and making the dividend collar impossible to open profitably.

Memorial Production (MEMP)—The stock ended at $16.89. The closest strike was 17.50, and the August call was valued AT 0.55, with the put at 1.60. This 1.05 debit offset a capital gain of only 0.61 upon exercise, and the dividend was 0.48. The 1.09 (0.61 + 0.48) was only 0.04 more than the option debit, which would be more than offset by transaction costs. The dividend collar will not work under these conditions.

MFA Financial (MFA)—The stock price closed at $7.89 per share. The next call was the July 8, and was worth only 0.05. The July 8 put was at 0.45, much too large a debit to be practical. The dividend was only 0.23 per share, so MFA was not a candidate.

National Retail Properties (NNN)—The stock price closed at $28.29. The next strike was 30, and the August call was worth only 0.25, while the put was valued at 2.65. The gap in value was too great, especially considering that the dividend was only 0.39. A marginal case could be made for the August 25 call, which was at 3.60. Upon exercise, a small credit would remain above the current price per share. However, the problem for a dividend collar remained the put side, which could not be provided at a profit. The 30 put was too expensive, and the 25 put (valued at 0.25) was too low to create a net profit if exercised.

QR Energy (QRE)—The closing price was $16.54. The August 17.50 was the next strike after the ex-dividend, and the 17.50 call was at 0.40. The 17.50 put was at 1.90. The debit was too large to justify a dividend collar on QRE.

R. R. Donnelly (RRD)—The stock price was $11.77 per share. The July 12 call was at 0.50, and the put at 1.30. The 0.80 debit was too great to justify a dividend collar in this case. A lower strike call could be employed (the July 11 was at 1.05, and the

July 10 at 2.20). However, this would increase the likelihood of exercise, which would create a net loss.

RAIT Financial Trust (RAS)—The closing price was $4.62. The July 5 call was worth only 0.05, and the put at 0.55. This is too great a debit to allow RAS to work for the dividend collar.

Senior Housing Properties (SNH)—The closing price was $22.32 per share. The July 22.50 call was at 0.20, and the put at 0.95. The 0.75 debit prohibited the creation of a dividend collar at SNH. It would not be profitable.

Suburban Propane (SPH)—The closing price was $41.27, and the August 40 call was at 1.95. The August 40 put was worth 1.20, creating a pretransaction cost credit of 0.75. However, the exercise price of either call or put would create a net loss of 1.27 points (current price of $41.27 less strike of 40). The next strike was 45, and the put was far too expensive to justify considering it for a dividend collar.

Teekay Corp. (TK)—The closing price was $29.28. The July 30 call was at 60, and the put at 1.60. The 1.00 debit was too high for a dividend collar. The 27.50 call was worth 2.10; this combined with the 30 put would create a 0.50 credit. However, upon exercise of the call, the capital loss would be 1.78, making TK impractical for a dividend collar.

Teekay LNG (TGP)—The stock closed at $38.55, At that time, the 40 call was worth only 0.25, while the put was at 2.75. This was an exceptionally large debit of 2.50. The 37.50 call was at 1.60, but even that would not have been rich enough to cover the cost of the put.

VOC Energy Trust (VOC)—The stock price was $18.20 at the close. The closest expiration was August, and the 17.50 call was 1.25. The 17.50 put was 0.90. This was a credit of 0.35 before transaction costs. However, exercise of either option would create a net capital loss on the underlying of 0.70, for a net loss of 0.35 before costs. The dividend was 0.69, making the overall profitable. However, reducing the net to 0.34 per share (dividend of 0.69 less capital loss of 0.35) reduces the return (based on strike of 17.50) to only 1.9%, annualizing to 7.6%. The goal in the dividend collar is to achieve double-digit returns. So even though the

VOC example would be profitable, it falls below this standard. Compared to other issues that exceed that standard, it would not make sense to tie up capital and margin on a VOC dividend collar.

A Few Put Aside for Later Study

Nine of the companies (18%) in the sample of 50 were identified as good candidates for variations on the strategy. These were:

Installment Collar

The installment approach is a variation in which one side of the option portion is opened with a long-term contract, to be offset by a series of short-term offsetting positions. This usually involves a long put held for many months, versus a series of short calls. A "reverse" installment collar involves opening a long-term short call and using the relatively rich premium to fund a series of short-term puts. Four of the companies were reserved for this chapter, demonstrating how this strategy works:

AT&T (T)—installment collar
Verizon (VZ)—installment collar
Enterprise Products (EPD)—reverse installment collar
Royal Bank of Canada (RY)—reverse installment collar

Ratio Write Dividend Collar

The ratio write is an expansion of the basic strategy in which the short-call side is developed as a ratio write. This means more calls are opened than are covered by stock. For example, if you own 300 shares and open four short calls, it creates a 4:3 ratio. This may be viewed as four short calls that are 75% covered, or as three covered calls and one uncovered call. While this strategy increases risks, many traders consider it manageable and acceptable. Two companies are used in the chapter to explain the ratio write dividend collar and evaluate its risks:

BP Prodhoe Bay (BPT)
Omega Healthcare (OHI)

VARIABLE RATIO WRITE DIVIDEND COLLAR

The variable ratio write is a variety of the ratio write; however, two strikes are employed instead of one. This vastly reduces the risk because, with both short-call strikes OTM (or one close to the money and the other OTM), the exercise risk is more easily managed. If the underlying price rises and approaches the money or moves ITM, the higher-strike calls can be rolled or closed. Because these consist of a high level of time value, as exercise nears, it is likely that these can be closed at a net profit or rolled forward. As long as the underlying price remains below the strikes, the calls can be held until they expire worthless. Two issues were held aside for analysis in the chapter on the variable ratio write dividend collar:

City Holding (CHCO)
Targa Resources (NGLS)

SYNTHETIC STOCK POSITIONS

The collar is usually defined as set up with both long-put and short-call OTM. However, the dividend collar at times works well with a synthetic stock position. This is the opening of a long and short option with the same strike. The combined positions mirror price movement in the underlying. As a variation of the dividend collar, the synthetic short stock is the most likely variety, which includes a long put and a short call at the same strike price. The other variety is a long call and a short put, and this will mirror stock movement with maximum profits if and when the stock price moves upward.

The synthetic short-stock strategy may stand alone; however, for the purpose of the dividend collar, it is a combination of a protective put and a covered call. Just as the position with different strikes will include cover of the short call, the synthetic short stock is distinguished only by the fact that the strikes are identical. One company was set aside to demonstrate how this works:

Legacy Reserves (LGCY)

THE SUCCESSES—ONLY A FEW, BUT YOU ONLY NEED ONE

Out of the 50 companies studied (and qualified as paying quarterly dividends at or above 4% with July expirations), only five (10%) fit the qualifications for a basic dividend collar. Following is a detailed examination of each, with the positions set up to approximate the same level of holdings, between $13,700 and $14,000 in stock offset by the appropriate number of long puts and short calls.

Calculating annualized returns is difficult in the following examples. Several issues arise. First of all, what basis should be used to calculate the return? The following are all based on the strike of the options. You may also use the purchase price of stock. As long as the comparisons are made consistently, the calculation of annualized return provides a means for judging how effective the dividend collar is in producing double-digit returns, so the same basis should be used in all cases.

A second question is whether or not to include the net income or loss from stock and option activity. In some cases, a net income is generated, and in others, a net loss. In the interest of expressing the most conservative outcome possible, when a net profit results from stock and option activity, it is not included in the calculation of annualized return. However, when a net loss results from stock and option activity, the dividend income is reduced by that loss, and the overall net is calculated and annualized.

FRANKLIN STREET PROPERTIES (FSP)

Closing price on June 29	$10.58
Dividend yield:	7.38%
Dividend amount per share:	0.19
Ex-dividend date:	July 25

Options expiring August 17 (49 days)	Aug 10 calls @ 4.50 Aug 10 puts @ 3.10

Actions:

Buy 1,300 shares @ 10.58 =	$13,754
Buy 13 puts @ 3.10 =	−$4,030
Sell 13 calls @ 4.50 =	$5,850
Net options credit	$1,820

Outcomes:

Calls or puts are exercised, Net capital loss, 0.58 per share =	−$754

Estimated transaction costs:[2]

Stock (buy and sell)	−$18
Options: 26 round trips each, 52 total; (8.95 x 4) + (0.75 x 52)	−75
Net total losses	$847
Net options credit, less total losses	$973
Dividend, 0.19 per share =	$247

Net return based on strikes:

$0.19 ÷ $10 = 1.9%.

Annualized:

(1.9% ÷ 49) x 365 = 14.2%.[3]

The three-month chart of FSP ended June 29 (figure 7.1).

Notice that the long-established resistance and support levels concluded with an upside breakout and gap. When this occurs, you cannot know whether the price move is going to retreat or continue. The advantage to the dividend collar in this example is that a profit is going to occur no matter which

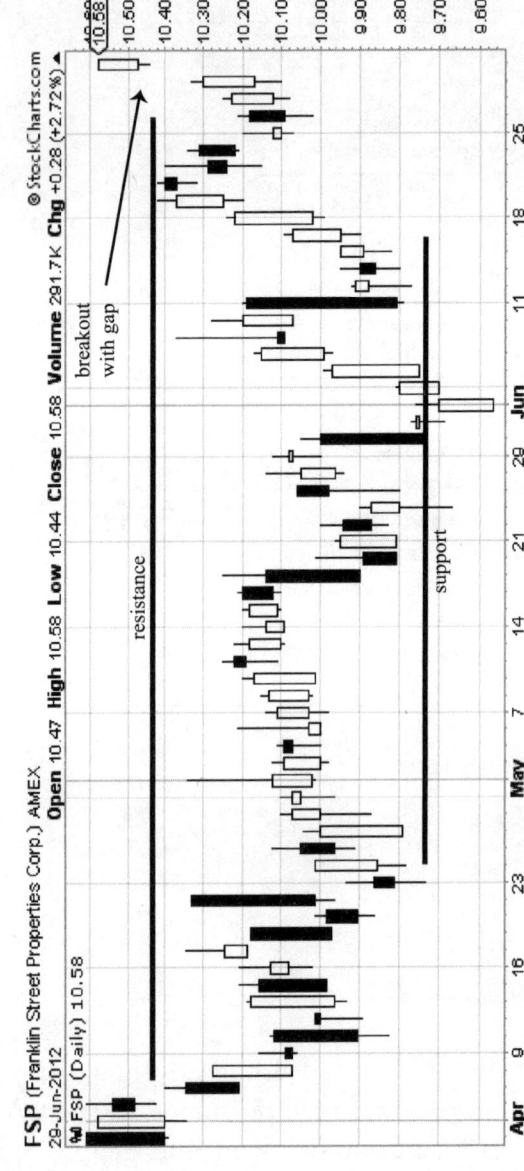

Figure 7.1 Franklin Street Properties
Source: StockCharts.com

option ends up exercised, and the dividend yield annualizes to double digits.

KITE REALTY (KRG)

Closing price on June 29	$4.99
Dividend yield:	4.81%
Dividend amount per share:	0.06
Ex-dividend date:	July 3
Options expiring July 20 (21 days)	July 5 calls @ 0.30 July 5 puts @ 0.30

Actions:

Buy 2,800 shares @ 4.99=	$13,972
Buy 28 puts @ 0.30 =	−$840
Sell 28 calls @ 0.30 =	$840
Net options credit	$0

Outcomes:

Calls or puts are exercised, Net capital gain, 0.01 per share =	$28

Estimated transaction costs:

Stock (buy and sell)	−$18
Options: 28 round trips each, 112 total; (8.95 x 4) + (0.75 x 112)	−120
Net total losses	−$110
Net options credit, less total losses	−$110
Dividend, 0.06 per share =	$168

Net return based on strikes, dividend only:

$0.06 ÷ $5 = 1.2%.

Annualized:

(1.2% ÷ 21) x 365 = 20.9%.

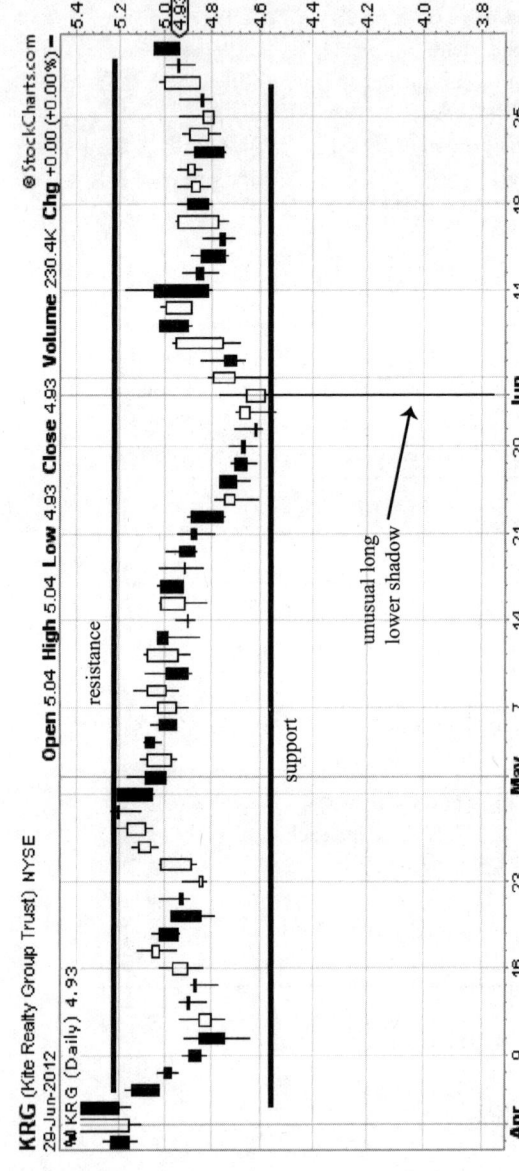

Figure 7.2 Kite Realty Group
Source: StockCharts.com

Annualized with stock/option losses deducted: [4]

Net loss: $168 − $110= $68
$68 ÷ $14,000 = 0.5%
(0.5% ÷ 21) x 365 = 8.7%.

The three-month chart of KRG ended June 29 (figure 7.2).

On this chart, the rather narrow trading range was long established. The exceptionally long lower shadow occurred only once, and is highlighted. However, note that trading returned immediately to the established trading range and remained there. This history indicates that the trading range is fairly strong and likely to remain within the borders.

PEOPLE'S UNITED FINANCIAL (PBCT)

Closing price on June 29	$11.61
Dividend yield:	5.58%
Dividend amount per share:	0.16
Ex-dividend date:	July 27
Options expiring August 17 (49 days)	Aug 11 calls @ 0.95
	Aug 11 puts @ 0.25

Actions:

Buy 1,200 shares @ 11.61=	$13,932
Buy 12 puts @ 0.25 =	−$300
Sell 12 calls @ 0.95 =	$1,140
Net options credit	$840

Outcomes:

Calls or puts are exercised, Net capital loss, 0.61 per share =	−$732

Estimated transaction costs:

Stock (buy and sell)	−$18
Options: 24 round trips each, 48 total; (8.95 x 4) + (0.75 x 48)	−72
Net total loss	−$822
Net options credit, less total loss	$18
Dividend, 0.16 per share =	$192

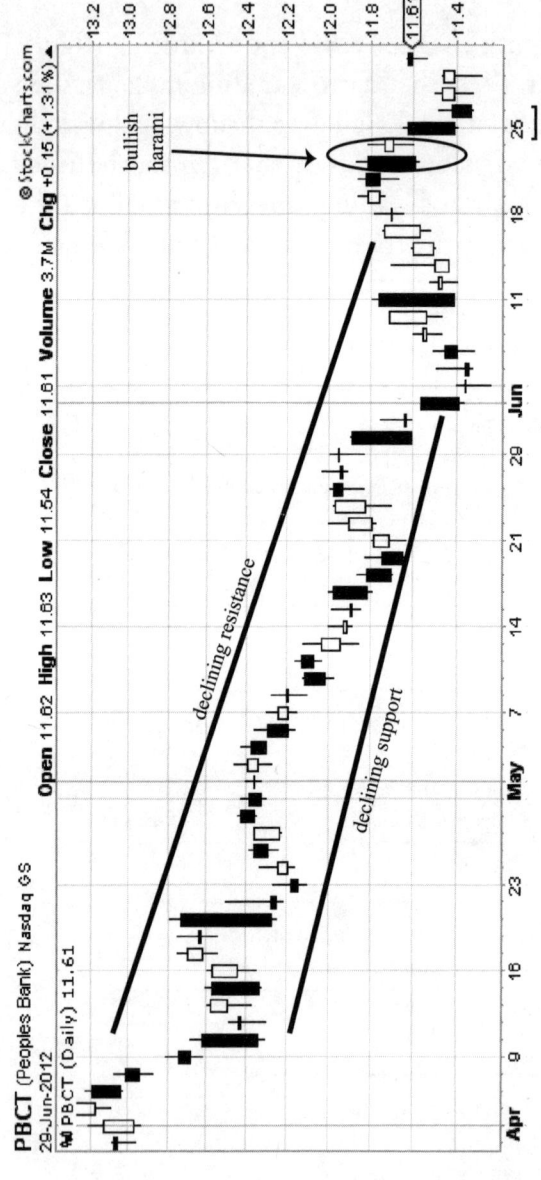

Figure 7.3 Peoples Bank
Source: StockCharts.com

Net return based on strikes, dividend only:

$0.16 ÷ $11 = 1.5%.

Annualized:

(1.5% ÷ 49) x 365 = 11.2%.

The three-month chart of PBCT ended June 29 (figure 7.3).

This chart reveals a declining trading range with a slight narrowing. This "triangle" formation indicates a coming bullish change as the triangle concludes. The candlestick pattern known as a "bullish harami" confirms this and signals a possible upward rally to follow. If that occurred, the dividend collar would remain profitable; if the downtrend continued, the long put would protect the long stock position and could be exercised to escape at the strike.

TEEKAY OFFSHORE (TOO)

Closing price on June 29	$27.95
Dividend yield:	7.40%
Dividend amount per share:	0.51
Ex-dividend date:	July 19
Options expiring August 17	July 28 calls @ 0.85
(49 days)	July 28 puts @ 0.85

Actions:

Buy 500 shares @ 27.95	$13,975
Buy 5 puts @ 0.85 =	–$425
Sell 5 calls @ 0.85 =	$425
Net options credit	$0

Outcomes:

Calls or puts are exercised,	
Net capital gain, 0.05 per share =	$25

Estimated transaction costs:

Stock (buy and sell)	–$ 18
Options: 10 round trips each, 20 total; (8.95 x 4) + (0.75 x 20)	–51
Net total losses	–$44
Net options credit, less total losses	–$44
Dividend, 0.51 per share =	$255

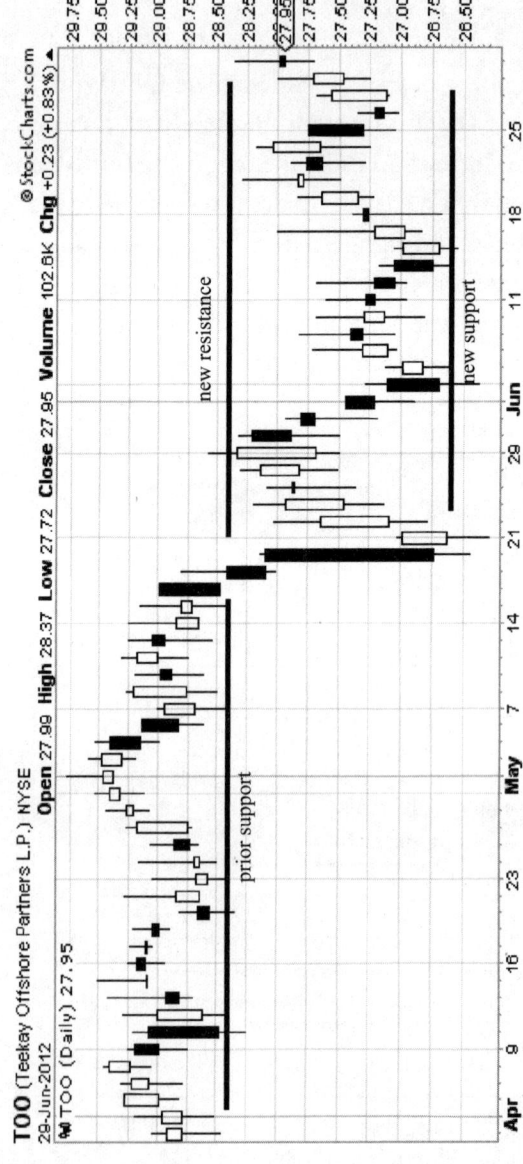

Figure 7.4 Teekay Offshore Partners
Source: StockCharts.com

Net return based on strikes, dividend only:

$0.51 ÷ $28 = 1.8%.

Annualized:

(1.8% ÷ 49) x 365 = 13.4%.

Annualized with stock/option losses deducted:

Net loss: $255 − $44 = $211
$211 ÷ $14,000 = 1.5%
(1.5% ÷ 49) x 365 = 11.2%.

The three-month chart of TOO ended June 29 (figure 7.4).

Here you see a familiar pattern in technical analysis when trading ranges evolve. The prior support level becomes the new resistance level, while a new, lower support is established. This indicates that the new trading range has been established for the moment. However, whether the underlying price moves above or below the 28 strike, market risk is eliminated and profits will occur in the form of the dividend yield.

UNIVERSAL CORP. (UVV)

Closing price on June 29	$46.33
Dividend yield:	4.22%
Dividend amount per share:	0.49
Ex-dividend date:	July 5
Options expiring July 20	Jul 45 calls @ 2.15
(21 days)	Jul 45 puts @ 0.50

Actions:

Buy 300 shares @ 46.33	$13,899
Buy 3 puts @ 0.50 =	−$150
Sell 3 calls @ 2.15 =	$645
Net options credit	$ 495

Outcomes:

Calls or puts are exercised,
Net capital loss, 1.33 per share = −$399

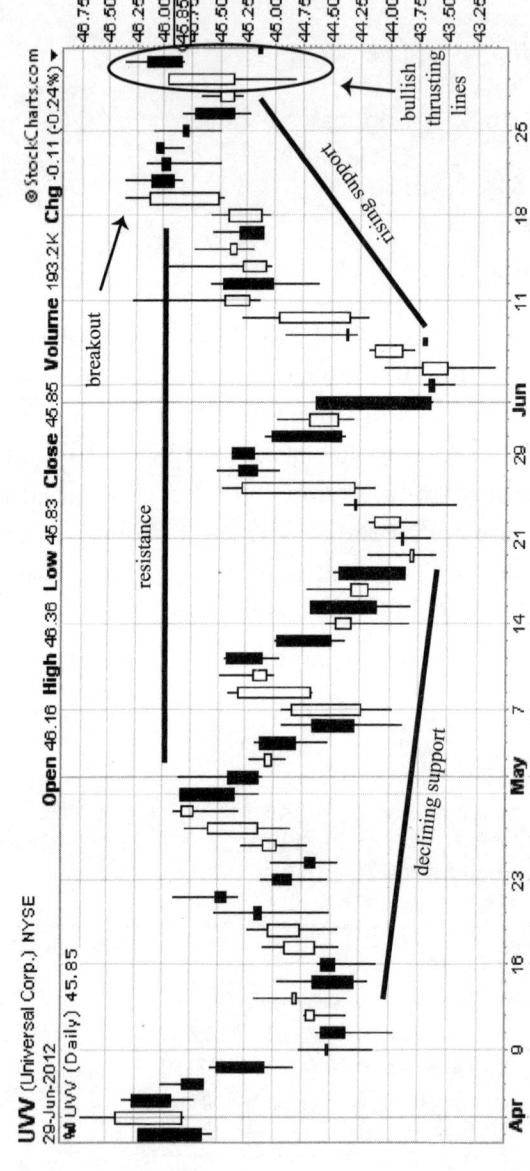

Figure 7.5 Franklin Street Properties
Source: StockCharts.com

Estimated transaction costs:

Stock (buy and sell)	−$18
Options: 6 round trips each, 12 total; (8.95 x 4) + (0.75 x 12)	−45
Net total losses	−$462
Net options credit, less total profit	$33
Dividend, 0.49 per share =	$147

Net return based on strikes, dividend only:

$0.49 ÷ $45 = 1.1%.

Annualized:

(1.1% ÷ 21) x 365 = 19.1%.

The three-month chart of UVV ended June 29 (figure 7.5).

This is a busy chart with a lot of signaling. First, the support level declines and then rises, indicating a turnaround in the trend and likely bullish movement. There are two confirmations of this. First is the breakout above resistance that appeared to hold through to the end of the charted period. Second was the two-session candlestick signal called bullish thrusting lines (a white candlestick followed by a higher black candlestick).

To summarize all five outcomes,

Franklin Street Properties (FSP)

Exercise produced a net profit in the stock/option trade, and this was not counted in the annualized return of dividend yield.

The dividend yield was 1.9% over 49 days, or annualized at 14.2%.

Kite Realty (KRG)

Exercise resulted in a net stock/option loss, and as a result, dividend yield was reduced by the amount of the loss.

The dividend yield alone was 1.2% over 21 days, or annualized at *20.9%*.

The net dividend yield with deduction of the stock/option loss was 0.5%, or annualized at *8.7%*.

PEOPLE'S UNITED FINANCIAL (PBCT)

Exercise produced a net profit in the stock/option trade, and this was not counted in the annualized return of the dividend yield.

The dividend yield was 15% over 49 days, or annualized at *11.2%*.

TEEKAY OFFSHORE (TOO)

Exercise resulted in a net stock/option loss, and as a result dividend yield was reduced by the amount of the loss.

The dividend yield alone was 1.8%, or annualized at *13.4%*.

The net dividend yield with deduction of the stock/option loss was 1.5% over 49 days, or annualized at *11.2%*.

UNIVERSAL CORP. (UVV)

Exercise resulted in a net profit in the stock/option trade, and this was not counted in the annualized return of the dividend yield.

The dividend yield was 1.1% over 21 days, or annualized at *19.1%*.

In each case, the annualized return was in double digits (exception: Kite Realty was under double digits when annualized with the net loss deducted from dividend yield). All other outcomes—exercise of either the calls or the puts—yielded net profits (or net losses, which reduced dividend yield but still yielded a double-digit return).

These five stocks had ex-dividend dates in July 2012. This is out of 740 total stocks yielding dividends of 4% or more. If an average of one-third reported dividends in July, it reduces the field to 247 issues. Of these, many paid irregular dividends or did not offer options trading. The field ended up with only 50 issues, and 10% of those worked profitably with the dividend collar.

In order to succeed with this basic strategy, you need only one issue per month. Arriving at these five is the result of hours of analysis and comparison; however, any of these yields double-digit annualized returns and eliminates all risk.

Assuming this is a typical outcome, you would find another approximately 240–250 issues with August expirations. Upon closing out a July transaction, this process is repeated, examining the August ex-dividend stocks to isolate their call-put relationship to find at least one more. It is always possible that none of the 240–250 issues will yield any for which the dividend collar will work, but this outcome is very unlikely. If that were to occur, you have a choice: Use a different strategy or continue monitoring the issues with potential, recognizing that with every price change, the status changes as well. The above examples were based on the close of June 29, 2012; it is certain that the close a day before or a day after would have yielded entirely different results. If you use a different strategy, you will probably need to accept higher risks. The installment collar, ratio write collar, variable ratio write collar, or synthetic short stock dividend collar are all alternatives. These are found in the following chapters.

CHAPTER 8

MODIFICATION: THE INSTALLMENT COLLAR APPROACH

> Patience is a necessary ingredient of genius.
> Benjamin Disraeli, *Contarini Fleming*, 1832

THE DIVIDEND COLLAR CONTAINS ELEGANCE AND SIMPLICITY because it eliminates market risk while providing high net returns. At the same time, because option profits are not the key, using soon-to-expire contracts is convenient and practical. Few other options strategies work as well.

Another distinct advantage is the fairly low margin requirements. The collar requires an initial margin of only 50% on the stock position and 100% of the put price, with no margin on the covered call. Maintenance is zero on both the call and the put. For the stock, maintenance is the lower of 10% of the put exercise price plus out-of-the-money (OTM) points on the stock, or 25% of the call exercise price.

Margin is complex, and deserves detailed study for all options strategies. The point of this discussion is that creating a collar does not add significantly to the margin demands placed on your portfolio. Compared to simply owning stock, margin is slightly higher initially, and then not much greater on the maintenance level. The Chicago Board Options Exchange (CBOE) provides an excellent reference explaining margin requirements for all options strategies.[1]

With margin advantage in mind, you can expand the basic dividend collar into several variations. Depending on the levels of implied volatility and your perceptions on an underlying over the long term, the *installment collar* is one strategy that modifies the dividend collar by adding long-term downside protection while creating potentially ongoing income from writing short calls. This strategy is not risk-free, however. If a current short call is exercised before the cost of the long-term put has been recovered, the strategy loses net value. To offset this risk, the installment collar should be designed so that any loss on the long put will be offset by two other factors: premium income from writing a series of short-term calls, and capital gains if and when the short calls are exercised.

Design of the Installment Collar

The installment collar modifies the basic strategy in one important manner: It replaces the short-term long put with a long-term put, and employs a series of short calls to recapture the cost of that put over the life of the put.

The rationale for the installment collar is that it provides long-term downside protection. However, because the put is more expensive than one expiring within one month, it has to be paid for by writing the short calls month after month. Because time value declines rapidly in the last month of a call's life, it is practical to employ this strategy, as long as you track the calls and avoid exercise, at least until the net cost of the put has been offset.

The short calls can be managed in one of three ways:

1. Hold until expiration and then replace. Options held until expiration will end up worthless in 75% of all cases. However, this does not mean exercise risk is always low. These same short calls may move in the money (ITM) even for a brief time, and if that time includes the period immediately prior to the ex-dividend date, your shares might be called away. (Exercise does not always occur. Long call holders will exercise only when the difference between the strike and the

current price is higher than the cost they paid for the call, so depending on the degree of price movement, not all calls are going to be exercised even when ITM.) If the call is ITM as expiration approaches, automatic exercise becomes a distinct possibility, and then a forward roll is more rational than allowing exercise to occur. However, exercise is always possible, so selection of the strike should ensure that in the event of exercise, it results in a net capital gain and not a loss.
2. Hold until value declines, and then buy to close and replace. This is the most likely action. As time value evaporates when the expiration date nears, the call becomes so cheap that it is easy to close and replace with another that is expiring the following month.
3. If these calls move ITM, roll forward to either the same strike or, when profitable, to a higher strike. The roll always provides additional income when the strike is the same, because later expiration adds time value. It is more difficult to roll forward and up to a higher strike, and still create a net profit (or at least avoid a debit). This is most likely when you restrict your selection for installment collars to underlyings with one-point strike increments. If the overall trading range does gradually move upward, your strike selection can track and "ladder up" as each expiration comes close, to be replaced by higher strikes in the following month.

Risk Attributes of the Installment Strategy

The precise selection of strikes does not matter as much as with many options strategies. For example, in the last chapter, all of the basic strategy examples had the same strike on both sides. This made them synthetic stock positions rather than strictly defined collars. A collar is actually a combination of a long OTM put and a short OTM call, plus 100 shares of stock. The dividend collar and its definition are more liberal because the outcome is the specific goal, not the placement of strikes.

For example, the installment collar may be more accurately classified as a diagonal spread, calendar spread, or diagonal calendar spread. None of these distinctions matter when you consider the purpose behind the dividend collar. Under the installment collar, the purpose is to create a longer-term insurance put and pay for it in short-call installments. The higher the put premium, the longer it will take to repay, and of course, the richer the call premium, the more rapidly the installments are applied.

Risk attributes of the insurance put are different than those in the basic strategy. The installment put is not risk-free, although its risks are manageable. The risks you face with this strategy change in the price structure of the underlying, in both directions.

If the underlying declines well below the put's strike, you will want to (1) exercise the put in order to sell shares at the fixed strike; or (2) sell the put to take profits that offset your loss and lower your net basis in the underlying. In a downside move, you are protected. However, the risk remains that the relatively expensive put will not be paid for in a short-call premium by the time the price decline occurs. In that case, the risk is a downside risk equal to the following: (1) the cost of the put minus any short-call premiums received to that point, and (2) the cost to buy in order to close any outstanding short calls at the time stock is sold. In the latter, even with a price decline, you may want to close the call rather than keep an uncovered position open. As an alternative, you can monitor to ensure that the underlying price does not rise above the call's strike, creating a different and potentially more serious market risk.

Another price change that creates risk occurs when the underlying price rises. In this case, the value of the put declines, but the risk of call exercise increases. Exercise will occur in most cases in one of two situations. First is when the call is ITM immediately before a quarterly ex-dividend date, and exercise is possible (although not a sure thing). Second is on the last trading day, when ITM calls are exercised automatically. You can roll forward to avoid exercise, but if the price is rising, you will also want to roll up to a higher strike. This might not be possible without a debit in the rolling transaction. Exercise can occur at any time when a short call is ITM, and the risk here is that it will occur prior to your having covered the cost of the put.

The risk is always offset, however, if and when the call's strike is high enough to cover the put cost upon exercise. In this case, exercise should be welcomed. For example, if your put costs 6 ($600) and to date you have collected 2 ($200) in call premium, exercise is acceptable as long as the call's strike is at least 4 points above your original basis in the underlying. Even though this represents a breakeven point in both stock and call, the dividend yield was earned during the period. A basic assumption of the installment collar—like all versions of the dividend collar—is that the strategy makes sense in order to ensure continued high dividend yield.

Unlike the basic dividend collar in which exercise is desirable and an essential aspect of the strategy, you may not always welcome call exercise with the installment put. The ideal situation would be to at least cover the put's cost over several months, while continuing to earn dividends, and then either to replace the position with another installment collar or allow exercise to occur. If the long-term goal is to continue the attractive dividend yield, there is no rush to achieve exercise. Once the put's cost has been covered, any subsequent call premium is extra income, and this will translate into ongoing covered call income with the long put providing ongoing downside protection. The combination of covered call income and dividends will be consistently double digits. This is possible simply with writing covered calls; however, without the protective put, covered calls face the same market risks as outright stock ownership, albeit on a discounted basis. For the covered call writer, a one-to-one call and protective put represent no income. So the essential value in the insurance put is realized when (1) the call's strike is higher than basis by at least as much as the outstanding and as yet unpaid put premium; (2) dividend yield is exceptional; and (3) income from covered calls continues to be attractive given the current value of the underlying and the premium level.

Another risk of the installment collar occurs if and when the dividend is changed during the installment period. This can mean the dividend is reduced or skipped. In either case, the whole purpose in focusing on high-yielding stocks is defeated, and this is a serious potential risk to the installment collar. You face the choice of either closing out the position and transferring to other underlying issues that pay dividends, or holding on without dividends until your call premium income matches or exceeds the cost of the put. In the latter, you may still earn double-digit annualized returns from covered call writing, and the longer-term long put continues to provide downside protection. So the loss of the dividend is not a total disaster.

One way to view the dividend risk is as a minor problem. As long as the put strike is higher than your original basis, and as long as call strikes are also higher and continue to track price levels above basis, you will profit upon exercise of either side. Covered call income will also annualize out to double digits. The main difference in the installment put is that once the put's premium has been covered, you continue earning double digits with no downside risk. That is eliminated by the put with its fixed strike.

The installment put contains risks and cannot be defined as risk-free. However, for anyone who enjoys the high income from writing covered calls, the installment eliminates the downside risk of holding long stock. This makes the covered call strategy truly risk-free, but *only* once the put has been paid for and *only* as long as the put remains open. If call premium income and dividends combine to cover the put's cost well before the put expires, you can create double-digit returns. The challenge is to create a net double-digit annualized return, considering that the cost of the long put has to be covered as well. It is possible, but that net double-digit return will not always materialize.

EXAMPLES OF THE STRATEGY

The higher level of market risk of the installment put is worthwhile for traders willing to accept the risks in exchange for ongoing higher-than-average dividends, longer-term downside risk coverage, and the ability to hold shares for the long term. This solves the problem every covered call writer faces, that of downside risk. The risk is the same as that of owning shares, although

Table 8.1 Stocks selected for analysis of the installment collar

Name	Ticker	July Ex-Dividend	Dividends Per share	%	Closing Price
AT & T	T	July 5	0.44	4.97%	$35.66
Verizon	VZ	July 6	0.50	4.55	44.44

Source: S&P Stock Reports.

call premium reduces the breakeven level in the underlying. When the price declines below this net basis (cost of shares minus income from covered calls), traders have to accept net losses or wait for prices to rebound. Because a rebound does not always occur quickly (or may not occur at all), this is a very serious risk. The installment dividend collar solves this problem for covered call writers.

Two of the 50 companies in the original analysis were set aside to provide examples here of the installment collar (table 8.1).

Because the installment collar involves offsetting current calls with long-term puts, a range of possible contracts has to be considered:

AT & T:

Month/Year	Strike	Calls	Puts
July 2012	35	0.62	
January 2013	35		1.99
April 2013	35		2.67
April 2013	36		3.20
January 2014	35		4.45

Verizon:

Month/Year	Strike	Calls	Puts
July 2012	44	0.65	
July 2012	45	0.22	
January 2013	45		3.25
April 2013	45		4.10
January 2014	45		6.35

In both of these cases, several choices have to be made. For purposes of the examples, the longest-term puts are selected, which are the January 2014 contracts. In the case of Verizon, the call selected depends on whether an ITM contract with a 0.65 premium is better than an OTM contract with only 0.22 premium. Going forward and estimating how the installment collar will work, a series of assumptions have to be made. These are all variable and have to be adjusted as the value of the underlying rises or falls, and as the premium of various levels of calls also changes.

At the close of July 3 (two sessions after the target close for all 50 stocks) both AT & T and Verizon had moved close to the money for the next-higher call. Premium values of the AT & T 36 calls for the next three expiration cycles were:

Month/strike	Premium	Return	Annualized
Jul 36	0.19	0.19 ÷ 36 = 0.5%	(0.5 ÷ 21) x 365 = 8.7%
Aug 36	0.48	0.48 ÷ 36 = 1.3%	(1.3 ÷ 49) x 365 = 9.7%
Sep 36	0.67	0.67 ÷ 36 = 1.9%	(1.9 ÷ 82) x 365 = 8.5%

For Verizon, the same analysis yielded the following results:

Month/strike	Premium	Return	Annualized
Jul 45	0.34	0.34 ÷ 45 = 0.8%	(0.8 ÷ 21) x 365 = 13.9%
Aug 45	0.55	0.55 ÷ 45 = 1.2%	(1.2 ÷ 49) x 365 = 8.9%
Sep 45	0.95	0.95 ÷ 45 = 2.1%	(2.1 ÷ 82) x 365 = 9.3%

For both companies, the one-month contracts are used even though, in the case of AT & T, the two-month calls yield more. The rationale is that you cannot know whether this better yield will continue for 19 months. In addition, using one-month calls limits exercise risk because time value declines most rapidly during this final month. The assumption going forward will be that maximum yield will be accomplished by writing a series of at-the-money (ATM) calls expiring in one month. Of course, because these are ATM, contracts will have to be closed or rolled forward if they go ITM immediately before the next ex-dividend date or right before the last trading day. So the analysis is going to be based on the assumption that a series of covered calls worth 0.19 will be available every month, and that the underlying price will remain at or below the strike price.

The same assumptions will be applied to Verizon, whose one-month calls yield the most desirable annualized returns. This analysis will assume the availability of a series of calls with 0.34 premium each month, and also that the underlying will remain at or below the strike.

ANALYSIS: AT & T

Actions: Buy 400 shares of AT & T on June 29 @ $35.66 = $14,264

		Debit/credit level
June 29, 2012		
Buy 4 Jan 2014, 35 puts @ 4.45 =		$–1,780
Sell 4 Jul 2012, 36 calls @ 0.19	$76	–1,704
July 23, 2012		
Sell 4 Aug 2012 36 calls @ 0.19	$76	–1,628
August 20, 2012		
Sell 4 Sep 2012 36 calls @ 0.19	$76	–1,552
September 24, 2012		
Sell 4 Oct 2012 36 calls @ 0.19	$76	–1,476
October 22, 2012		
Sell 4 Nov 2012 36 calls @ 0.19	$76	–1,400
November 19, 2012		
Sell 4 Dec 2012 36 calls @ 0.19	$76	–1,324
December 24, 2012		
Sell 4 Jan 2013 36 calls @ 0.19	$76	–1,248
January 21, 2013		
Sell 4 Feb 2013 36 calls @ 0.19	$76	–1,172
February 18, 2013		
Sell 4 Mar 2013 36 calls @ 0.19	$76	–1,096
March 18, 2013		
Sell 4 Apr 2013 36 calls @ 0.19	$76	–1,020
April 22, 2013		
Sell 4 May 2013 36 calls @ 0.19	$76	–944
May 20, 2013		

Continued

		Debit/credit level
Sell 4 Jun 2013 36 calls @ 0.19	$76	–868
June 24, 2013		
Sell 4 Jul 2013 36 calls @ 0.19	$76	–792
July 22, 2013		
Sell 4 Aug 2013 36 calls @ 0.19	$76	–716
August 19, 2013		
Sell 4 Sep 2013 36 calls @ 0.19	$76	–640
September 23, 2013		
Sell 4 Oct 2013 36 calls @ 0.19	$76	–564
October 21, 2013		
Sell 4 Nov 2013 36 calls @ 0.19	$76	–488
November 18, 2013		
Sell 4 Dec 2013 36 calls @ 0.19	$76	–412
December 23, 2013		
Sell 4 Jan 2014 36 calls @ 0.19	$76	–336

This summary is not adjusted for transaction costs of approximately $12 per trade. It is also based on three variables, and the longer the period, the more likely that these three variables will no longer apply (however, conditions could either improve or worsen). The variable assumptions are:

1. All of the short calls will be held until expiration and will expire worthless.
2. The premium amount each month will remain approximately the same.
3. The underlying price will remain ATM or slightly below.

While none of these assumptions are realistic, they provide a baseline for understanding the installment collar. In this example, after 19 months, a net debit remains between the long put and the series of short calls. You can look at this net as the cost of downside protection. However, it remains a problem that the net was a debit. In other words, option income during those 19 months was zero since the call premium was used to offset part of the cost of the put.

During the same period, seven quarterly ex-dividend dates occur. The quarterly dividend was 0.44 per share per quarter. So for 400 shares, total dividend income over these 19 months is:

7 x 0.44 x 400 = $1,232.

Dividend yield minus the net loss on options was:

$1,232 − $336 = $896.

Based on the put strike of 35 for 400 shares ($14,000), annualized yield was:

(($896 ÷ $14,000) ÷ 19) x 12 = 4.0%.

So the combined net yield on the installment collar was only 4.0%. This was lower than the 4.97% dividend yield, because the net loss on option premium had to be deducted.

This analysis demonstrates that the installment dividend collar is not an exceptionally high-yielding strategy. However, for covered call writers, the lower annualized yield may be viewed as the cost for providing 19 months of eliminating downside market risk.

If the trader had purchased shares below the June 29 price of $35.66, the overall outcome would be vastly improved. It would also provide the assurance of net profits if the short calls were exercised. In this case, the installment collar may be viewed as a way to generate acceptable annual returns with zero downside market risk over the long term.

The three-month chart for T is shown in figure 8.1.

This chart reveals a rising trading range but with narrow breadth. This signals the possibility of a continuing upward tendency in price; however, if price does continues trending upward, the wise reaction would be to write subsequent covered calls at ever-higher strikes, thus "riding" the trend. If the price range were to fall, strikes could be written that are lower but still at profitable levels if exercised. If the price did fall below the mid-level trading

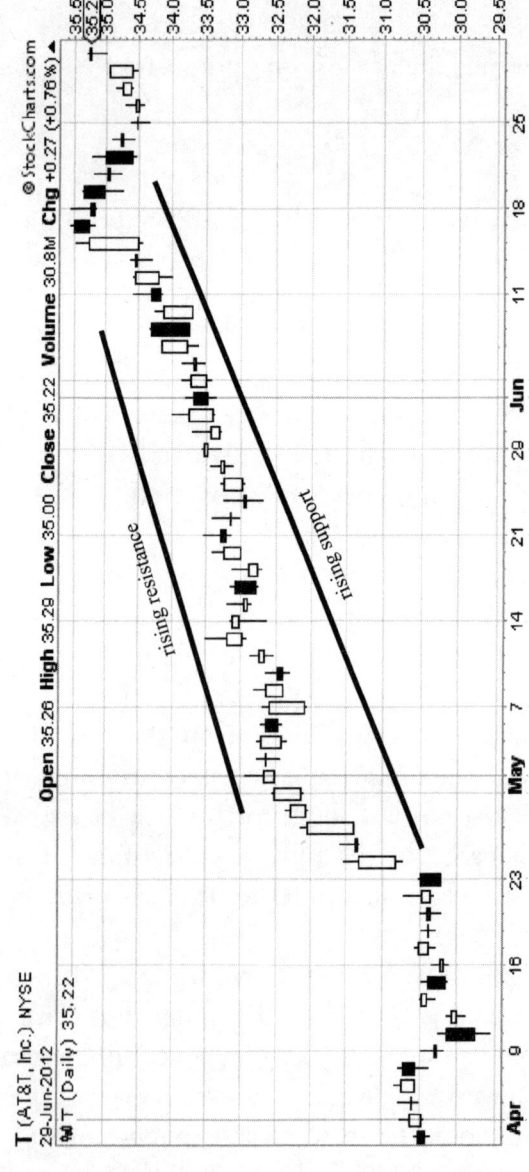

Figure 8.1 AT&T
Source: StockCharts.com.

range, the put could be exercised at any time, or the installment plan suspended until prices return to an uptrend.

Analysis: Verizon

Actions: Buy 300 shares of Verizon on June 29 @ $44.44 = $13,332

June 29, 2012		Debit/credit level
Buy 3 Jan 2014 45 puts @ 6.35 =		$–1,905
Sell 3 Jul 2012 44 calls @ 0.65	$195	–1,710
July 23, 2012		
Sell 3 Aug 2012 44 calls @ 0.65	$195	–1,515
August 20, 2012		
Sell 3 Sep 2012 44 calls @ 0.65	$195	–1,320
September 24, 2012		
Sell 3 Oct 2012 44 calls @ 0.65	$195	–1,125
October 22, 2012		
Sell 3 Nov 2012 44 calls @ 0.65	$195	–930
November 19, 2012		
Sell 3 Dec 2012 44 calls @ 0.65	$195	–735
December 24, 2012		
Sell 3 Jan 2013 44 calls @ 0.65	$195	–540
January 21, 2013		
Sell 3 Feb 2013 44 calls @ 0.65	$195	–345
February 18, 2013		
Sell 3 Mar 2013 44 calls @ 0.65	$195	–150
March 18, 2013		
Sell 3 Apr 2013 44 calls @ 0.65	$195	45
April 22, 2013		
Sell 3 May 2013 44 calls @ 0.65	$195	240
May 20, 2013		
Sell 3 Jun 2013 44 calls @ 0.65	$195	435
June 24, 2013		
Sell 3 Jul 2013 44 calls @ 0.65	$195	630
July 22, 2013		
Sell 3 Aug 2013 44 calls @ 0.65	$195	825
August 19, 2013		
Sell 3 Sep 2013 44 calls @ 0.65	$195	1,020
September 23, 2013		
Sell 3 Oct 2013 44 calls @ 0.65	$195	1,215
October 21, 2013		
Sell 3 Nov 2013 44 calls @ 0.65	$195	1,410

Continued

June 29, 2012		Debit/credit level
November 18, 2013		
Sell 3 Dec 2013 44 calls @ 0.65	$195	1,605
December 23, 2013		
Sell 3 Jan 2014 44 calls @ 0.65	$195	1,800

In this example, the overall strategy results in a credit after 19 months, with breakeven in approximately 10 months. The $1,800 net can be annualized based on 300 shares and with the put strikes of 45 for 300 shares:

$$((\$1{,}800 \div \$13{,}500) \div 19) \times 12 = 8.4\%.$$

When this annualized return is added to the annual dividend yield of 4.55%, double digit is achieved:

$$8.4\% + 4.55\% = 12.95\%.$$

The installment collar produces a desirable double-digit return while providing downside risk-free status for 19 months. The only upside risk exists for the period of the first 10 months. The call strikes used in this example were 0.44 ITM, representing a capital loss risk of $132 for three shares. However, once the short calls begin earning above breakeven, this—and transaction costs averaging $11 per transaction—is quickly offset.

The outcome is even more desirable if the basis in stock was lower than the closing price on June 29, 2012, of $44.44 per share. For example, if the original basis was $40 per share, then exercise of the 45 puts would have created net capital gains of $1,500 more (five points for 300 shares), and exercise of the 44 calls would have produced additional capital gains of $1,200 (four points for 2300 shares).

The three-month chart for VZ is found in figure 8.2.

VZ's trading range narrowed considerably during this period, indicating the possibility of a downtrend reversal. However, this cannot be known for certain. The overall trend was upward,

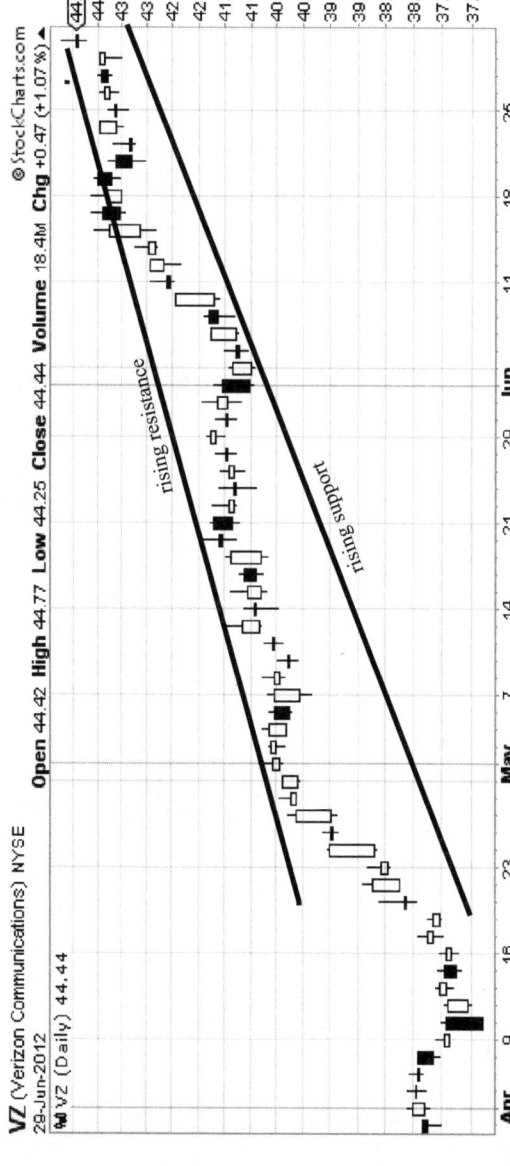

Figure 8.2 Verizon Communications
Source: StockCharts.com.

which is desirable for the installment strategy. If the trend did continue to rise, subsequent calls could be written with higher strikes in the future.

USING THE RATIO WRITE OR VARIABLE RATIO WRITE ON THE CALL SIDE

The installment collar can be expanded with the use of either the ratio write or the variable ratio write. This increases the exercise risk of calls; however, the variable format is much less risky because two different strikes are employed. If the underlying begins moving to the money, some or all of the calls are to be closed or rolled. Because time value falls rapidly in the final month, this is very likely even if the calls have already moved in the money. As long as the move is not too fast or too extreme, it is usually not difficult to avoid exercise.

The risk remains, however, for both the ratio write and the variable ratio write. Exercise and a resulting loss are always a possibility if the calls move ITM. So this is not a risk-free version of the installment dividend collar.

Using the same examples as previously presented in this chapter, both AT & T and Verizon can be subjected to both of these expansions of the strategy. AT & T reported July 36 calls at 0.19, as shown in the previous example. The installment collar could be based on a 3:2 ratio consisting of 400 shares and six short calls instead of 4. The same put is used as well. The risk here is that with the same assumptions in place, the starting price of the underlying is only 0.34 below the money. Any movement into the money requires closing the excess positions or rolling them forward. However, as long as the underlying remains ATM or OTM, this ratio write over 10 months looks like this:

ANALYSIS: AT & T

Actions: Buy 400 shares of AT & T on June 29 @ $35.66 = $14,264

		Debit/credit level
June 29, 2012		
Buy 4 Jan 2014 35 puts @ 4.45 =	$–1,780	
Sell 6 Jul 2012 36 calls @ 0.19	$114	–1,666
July 23, 2012		
Sell 6 Aug 2012 36 calls @ 0.19	$114	–1,552
August 20, 2012		
Sell 6 Sep 2012 36 calls @ 0.19	$114	–1,438
September 24, 2012		
Sell 6 Oct 2012 36 calls @ 0.19	$114	–1,324
October 22, 2012		
Sell 6 Nov 2012 36 calls @ 0.19	$114	–1,210
November 19, 2012		
Sell 6 Dec 2012 36 calls @ 0.19	$114	–1,096
December 24, 2012		
Sell 6 Jan 2013 36 calls @ 0.19	$114	–982
January 21, 2013		
Sell 6 Feb 2013 36 calls @ 0.19	$114	–868
February 18, 2013		
Sell 6 Mar 2013 36 calls @ 0.19	$114	–754
March 18, 2013		
Sell 6 Apr 2013 36 calls @ 0.19	$114	–640
April 22, 2013		
Sell 6 May 2013 36 calls @ 0.19	$114	–526
May 20, 2013		
Sell 6 Jun 2013 36 calls @ 0.19	$114	–412
June 24, 2013		
Sell 6 Jul 2013 36 calls @ 0.19	$114	–298
July 22, 2013		
Sell 6 Aug 2013 36 calls @ 0.19	$114	–184
August 19, 2013		
Sell 6 Sep 2013 36 calls @ 0.19	$114	–70
September 23, 2013		
Sell 6 Oct 2013 36 calls @ 0.19	$114	44
October 21, 2013		
Sell 6 Nov 2013 36 calls @ 0.19	$114	158
November 18, 2013		
Sell 6 Dec 2013 36 calls @ 0.19	$114	272
December 23, 2013		
Sell 6 Jan 2014 36 calls @ 0.19	$114	386

Unlike the straightforward one-to-one matched covered calls, the ratio write creates a net credit over 19 months. It still provides the same elimination of downside risk, but exercise risk is considerable if and when the calls move ITM. So this position has to be monitored and adjusted to ensure exercise does not take place.

The return calculation has to first be annualized, and then the dividend yield is added. The $386 profit is a return of:

$386 ÷ $14,000 = 2.8%.

Annualized:

(2.8 ÷ 19) x 12 = 1.8%.

When this is added to the dividend yield of 4.97% per year:

1.8% + 4.97% = 6.77%.

This annualized return is not double digits, and it is much less than a straightforward covered call strategy. However, this approach also includes complete elimination of downside risk below the put's strike for the entire period. So covered call writers who are concerned about downside risk may employ the ratio write dividend collar to reduce risk, in exchange for a reduced annual return.

In the case of Verizon, the outcome will be quite different. The company's options as of June 29 included the 44 call at 0.65. With 300 shares bought, selling four calls per month, creates a 4:3 ratio write. The outcome:

ANALYSIS: VERIZON

Actions: Buy 300 shares of Verizon on June 29 @ $44.44 = $13,332

		Debit/credit level
June 29, 2012		
Buy 3 Jan 2014 45 puts @ 6.35 =		$–1,905
Sell 4 Jul 2012 44 calls @ 0.65	$260	–1,645
July 23, 2012		
Sell 4 Aug 2012 44 calls @ 0.65	$260	–1,385

		Debit/credit level
August 20, 2012		
Sell 4 Sep 2012 44 calls @ 0.65	$260	–1,125
September 24, 2012		
Sell 4 Oct 2012 44 calls @ 0.65	$260	–865
October 22, 2012		
Sell 4 Nov 2012 44 calls @ 0.65	$260	–605
November 19, 2012		
Sell 4 Dec 2012 44 calls @ 0.65	$260	–345
December 24, 2012		
Sell 4 Jan 2013 44 calls @ 0.65	$260	–85
January 21, 2013		
Sell 4 Feb 2013 44 calls @ 0.65	$260	175
February 18, 2013		
Sell 4 Mar 2013 44 calls @ 0.65	$260	435
March 18, 2013		
Sell 4 Apr 2013 44 calls @ 0.65	$260	695
April 22, 2013		
Sell 4 May 2013 44 calls @ 0.65	$260	955
May 20, 2013		
Sell 4 Jun 2013 44 calls @ 0.65	$260	1,215
June 24, 2013		
Sell 4 Jul 2013 44 calls @ 0.65	$260	1,475
July 22, 2013		
Sell 4 Aug 2013 44 calls @ 0.65	$260	1,735
August 19, 2013		
Sell 4 Sep 2013 44 calls @ 0.65	$260	1,995
September 23, 2013		
Sell 4 Oct 2013 44 calls @ 0.65	$260	2,255
October 21, 2013		
Sell 4 Nov 2013 44 calls @ 0.65	$260	2,515
November 18, 2013		
Sell 4 Dec 2013 44 calls @ 0.65	$260	2,775
December 23, 2013		
Sell 4 Jan 2014 44 calls @ 0.65	$260	3,035

The return calculation is first annualized based on the put strike of 45 for 300 shares, and then added to the dividend yield. The $3,035 profit is a return of:

$3,035 ÷ $13,500 = 22.5%.

Annualized:

(22.5 ÷ 19) x 12 = 14.2%.

When this is added to the dividend yield of 4.55% per year:

14.2% + 4.55% = 18.75%.

In the case of Verizon, the addition of one extra call in the ratio write increases exercise risk. However, it continues to eliminate all downside risk. The substantial annualized return may be worth the added risk to many traders, especially since all downside risk is gone for 19 months.

The variable ratio write changes the equation considerably because upside risks are lowered. This is achieved with the use of two strikes instead of one. To enhance income even further, a higher strike may also be extended for an additional amount time. For example, AT & T had the following calls available on June 29:

Jul 35	0.62
Sep 36	0.50

A variable ratio write can be constructed in several ways. In this case, the four July 36 calls will be matched to the 400 shares purchased at the same time. If exercised, the capital loss on the underlying will be 0.04 per share (value of $35.66 less strike of 35–0.66 loss; 0.66 less 0.62 call premium = 0.04 per share). This represents a potential loss of only $16 before transaction costs. However, adding another two of the September 36 calls at 0.50 adds $100 of profit. This strategy comes out as follows:

ANALYSIS: AT & T

Actions: Buy 400 shares of AT & T on June 29 @ $35.66 = $14,264

MODIFICATION

		Debit/credit level
June 29, 2012		
Buy 4 Jan 2014 35 puts @ 4.45 =		$–1,780
Sell 4 Jul 2012 35 calls @ 0.62	$248	
Sell 2 Sep 2012 36 calls @ 0.50	100	–1,432
July 23, 2012		
Sell 4 Aug 2012 35 calls @ 0.62	$248	
Sell 2 Oct 2012 36 calls @ 0.50	100	–1,084
August 20, 2012		
Sell 4 Sep 2012 35 calls @ 0.62	$248	
Sell 2 Nov 2013 36 calls @ 0.50	100	–736
September 24, 2012		
Sell 4 Oct 2012 35 calls @ 0.62	$248	
Sell 2 Dec 2012 36 calls @ 0.50	100	–388
October 22, 2012		
Sell 4 Nov 2012 35 calls @ 0.62	$248	
Sell 2 Jan 2013 36 calls @ 0.50	100	–40
November 19, 2012		
Sell 4 Dec 2012 35 calls @ 0.62	$248	
Sell 2 Feb 2013 36 calls @ 0.50	100	308
December 24, 2012		
Sell 4 Jan 2013 35 calls @ 0.62	$248	
Sell 2 Mar 2013 36 calls @ 0.50	100	656
January 21, 2013		
Sell 4 Feb 2013 35 calls @ 0.62	$248	
Sell 2 Apr 2013 36 calls @ 0.50	100	1,004
February 18, 2013		
Sell 4 Mar 2013 35 calls @ 0.62	$248	
Sell 2 May 2013 36 calls @ 0.50	100	1,352
March 18, 2013		
Sell 4 Apr 2013 35 calls @ 0.62	$248	
Sell 2 Jun 2013 36 calls @ 0.50	100	1,700
April 22, 2013		
Sell 4 May 2013 35 calls @ 0.62	$248	
Sell 2 Jul 2013 36 calls @ 0.50	100	2,048
May 20, 2013		
Sell 4 Jun 2013 35 calls @ 0.62	$248	
Sell 2 Aug 2013 36 calls @ 0.50	100	2,396
June 24, 2013		
Sell 4 Jul 2013 35 calls @ 0.62	$248	
Sell 2 Sep 2013 36 calls @ 0.50	100	2,744
July 22, 2013		
Sell 4 Aug 2013 35 calls @ 0.62	$248	

Continued

		Debit/credit level
Sell 2 Oct 2013 36 calls @ 0.50	100	3,092
August 19, 2013		
Sell 4 Sep 2013 35 calls @ 0.62	$248	
Sell 2 Nov 2013 36 calls @ 0.50	100	3,440
September 23, 2013		
Sell 4 Oct 2013 35 calls @ 0.62	$248	
Sell 2 Dec 2013 36 calls @ 0.50	100	3,788
October 21, 2013		
Sell 4 Jan 2014 35 calls @ 0.62	$248	
Sell 2 Sep 36 2012 36 calls @ 0.50	100	4,136
November 18, 2013		
Sell 4 Dec 2013 35 calls @ 0.62	$248	
Sell 2 Feb 2013 36 calls @ 0.50	100	4,484
December 23, 2013		
Sell 4 Jan 2014 35 calls @ 0.62	$248	
Sell 2 Mar 2013 36 calls @ 0.50	100	4,832

The return calculation has to first be annualized, and then the dividend yield is added. The $4,832 profit is a return of:

$4,832 ÷ $14,000 = 35.5%.

Annualized:

(35.5 ÷ 19) x 12 = 22.4%.

When this is added to the dividend yield of 4.97% per year:

22.4% + 4.97% = 27.37%.

Verizon, in comparison, offered the following calls on June 29:

| Jul 44 | 0.65 |
| Jul 45 | 0.22 |

The Verizon model was designed for 300 shares, so a variable ratio write consists of two of each of these options. The outcome:

Analysis: Verizon

Actions: Buy 300 shares of Verizon on June 29 @ $44.44 = $13,332

		Debit/credit level
June 29, 2012		
Buy 3 Jan 2014 45 puts @ 6.35 =		$–1,905
Sell 2 Jul 2012 44 calls @ 0.65	$130	
Sell 2 Jul 2012 45 calls @ 0.22	44	–1,731
July 23, 2012		
Sell 2 Aug 2012 44 calls @ 0.65	$130	
Sell 2 Aug 2012 45 calls @ 0.22	44	–1,557
August 20, 2012		
Sell 2 Sep 2012 44 calls @ 0.65	$130	
Sell 2 Sep 2012 45 calls @ 0.22	44	–1,383
September 24, 2012		
Sell 2 Oct 2012 44 calls @ 0.65	$130	
Sell 2 Oct 2012 45 calls @ 0.22	44	–1,209
October 22, 2012		
Sell 2 Nov 2012 44 calls @ 0.65	$130	
Sell 2 Nov 2012 45 calls @ 0.22	44	–1,035
November 19, 2012		
Sell 2 Dec 2012 44 calls @ 0.65	$130	
Sell 2 Dec 2012 45 calls @ 0.22	44	–861
December 24, 2012		
Sell 2 Jan 2013 44 calls @ 0.65	$130	
Sell 2 Jan 2013 45 calls @ 0.22	44	–687
January 21, 2013		
Sell 2 Feb 2013 44 calls @ 0.65	$130	
Sell 2 Feb 2013 45 calls @ 0.22	44	–513
February 18, 2013		
Sell 2 Mar 2013 44 calls @ 0.65	$130	
Sell 2 Mar 2013 45 calls @ 0.22	44	–339
March 18, 2013		
Sell 2 Apr 2013 44 calls @ 0.65	$130	
Sell 2 Apr 2013 45 calls @ 0.22	44	–165
April 22, 2013		
Sell 2 May 2013 44 calls @ 0.65	$130	
Sell 2 May 2013 45 calls @ 0.22	44	9
May 20, 2013		
Sell 2 Jun 2013 44 calls @ 0.65	$130	
Sell 2 Jun 2013 45 calls @ 0.22	44	183

Continued

		Debit/credit level
June 24, 2013		
Sell 2 Jul 2013 44 calls @ 0.65	$130	
Sell 2 Jul 2013 45 calls @ 0.22	44	357
July 22, 2013		
Sell 2 Aug 2013 44 calls @ 0.65	$130	
Sell 2 Aug 2013 45 calls @ 0.22	44	531
August 19, 2013		
Sell 2 Sep 2013 44 calls @ 0.65	$130	
Sell 2 Sep 2013 45 calls @ 0.22	44	705
September 23, 2013		
Sell 2 Oct 2013 44 calls @ 0.65	$130	
Sell 2 Oct 2013 45 calls @ 0.22	44	879
October 21, 2013		
Sell 2 Nov 2013 44 calls @ 0.65	$130	
Sell 2 Nov 2013 45 calls @ 0.22	44	1,053
November 18, 2013		
Sell 2 Dec 2013 44 calls @ 0.65	$130	
Sell 2 Dec 2013 45 calls @ 0.22	44	1,227
December 23, 2013		
Sell 2 Jan 2014 44 calls @ 0.65	$130	
Sell 2 Jan 2014 45 calls @ 0.22	44	1,401

Although the dollar amount of return is lower in this example than for the nonvariable ratio write dividend collar, risks are substantially lower as well, due to the use of a higher strike. The return calculation is first annualized based on the put strike of 45 for 300 shares, and then added to the dividend yield. The $1,401 profit is a return of:

$1,401 ÷ $13,500 = 10.4%.

Annualized:

(10.4 ÷ 19) x 12 = 6.6%.

When this is added to the dividend yield of 4.55% per year:

6.6% + 4.55% = 11.15%.

This is a good example of how a variable ratio write dividend collar produces double-digit returns while accomplishing two important goals. First, all downside risk is eliminated for 19 months without net cost. In fact, even with the cost of the put, the strategy yields a net profit. The first 10 months are at risk of a net loss overall, due to the net debit remaining until that point. If all of the calls were exercised prior to the installment turning into a net credit, a loss would be realized. However, because the higher strike is OTM and two strikes are in use, exercise can be avoided through closing one or more of the contracts or by rolling forward. This could mean it will take longer to achieve the goal; however, once a short position has been closed, a new one can be opened after underlying movement establishes a higher base price. This creates a new variable ratio write while keeping the long puts in place.

THE REVERSE INSTALLMENT DIVIDEND COLLAR

Another variation on the installment collar is the *reverse* version. In this strategy, you start out selling a long-term call, which creates a healthy credit, and then you buy a series of short-term puts each month. The "budget" for these puts is equal to the credit earned on the short calls. The big question in this version is: Will there be enough call credit to fund the purchase of a series of puts? If not, there are three choices facing you: First, you can continue to own stock and the short call without downside protection. Second, once the credit is used up, you can close the call and either keep the stock or sell it. Or third, you can close the short call and create a new dividend collar in one of its varieties.

Two of the fifty companies in the original analysis were identified as potential candidates for a reverse installment dividend collar:

Name	Ticker	Ex-Dividend	July Per share	Dividends %	Closing Price
Royal Bank of Canada	RY	July 12	0.55	4.45%	$51.22
Enterprise Products	EPD	July 26	0.63	5.01	51.24

The reverse installment collar involves offsetting current long puts with long-term short calls, and so the following contracts are in play:

Royal Bank of Canada:

Month/Year	Strike	Calls	Puts
October 2012	50		1.80
January 2013	50	4.00	

Enterprise Products:

Month/Year	Strike	Calls	Puts
August 2012	50		1.00
January 2013	50	2.65	

The reverse expansion of this strategy can never be as profitable as the previous variety, in which a series of short-term calls were written against one long-term put. This is due to the richer premium levels of puts. A month-to-month version of the reverse installment would not work. Even this example, in which a seven-month long put is opened versus a seven-month call (RY) or a six-month call (EPD), ends with marginal outcomes. So the only value to the reverse installment method is the elimination of all downside risk for a period of time. The question you need to address is whether this strategy is worthwhile. It is if you want to continue earning dividends on the stocks in your portfolio, but without significant exercise risk. Furthermore, the strategy requires that you give up a chance for option-based income or capital gains (if the call is eventually exercised).

RY's situation requires a long put three months away. Assuming the same price would be available in October, a January 2013 put would cost an additional 1.80, so the total long side would be 3.60, versus the short call of 4.00 expiring the same month. This is approximately a breakeven scenario over seven months. However, during that time, all downside risk has been eliminated.

And there would be three dividend earning periods paying 0.55 per share. So a 100-share strategy (with one long put and one short call) would yield $55, a 4.45% return. In this case, the reverse installment allows you to protect the equity against potential downside movement while earning a respectable dividend. The risk includes the possibility that a long put might cost more in the October period, meaning the net cost of options would be higher, eroding the dividend income or, in the alternative, making it necessary to give up the downside protection by opening another put.

The three-month chart for RY is in figure 8.3.

The RY chart showed a declining trading range, followed by a rising one, and a three-session failed breakout. The trend could go in either direction at this point, so a reverse installment strategy is a very uncertain one in this situation.

EPD involved a two-month put costing 1.00. If in August, an October position was to be opened costing another 1.00, the total long cost would be 2.00. Considering that the call premium was 2.65, it would be unlikely that downside protection could be funded with a short call premium through the entire period. In this case, the reverse installment would not work. An alternative might include making a ratio write on the call side or, to reduce risks, a variable ratio write. However, given the proximity of the call and put premium over the seven-month period, it would make more sense to write an installment collar on EPD, or to abandon this underlying as a viable candidate.

The installment collar will work out profitably in numerous cases; however, to execute it, you have to accept a period of risk exposure. As long as the net debit continues, exercise will result in a net loss. The ratio write and variable ratio write versions can improve the overall profitability, but higher risks also have to be accepted. The reverse installment is the least likely among all of these selections to offer profitable results. It is most useful when you want to protect against downside risks and you are willing to give up potential capital gains in exchange for ongoing dividend yield.

Figure 8.4 shows the three-month chart for EPD.

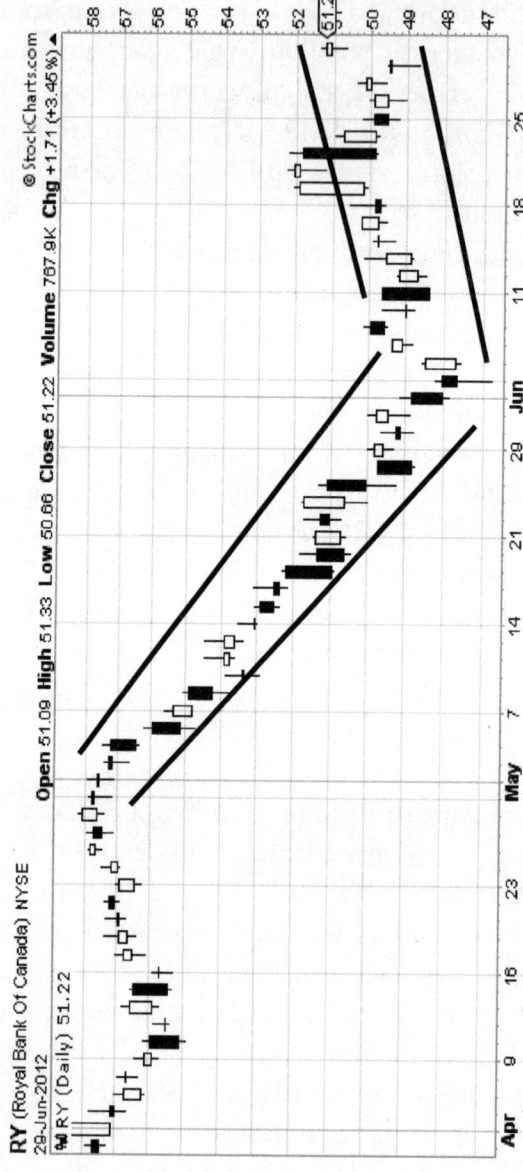

Figure 8.3 Royal Bank of Canada
Source: StockCharts.com.

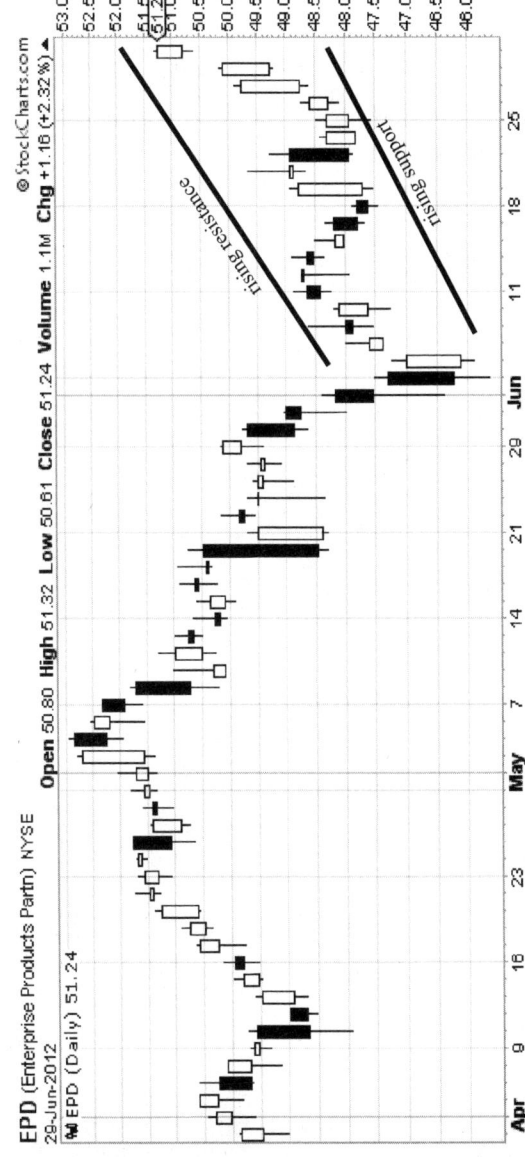

Figure 8.4 Enterprise Products
Source: StockCharts.com.

The RY chart showed a declining trading range, followed by a rising one, and a three-session failed breakout. The trend could go in either direction at this point, so a reverse installment strategy is a very uncertain one in this situation.

The next chapter returns to the theme of the ratio write, not for installment strategies, but as a variety of the basic dividend collar. It demonstrates how a dividend collar can be made more profitable in exchange for additional market risk, and how the rapidly declining time value of short calls mitigates that risk during the last month before expiration.

CHAPTER 9

Expanding into the Ratio Write Dividend Collar

> Imagination, not invention, is the supreme master of art as of life.
> Joseph Conrad, *A Personal Record*, 1912

THE BASIC DIVIDEND COLLAR WORKS TO (1) ELIMINATE DOWNSIDE risk, (2) create double-digit income from dividend yield, and (3) use short-term expiration to your advantage. It is one of the few option strategies in which exercise is welcomed (after the ex-dividend date).

Even so, one of the chronic problems with the dividend collar is that it works on only a few companies per month. Out of the approximately 720 companies yielding 4% or more in dividends, many have to be eliminated, due to:

1. *Irregular dividend schedule* (monthly, semiannually, or annually). Why should these not be used? You could set up a dividend collar based on any of these, but some problems arose in researching them. Monthly paying companies did not provide adequate ranges of options to justify the dividend collar in a majority of cases. Others (semiannual and annual) did not appear often enough to rely on finding monthly candidates, and those that were available also tended to have sparse option selections. Only the quarterly issues were used in the study on which this book is based. However, when you

expand into strategies like the ratio write, some of these irregular dividend-paying companies could work in the strategy.
2. *Skipped dividends.* Some companies declare dividends quarterly, but skip a payment due to cash flow and profit disappointments. As a risk standard, any companies that skipped a dividend during the past year were excluded. Once the ex-dividend date is set to occur within one month and no announcements have been made, the dividend is most likely to occur as scheduled. However, if the company has announced that the dividend will be skipped (or reduced), it makes sense to move on to other companies.
3. *No options available.* A large portion of the companies paying attractive dividends do not offer options trading, and so are not acceptable candidates for any of the dividend collar strategies.
4. *Inadequate option trading.* Even among companies paying dividends on a quarterly schedule, some do not offer enough of a range or premium level to justify the strategy.
5. *Oddities in listed premium values.* If option premium listings appear far too high given the current underlying value, it usually means that upon entering a trade, you will not get that premium. This occurs because a particular value was entered at a point when the underlying value was quite different, and due to a low volume of trades (or no option trades) the listed bid or offer price is wrong. If you see a very high bid and ask, but the "latest trade" is listed at zero, you cannot depend on the premium values shown. Also, if higher or lower strikes moving away from the money are all listed at the same value, it also indicates a lack of trades and inaccuracy in what you see in the listing. Those issues with premium values that seemed odd were excluded from the list of possible candidates.
6. *Companies paying dividends in noncash form.* Some companies pay dividends in additional shares, and for these, special rules apply. You might not be entitled to the dividend if you do not hold stock through the payment date, so stock dividends also have been excluded from this study.

In the study undertaken for this book, approximately one-third of the 740 candidates had ex-dividend dates in July 2012. So about

250 companies fell into this range. Of these, about 200 failed one of the tests above, leaving only 50 candidates.

This process of elimination points out a problem with the basic strategy. Of the 50 stocks that survived the analysis, only 5 were used to demonstrate profitable dividend collars. Four of the five yielded double-digit returns, and the last one yielded 8.7% on an annualized basis. This is not a bad outcome, considering that you only need one per month. As long as you find one in July, August, and September, each annualizing in double digits, you can continue the research for the next three cycles (Oct–Nov–Dec; Jan–Feb–Mar; and Apr–May–Jun) and create that minimum outcome every month. As long as you are able to eliminate downside risk and create the desired outcome in each case, you do not need diversification; risks do not have to be managed or reduced if they can be eliminated completely.

The research effort demands a lot of time and, as the previous summary points out, it ended up with only five candidates for the strategy. However, if you expand the basic idea into a ratio write, the possibilities are much more plentiful. With a ratio write, you increase your short-call income, so many more underlying stocks are going to produce net profits. Even so, the ratio write also involves market risk; therefore, you need to (1) understand the degree of risk involved with this strategy and (2) be willing to accept those risks.

RISKS AND BENEFITS OF THE RATIO WRITE

The ratio write consists of writing more calls against stock than you can cover. For example, if you own 200 shares and sell three calls, you create a 3:2 ratio write. With 300 shares in your portfolio, selling four calls creates a 4:3 ratio write.

The higher the ratio, the lower the risk. Owning more increments of 100 shares reduces the exercise risk and consequence as a result. For example, in the 3:2 ratio write, you are covered by 67%, but with a 4:3 ratio write, even though you still have one uncovered call in the mix, the cover rate is 75%. So you can view the ratio write as a combination of covered and uncovered calls, or as a mitigation of the uncovered risk based on the ratio.[1]

The purpose to the ratio write is to increase current income. In exchange, you have to be willing to accept the added risk that appears whenever a portion of the position is uncovered. The benefit is greater whenever premium levels are higher. If you increase the ratio beyond a single contract, the covered and exposed relationship changes as well.[2]

Risk is mitigated in two ways. First, by writing a higher number of exposed contracts against more increments of 100 shares, you create higher "excess" premium income, while the exposure rate is the same. This reduces risk because, for the same or less exposure, you earn higher premium. The second way to reduce or manage risk is through strike and expiration selection. Expiration within one to two months will create the most rapid time-value decay. The ratio write should be opened using one of three methods:

1. Strikes are out of the money (OTM). Time value will decline rapidly if you select one-month or two-month options, and, even if the price moves in the money (ITM), time decay might outpace the rise in intrinsic value.
2. Strikes are at the money (ATM). Time decay will also offset upward price movement in the underlying, but as with the first case, exercise then becomes a possibility. You may want to close the exposed portion of the position, cover it, or roll it forward.
3. Strikes are ITM, but the income from the calls exceeds the net difference between the strike and the current price. In this case, the point spread is critical in assessing the profitability of the ratio write. For example, if the strike is two points below current value but premium is 4.5 points, exercise of the covered portion produces a 2.5-point net profit (before transaction costs). However, the uncovered portion remains a problem and will have to be closed or rolled to avoid exercise. Or, if the overall net profit from the option premium exceeds the net cost of exercise, then exercise may yet produce a net profit. The danger in this approach is that the higher the underlying price moves, the more expensive exercise will be for those uncovered portions of the strategy. You will be wiser to close or roll exposed contracts if they remain ITM.

The two most dangerous dates are the last trading day (when exercise of ITM calls is certain) and the day before the ex-dividend date (when exercise is possible but not certain).

In recognition of the risks involved with a ratio write, you need to be convinced that the level of premium income provides enough cushion; that the proximity between the current price of the underlying and the strikes is comfortable in terms of exercise risk; that expiration is going to occur within one to two months; and most important of all, that the amount of additional income justifies the exercise risk.

The ratio write has limited profit potential above and beyond the covered call (represented by the additional premium received for the exposed portion of the position) but unlimited risk (represented by exercise of the exposed portion with the threat of the underlying price rising above that fixed strike level). Because of this, the risk has to be managed, anticipated, and eliminated once it begins to materialize—by rolling, closing, or covering.

TWO UNDERLYING STOCKS AND HOW THE RATIO WRITE WORKS

The study of 50 companies led to two companies on which a ratio write will work, as a stand-alone strategy as well as for a modified dividend collar. These two companies present very different situations, making the study of them all the more interesting:

Name	Ticker	Ex-Dividend	July Per share	Dividends %	Closing Price
BP Prudhoe Bay	BPT	July 12	2.64	8.48%	$116.47
Omega Healthcare	OHI	July 26	0.42	7.42	22.50

The first step is to evaluate the viability of a ratio write, based on the assumption that a trader has purchased shares and wants to augment current income (without initial consideration of a dividend collar). The reason for buying these in the first place may well be the high-dividend yields. However, high yield might also represent high volatility, so selection of high yield is not adequate by itself to justify purchasing high-dividend yielding stocks. This is why the dividend collar presents a solution in so many high-yielding examples. In fact, however, in both of these examples, the stock price had not fallen dramatically. Over the prior 12-month period, BPT ranged from a high of $129 to a low of $96, and OHI ranged from a high of $24 to a low of $14. Given these ranges, the price-specific trend did not provide any indications of exceptional volatility and, specifically, did not point to the current price as a dramatic decline from historical high price levels.

Even so, conservative investors, even those focused on covered call activity, will be attracted to the ratio write as a source for augmenting options-based income, and will also find the ratio write dividend collar to be a lucrative and safe method for eliminating downside risk while increasing income and at the same time accepting the exercise risk, given the potential for exercise of a short, uncovered call. The exercise risk is limited in time, however, as long as short calls are selected with expiration within one to two months. With rapid time decay in this period, the likelihood of exercise is diminished in three ways. First, the price might move OTM and remain there. Second, a short position with declining time value can be closed at breakeven or a profit, even if the call has moved ITM. Third, the short call can be rolled forward to defer exercise.

The BPT version of a ratio write is unusual because at the time it was studied (the close at the end of June 2012), the calls studied were ITM. However, they were rich enough so that exercise at the strike could produce a positive outcome. This means the risk level was mitigated, but not removed. For example, the following calls are part of this analysis:
BP Prudhoe Bay

Month/Year	Strike	Calls
Jul 2012	110	7.00
Jul 2012	115	2.75

The 110 calls produce a net profit between the call premium and strike; however, because a ratio write involves short portions, the 100 contracts are not used. They represent a 6.57-point gap but only a 7-point premium, not enough to justify going that deep ITM.

If the 115 call is sold as part of a ratio write, it produces a 2.75-point income, but the difference between the 115 strike and the price of $116.57 at this point is only 1.57 points. At the strike, the net positive was 1.18 points (2.75–1.57). So if the call were exercised at 115, the net capital loss on the stock would be 1.57 points, but the call premium was 2.75 points. The true market risk is going to be found if exercise occurs when the stock price had risen above these levels. For example, if BPT moved up to $117.75 per share, the outcome of exercise would be:

Current price at exercise	$117.75
Less: strike price	–115
Net exercise loss	$2.75
Less: call premium earned	–2.75
Net pretransaction cost	$0.00

Given the current price of the underlying at $116.57, this represents a "cushion" of only 0.43 per share, not a very comfortable margin. However, the expected decline of time value and extrinsic (or, volatility) value represented 1.18 points, so if this declines and offsets any upward price movement in the underlying, the risk will be manageable. If the underlying price exceeds the breakeven, then market risk will lead to a net loss.

The intentional sale of an ITM ratio write will be seen as reckless by the most conservative traders. However, the deciding point may also be based on a study of the underlying and a belief about likely price direction. The ratio write may provide great benefit as part of a dividend collar if and when the underlying price declines. The high short-call income becomes profitable, and the long put is exercised to offset the underlying capital loss.

As an example of a ratio write, assume you purchased 300 shares of BPT and sold four of the 115 calls:

BP Prudhoe Bay	
Buy 300 shares @ $116.57	$34,971
Sell 4 Jul 2012 115 calls @ 2.75	$1,100

Outcomes:

1. *Stock price falls to or below $115 per share:*
   The ratio write is profitable, and all of the calls may expire worthless, or when they decline below the 2.75 price, can be closed at a profit. The dividend of 2.64 per share, for a total of $792, is earned as well. Over 22 days, the total dividend profit of $792 represents a return of 2.3% (based on stock price). Annualized: (2.3% ÷ 21) x 365 = *40.0%*. This excludes the return from the options.

2. *Stock price rises above the strike, but remains at $117.75 or below:*
   The ratio write remains at breakeven or better; however, given the narrow range of profit, transaction costs will be likely to exceed any minimal net remaining upon exercise. As long as the calls are ITM, positions should be closed or rolled to avoid exercise. The risk of exercise is most severe on the last trading day, with somewhat lower risk before the ex-dividend date. ITM calls may be exercised at this point, but only if the long call owner's basis is less than the dividend to be earned. If the calls are not exercised, the same annualized 40.0% return is earned. However, the risk of exercise for the uncovered portion rises with each point rise in the underlying.

3. *Stock price rises above $117.75 per share:*
   The ratio write creates a net capital loss. This is the risk of the position, and given the problem of having started out with ITM positions, the risk of loss is only made worse. The best course of action if and when the underlying rises, would be to (1) close at least the one excess contract to avoid the potential for severe loss and (2) roll one or more of the positions forward or, if possible, forward and up to the next strike increment. This will be difficult for this underlying, since strike increments are at five points. The calculated breakeven in the stock price did not include dividend income. If the calls are not exercised prior to the ex-dividend date, the profit in the form of the current dividend remains intact, and would have to be compared to the potential capital loss on the underlying if exercised.

To demonstrate how important timing is in constructing a ratio write, as of July 10, the price of the underlying and the value of options had changed significantly. The underlying price was $12.99 during the trading day, and the July 120 calls were at 2.20. At these prices, a ratio write could be constructed consisting of:

BP Prudhoe Bay	
Buy 300 shares @ $120.99	$36,297
Sell 4 Jul 2012 120 calls @ 2.20	$880

Although the premium total is less, the difference between the current price and the strike was 1.21 (2.20–0.99). This creates a lower exercise risk because the stock price may more easily fall to or below the 120 level and move OTM. This increases the opportunity for closing at a profit or for rolling forward. However, as with all options positions, the viability of a ratio write relies on the timing, risk exposure, and your willingness to accept the short-term market risk. In this example, there remained only eight trading days until the July expiration. Thus, even if the stock price were to remain ITM, it is very likely that the 120 call premium values would drop rapidly within that short time, enabling you to close the excess position at a profit. That would leave the three remaining calls at risk of exercise, each creating a 0.99 loss. These too can be closed at a profit or rolled forward to avoid exercise if the underlying price remains ITM. The dividend yield in this example is additional profit (or reduction of loss).

The second underlying is Omega Healthcare. Calls to be considered for this example of a ratio write are limited to only one:

Month/Year	Strike	Calls
Aug 2012	22.50	0.60

This is interesting as a ratio write candidate, since the strike and underlying price are identical. For those interested in writing covered calls, exercise produces breakeven on the underlying (actually a loss due to transaction costs) and a profit on the short call of 0.60. This is marginal, due not only to transaction costs but also because the call premium is not necessarily high enough to justify the possibility of the stock being called away.

For example, assume that you bought 1,500 shares of OHI and then sold 20 calls (this creates a 4:3 ratio write, 15 sets of 100 shares versus 20 short calls, 20:15, or 4:3):

Buy 1,500 shares @ $22.50	$33,750
Sell 20 Aug 2012 22.50 calls @ 0.60	$1,200

Outcomes:

1. *Stock price falls to or below $22.50 per share:*
   The short calls are allowed to expire worthless or can be bought to close at a profit. However, if stock price falls lower than $21.70, a net loss is realized (before transaction costs:

Basis in stock, 1,500 shares	$33,750
Less: Value of 1,500 @ $2.170 =	32,500
Net loss	$1,200

This is the downside breakeven point. So with a straightforward ratio write, only 0.80 of downside protection is provided. However, the dividend of 0.42 per share equals $630 for 1,500 shares. As long as the stock price remains at or above $21.70, the dividend yield is additional profit. It is 1.9% over 49 days, or annualized at: $(1.9 \div 49) \times 365 = 14.2\%$.

If the underlying price fell to $21.28, it would represent the overall breakeven point including dividend yield ($1,200 + $630):

Basis in stock, 1,500 shares	$33,750
Less: Value of 1,500 @ $2,128 =	31,920
Net loss	$ 1,830

2. *Stock price rises above the strike of $22.50:*
   In this case, the calls will all be exercised unless later action is taken. This may be in the form of closing at least one position

at a profit or at a loss, or rolling one or more calls forward or forward and up a strike increment. The potential to roll forward and up is higher with this underlying than with the previous one, because strike increments are at 2.5 points rather than at 5 points. The dividend yield of 14.2% annualized remains intact unless calls are exercised before the ex-dividend date.

Adding Puts to Create the Ratio Write Dividend Collar

The preceding analysis shows that a ratio write, even with a favorably high ratio level, may be difficult to create profitably. This is especially true when the margin or profit is small, and the rise of a few points in the underlying could pose a significant exercise risk. With this in mind, the viability of a ratio write has to be evaluated on its own risk-related merits. As a dividend collar alternative, the position takes on a different appearance.

In the ratio write dividend collar, the two-sided purpose is to augment income and also to eliminate downside risk. This requires that you accept the exercise risk on the upside. Even so, however, with short-term expiration, time decay will be rapid and even ITM results may be closed profitably or rolled forward.

The same two issues are analyzed as candidates for the ratio write dividend collar. Because both have exceptionally high dividend yield, exercise is not a negative as long as it can be avoided on the uncovered portion of the strategy; as long as the risk is acceptable; and as long as you are able to earn the quarterly dividend. However, this evaluation cannot be applied in every situation. The added risk needs to be assessed in comparison to the dividend yield and profit level from selling calls:

Name	Ticker	July Ex-Dividend	Dividends Per share	%	Closing Price
BP Prudhoe Bay	BPT	Jul 12	2.64	8.48%	$116.47
Omega Healthcare	OHI	Jul 26	0.42	7.42	22.50

For BPT, the following option contracts are studied as candidates for the ratio write dividend collar:

Month/Year	Strike	Calls	Puts
Jul 2012	115	2.75	
Jul 2012	115		3.90

The transaction involving the same 300 shares and four calls is summarized as:

BP Prudhoe Bay	
Buy 300 shares @ $116.57	$34,971
Sell 4 Jul 2012 115 calls @ 2.75	$1,100
Buy 3 Jul 2012 115 puts @ 3.90	1,170
Net debit	$70

The problem with this version of the ratio write dividend collar is that exercise of the long puts will produce a net loss of $471 (300 shares @ 1.57) plus the debit of $70, and plus the transaction costs. At the same time, if the stock price remains above the 115 strike, the four short calls will be exercised, creating a loss (and a loss that expands with the exposed fourth short call as the price moves higher). So even though the net debit is small, the income potential is nonexistent. This is a case in which the position is created for a small cost, but downside protection and upside risk both contain flaws.

The dividend of $2.64 per share, or $792, creates a cushion on both sides; however, if the purpose of employing the ratio write dividend collar is to earn the dividend while eliminating market risk, the need to absorb losses with the dividend income is contrary to the intended purpose.

Figure 9.1 shows the three-month chart for BPT.

This pattern is typical of the changing trend over time. BPT trended downward from mid-April until the end of June, and then upward for the month of July. The uncertainty of the pattern does not help to determine whether a ratio write is sensible or too risky.

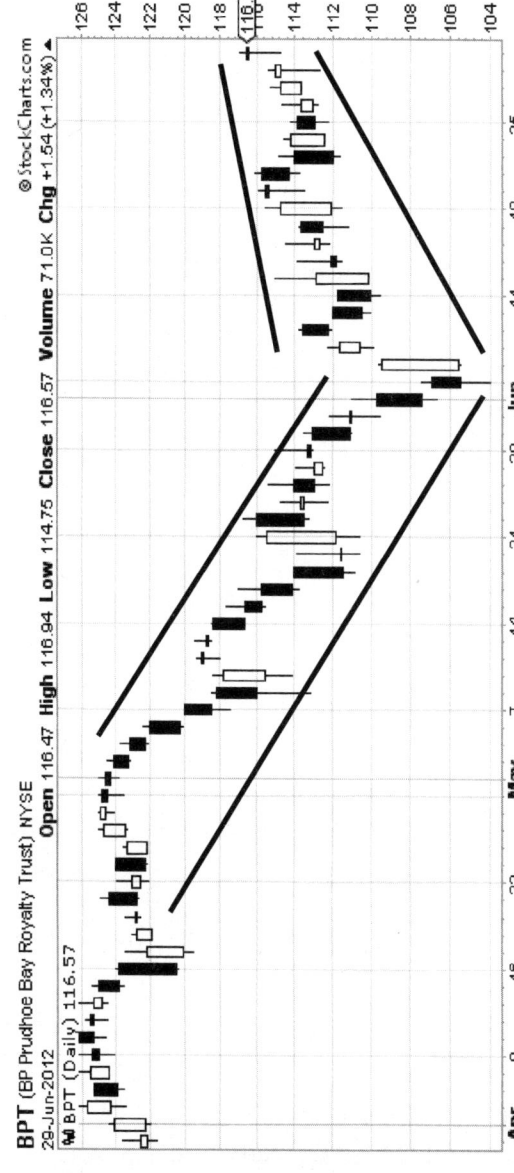

Figure 9.1 BP Prudhoe Bay Royalty Trust

Source: StockCharts.com.

The Omega Healthcare ratio write dividend collar is based on the following values of options contracts:

Month/Year	Strike	Calls	Puts
Aug 2012	22.50	0.60	
Aug 2012	22.50		0.60

This is an unusual situation because the calls and puts are valued equally, and the strike is identical to the underlying price. Why not a simple dividend collar? Exercise of either side produces no profit whatsoever, and the net loss would be the sum of transaction costs. So the alternative of the ratio write dividend collar needs to be studied. It could consist of a 4:3 ratio on the call side:

Buy 1,500 shares @ $22.50	$33,750
Sell 20 Aug 2012 22.50 calls @ 0.60	$1,200
Buy 15 Aug 2012 22.50 puts @ 0.60	900
Net credit	$300
Trading costs are estimated as follows:	
$8.95 @ 2 stock transactions	−18
35 option trades @ two x 8.95 plus 0.75 per contract =	−44
Net credit after trading costs	$238

Now the potential for profit is more realistic. As long as the calls are not exercised before the ex-dividend date, you will earn the dividend of $630 (0.42 per share x 1,500 shares). This provides a modest cushion on both sides. However, the wise course in the event of an upside move would be to close or roll the five exposed contracts and take the dividend yield as the primary source of profits. On the downside, the market risk is covered with the combined long put, and income will consist of the $238 net credit plus $630 dividend, for a total of $868.

The three-month chart for OHI is shown in figure 9.2.

The chart began with a very steady and predictable trading range. This evolved into a rising trading range, introducing more volatility to the picture. However, at the last entry, a bearish piercing-lines pattern indicated a likely downside reversal.

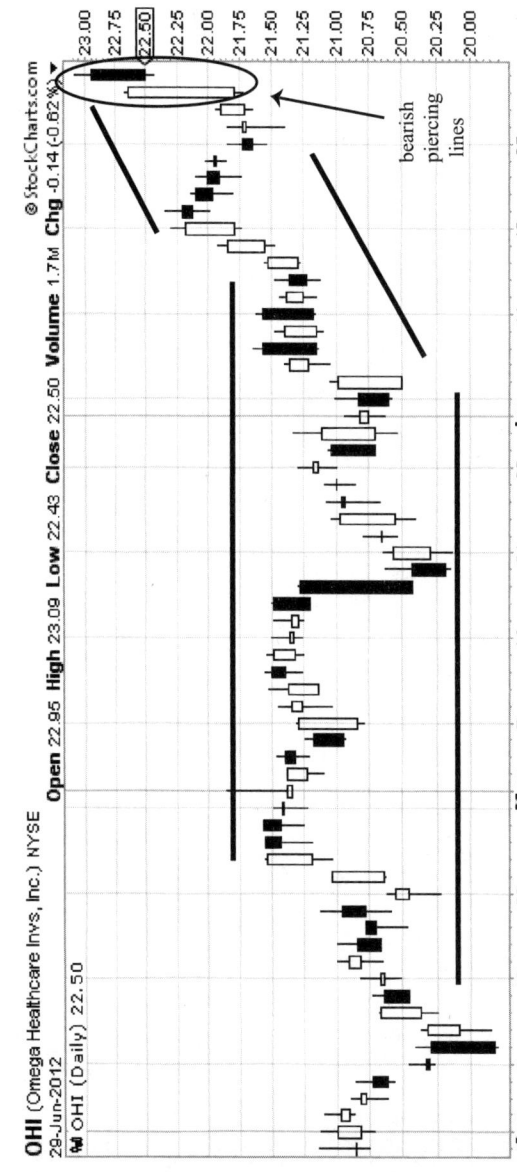

Figure 9.2 Omega Healthcare
Source: StockCharts.com.

An "Ideal" Ratio Write

The greatest challenge in the ratio write is creating a situation with acceptable risks. Ideally, this means the call strikes are far enough OTM that exercise is not an imminent threat. However, matching this with an ATM or ITM put that remains affordable is a considerable challenge.

One candidate for which the ratio write was ideal in these terms is the topic of the next chapter, the *variable* ratio write dividend collar. However, you can also review this for the ratio write without that dividend feature, based on the proximity of the call strike to the value as of the end of June. City Holding (CHCO) closed at $33.69 and yielded a dividend of 0.35 per share, which was 4.23%. On that same date, the 35 call was valued at 1.45. Here is an example of the ratio write based on CHCO:

Buy 1,000 shares of CHCO @ 33.69 =	$33,690
Sell 15 Jul 35 calls @ 1.45 =	$2,175

The initial transaction in short calls yielded 6.5% over 21 days to expiration; this return, when annualized, was: (6.5 ÷ 21) x 365 = *113.0%*.

However, exercise risk is also present. With the call strikes 1.31 points OTM, the opportunity to close one or more of the calls at a profit is quite healthy. The ex-dividend date was July 11, so six trading days after the June 29 close, or July 10, was the ex-dividend date. If the calls moved ITM by then, exercise would be possible for some or all of the positions. Given the OTM status, exercise would have produced a pretransaction cost profit of $524 in 10 days, or 1.6%, annualized as: (1.6% ÷ 10) x 365 = *58.4%*. This is an acceptable outcome considering the short holding period. The dividend was 0.35 per share, or $350. So the combination of the call premium and dividend is $2,525; this creates an upside breakeven point of $37.525 per share for the 1,000 shares (assuming the exposed 5 calls were closed or rolled):

1,000 shares, breakeven $37.525, market value =	$37,525
Less: Exercise price	−35,000
	$2,525

As long as the stock price remains at or below $37.53 per share for the next 10 days after opening the position on June 29, the position will be profitable (before transaction costs). On the downside, the breakeven is $32.475:

1000 shares, exercise @ 35	$35,000
Less: breakeven price, $32.475 x 1,000 shares =	−32,475
Net loss	$2,525

The net loss is equal to the income from the call premium and dividend. As of July 10, the price of the underlying was close to $34. So there was no risk of exercise prior to the ex-dividend date, and the stock price remained within the profit zone between $37.525 and $32.475 per share.

After the July 10 day before the ex-dividend date, you could close one or more of the short calls, wait out expiration on July 21, or be prepared to roll forward if the underlying price crossed the $35-per-share level. On July 10, the underlying price closed at $34.31 per share, so there was no risk of being exercised right before the ex-dividend date. In addition, the 35 calls had fallen from 1.45 down to 0.35, a loss of 1.10. Any or all of the short calls could have been closed at a profit of 1.10 each, or about 1.00 after trading fees, or simply left in place to expire worthless eight trading days later. Given the proximity of price to the strike, it would have made sense to close them, take the profits, and write later-expiring covered calls. Or, selling the 1,000 shares would produce a net profit of $620 on the 1,000 shares. Adding the dividend and the call profit to the capital gain, the overall profit would be $1,370 ($350 + $400 + $620). Based on the original purchase price of $33,690, this is a return of 4.1% ($1,370 ÷ $33,690). If this close were executed on the 11th (the ex-dividend date), you would be stockholder of record and would have held the shares for 12 days. So annualized, this return would be: (4.1% ÷ 12) x 365 = *124.7%*.

The desirability of a position such as this makes ratio writing profitable, especially with a higher than average dividend. In this example the dividend yield was 4.23%. However, such situations are not easy to find. They exist, momentarily and at various times within the option cycle, so finding them requires patience.

The same issue is well suited for a ratio write dividend collar, since calls and puts are both priced at 1.45. Whenever the strike of both the call and the put are higher than the purchase price of shares, the exercise of either is going to produce a net capital gain. This, added to the credit you earn for setting up the ratio write, has potential for significant short-term profits:

Buy 1,000 shares of CHCO @ 33.69 =	$33,690
Sell 15 Jul 35 calls @ 1.45 =	$2,175
Buy 10 Jul 35 puts @ 1.45 =	$–1,450
Net credit	$725

As long as you continuously monitor the underlying to ensure that the exposed calls do not move in the money, the risks of this strategy can be managed; however, there are exercise risks, and these calls were only 1.31 points OTM. The rapidly approaching expiration date works in your favor, however.

Assuming you will be able to dispose of the five exposed calls at a profit, you will be able to add the capital gain to option and dividend profits as well. In either case of exercise (your short calls are assigned, or you exercise your long puts), the gain will be $1,310 (strike of 35 minus cost of 33.69 per share, total of 1,000 shares). If you would prefer to hold onto your shares, an alternative to put exercise is to sell the puts. A profit will be generated because the net of the short call credits, your basis in the puts, was zero. For example, if the puts were valued at 1 each by the last trading day, you could sell and gain $1,000 before transaction costs.

The ratio write dividend collar in this instance yields huge benefits, but two important provisions have to be kept in mind. First, you are at risk for the exposed portion of the short call ratio until you buy to close or allow those positions to expire worthless. Second, these situations are difficult to find. The identical price of calls and puts above current value is going to occur only as an aberration to the more typical situation, in which ITM puts are much more expensive than OTM calls.

The short-call risks can be lowered substantially be reducing the number you open. For example, opening 12 instead of two creates a net credit of 2.90, more than enough to cover all of your trading fees. Given the inevitable capital gains no matter which direction the underlying moves, plus the attractive dividend, this risk-reduction approach makes the strategy relatively conservative when viewed next to the 3:2 (33% exposure) variety, at a 6:5 ratio with only 17% exposure.

Recovery Strategies Based on Rising Prices

The ratio write might look better on paper than it does in practice in a majority of situations. There is a likelihood of creating a loss if the strikes are not chosen well; if the underlying price moves upward unexpectedly; or if you fail to monitor positions often enough and miss the opportunity to exit with a small profit or a reduced loss.

In these situations, or in the time leading up to likely loss, you can take a number of actions designed to work as recovery strategies. First, when paper losses appear, it could make sense to close and take a small loss, in the event that a larger loss might occur if this action is not taken. Closing to mitigate possible losses is painful, but options traders might easily suffer from the stubborn "requirement" that a loss reverse itself and become breakeven or profitable. This view can be expensive.

To avoid losses in the first place, consider closing exposed short calls as part of the ratio write, once they become even marginally profitable. However, given the balance between the benefit of short calls, the cost of long puts, and the overall transaction fees, calculate the required level of profits that is affordable within the position. If the overall goal is to create a short-term dividend collar, getting to breakeven on both underlying capital gains/losses and option positions is acceptable. A buy-to-close of exposed short calls not only accomplishes this, but also eliminates the market risk itself. The ratio write contains unavoidable market risks, and because of this, the dividend collar is profitable only if losses are not generated due to unexpected exercise.

The short positions might not become profitable enough to close with offsetting costs. In these cases, as those calls move to the money, you need to calculate whether it is worthwhile to close and take a small loss, or roll forward. The roll forward creates additional credit because greater time value is accumulated in the new position; however, the forward roll presents a new dilemma as well: If the purpose of the dividend collar is to move in and out of underlying and option positions every month to maximize dividend income, does the forward roll not contradict this goal? In fact, it does. The roll keeps the short call alive for a longer period, even if only one month. At this point, what happens if the covered call portion is exercised and shares are called away? In this outcome, you are left with an uncovered call. The theoretical risk-free or manageable risk position then becomes a high-risk position that can be closed only by accepting a net loss.

This scenario is the worst case for the ratio write. Exercise itself is not as severe as long as the small loss in uncovered calls is offset by option and dividend profits. Being left with an uncovered call with no ratio write left is an entirely different situation and quite a dilemma. It raises the question of whether the ratio write is a logical choice. When this situation does occur, you need a new strategy to mitigate or remove the risk. Either the ratio write itself contains too much risk, given the potential for exercise of covered calls leading to uncovered leftover contracts, or you need to cover the positions.

You can cover the remaining calls by repurchasing shares of the underlying. However, this also contradicts the purpose of the dividend collar. In this outcome, you purchase shares of an underlying whose next ex-dividend date is three months away. This decision is typical of a problem options often face: An initial strategy appears manageable, but subsequent changes in the underlying price make it high risk and unprofitable. While purchasing shares to cover eliminates the uncovered call risk, it also ruins the purpose of the initial strategy.

A second method of covering is to open long call positions that either have a higher strike or expire later. Either selection will create a net debit; however, it has to be viewed as a mitigation strategy in which the potentially large loss is reduced to a smaller loss. The higher-strike approach might be less expensive, especially if the underlying provides one-point strike increments. In this case, the loss is reduced from an unknown exercise loss of many points, to a maximum loss of one point per contract.

One situation in which covering the exposed calls with more stock will become profitable is when the call premium is so rich that a covered call makes sense. For example, if you have two remaining uncovered calls after exercise of the covered portion of the position, buying 300 shares and selling an additional call could create a desirable mitigation of potential loss, plus additional covered call income. The problem with this approach is that at the time you buy those shares, the exposed short calls will already be in the money. As a consequence, exercise will program in a net loss on the newly acquired shares. It is unlikely that this strategy can be created profitably, unless the purchase of additional shares is executed when the exposed calls are at or below the strike.

Give the dismal prospects for profitable outcome from rolling or covering exposed positions, the only remaining choice is to accept exercise and take the loss. This is not unreasonable as long as the ITM points are minimal, but when the underlying has soared far above strike, exercise could be very expensive. This scenario leaves you no choice but to roll forward and hope to avoid exercise. The holder of a long call has no rational cause to exercise until the last trading day or, if this situation goes on for three months, until before the ex-dividend date. However, whenever you are holding short calls, exercise can occur at any time. In a situation such as this, forward rolling should be accompanied with stepped-up strikes, even if that creates a small debit. The debit is preferable to taking a large exercise loss.

The stark reality is that ratio write dividend collars are not risk-free. You can easily remove downside market risk with the purchase of puts at or above current value, and ratio writes are justified in the minds of traders in order to fund the cost of the long puts. However, the upside exercise risk could make the strategy ill-advised. Most traders only consider the possibility that exercise may occur while the entire position remains open. In that case, exercise might involve only a small portion of the overall short-call positions. However, if all of the covered positions are called away and the exposed calls are rolled forward, the leftover uncovered calls could be a wake-up call to the trader. The original belief that the ratio write is a low-risk strategy is contradicted once the long stock and covered calls are gone, and the rolled uncovered calls remain and are ITM.

This market risk can be mitigated substantially through the creation of a dividend collar using not a one-strike ratio write, but a *variable ratio write*. In this version of the strategy, two strikes are used. In the event that the calls move ITM, strikes can be rolled forward or closed, and the use of multiple OTM strikes at the origin of the strategy provides you with greater flexibility and rapidly declining time value. The next chapter examines and analyzes the variable ratio write dividend collar.

CHAPTER 10

MORE EXPANSION, CREATING THE VARIABLE RATIO WRITE DIVIDEND COLLAR

> Information's pretty thin stuff, unless mixed with experience.
> Clarence Day, *The Crow's Nest*, 1921

THE LAST CHAPTER DEMONSTRATED THAT ONLY IN RARE instances is a ratio write likely to combine high dividend yield with relatively low risk. The risk level is unavoidable, and even the fact that expiration will occur in less than one month might not be reason enough to accept the risk level.

At the same time, creating high call premium income as a means for creating a workable dividend collar is desirable. Workable situations are not common, and although the basic dividend collar can be found in a few issues each month, an alternative that expands the field of possibilities is attractive. The *variable ratio write* enables you to add greater flexibility to the ratio write while also reducing risk exposure. Like the ratio write, with the variable version you write more calls than you can cover, but you use more than one strike.

THE VARIABLE RATIO WRITE STRATEGY—LIMITED PROFIT AND LOSS

Because the strategy includes short calls, a popular criticism of it is that upside profit potential is limited. The argument is, "Why undertake the risk when the chances of exercise are high, meaning you can never profit beyond the higher strike?" The criticism is valid; however, keep in mind that the purpose in seeking a dividend collar is not to make a profit in either the underlying security or the options, but to eliminate downside risks while earning dividends every month (instead of every quarter).

The risk-free basic dividend collar accomplishes this, and several examples were provided in earlier chapters. The variable ratio write approach gives you two benefits: First, it also allows you to eliminate downside risk completely and for an expanded field of possible issues, and second, it reduces the risk of using a ratio write in the strategy. It does not eliminate the exercise risk that is the most important negative attribute when using the ratio write, but it does reduce the risk to a level many traders will find acceptable (especially since expiration will occur in one month or less, meaning time decay will be rapid).

In the typical variable ratio write, you own a specific number of shares and write more calls than you can cover, using two strikes. For example, if you own 300 shares at $29 per share, you create a variable ratio write if you sell two 30 calls and two 31 calls (or two 32.50 calls). The risk-reduction aspect of this is easily spotted. The higher strikes are out of the money (OTM) so that, if the price begins to move upward toward the money, the lower strikes can be rolled or closed, and the upper strikes can be closed, usually at a profit (because they are OTM and expiration is very close). So as long as the positions are monitored, the variable ratio write has much lower risk than the ratio write.

The fact that the potential profit on the underlying is limited by the use of covered calls—the popular criticism of this strategy—is not applicable, since the purpose here is to create a net breakeven or credit in option and stock while eliminating downside risk (and limiting upside risk) so that exceptionally high-yielding dividends can be earned each and every month.

The limited profit, with all of this in mind, is acceptable and even desired. Elimination of risk is far more important than earning higher short-term income or speculating on the possibility that the stock price might rise and create an exceptional profit. In fact, comparing various dividend collar strategies to that of just owning stock, the dividend-based strategy is far more profitable. If you simply own stock, you have to accept the downside risk in exchange for the upside profit potential. One or the other is going to occur and, while you earn the dividend in either case, the prospects for earning profits consistently with long stock are dismal, especially in volatile markets. It is possible, but it takes time, and the risk exposure is a constant.

Strategies like the variable ratio write dividend collar solve a good portion of the market-risk problem faced by every stockholder. It does eliminate downside market risk below the put's strike, and provides low risk on the upside with limited (or zero) profit potential on the underlying or on options. However, as long as the underlying yields a healthy dividend, you can make your annualized double-digit return with a level of risk that may be acceptable to you. (If the level of risk in the variable ratio write is not acceptable, then it makes more sense to restrict trading to the basic dividend collar strategy, where all market risk is eliminated.)

Selecting the Precise Strategy

You have choices in specifically how you set up a variable ratio write, even before seeking a dividend collar based on this strategy. The standard variable ratio write contains two strikes, either both OTM or one OTM and one at the money (ATM). You match one set of 100 shares per covered option and then decide how many exposed extra contracts to open. In the most aggressive form, a 2:1 ratio (100 shares and two short calls, or multiples of this) will enable you to manage the short calls based on short-term until expiration, and on careful monitoring of the positions.

The ideal situation is short-term expiration because time decay is most rapid. For example, during the last month before expiration, OTM and even ATM positions will lose considerable value. It is possible to create profitable outcomes by closing short calls even when they have moved in the money (ITM). As long as the rate of time decay outpaces the increase in the intrinsic value of the ITM call, profits can be realized. However, if the underlying price moves too quickly, a breakeven or profit-based scenario can turn quickly to a loss position. It is prudent to prepare for this danger by either closing or rolling exposed positions before they go ITM.

A problem with rolling occurs if the remaining, covered calls are exercised. For example, with 100 shares and two calls (at different strikes) you might roll the higher strike forward because the underlying price is approaching the money. The lower-strike call is exercised, and the 100 shares are called away. This leaves you with an uncovered call. Before this occurs, remember that rolling forward presents this specific danger. It often makes much more sense to just close the excess position if the underlying price continues to rise.

The variable write market risk is reduced when the ratio increases. Thus, a 3:2 ratio is less risky than a 2:1, and a 4:3 is less risky than a 3:2. This is because the percentage of total short calls that are exposed declines as the ratio expands. A 2:1 is 50% exposed (and 50% covered); a 3:2 is 33% exposed (and 67% covered); and a 4:3 is 25% exposed (and 75% covered).

THE RISKS OF THE VARIABLE RATIO WRITE

The risks vary based on the ratio. However, with all variable ratio writes, the risk itself is going to be determined by (1) time to expiration and, as a related factor, the rate of decline in time-value premium, and (2) the "moneyness" of each position. An OTM call contains less risk than at ATM, and of course an ATM is less risky than an ITM. So the risk is scaled to both time and proximity.

A short call that is both OTM and due to expire in one month or less presents a relatively small degree of market risk. It is likely that even as the underlying price rises, the ATM option will be unresponsive and certainly will not rise point-for-point with the underlying. As the underlying price approaches the call's strike, the delta will begin rising toward 1.00. And the faster the underlying price rises, the faster the change occurs. This rate of change, or gamma, is an indication of the changing risk of the short call as the underlying nears the strike. Depending on a comparison between the original sale to the open price and the current price, the timing of a buy to close for the exposed position has to be determined based on all of the factors (profit or loss, proximity, and time to expiration).

The theory of the variable ratio write tells you that you should be able to hold an open and exposed short call until expiration, when it will expire worthless. Exercise risk is present, though, and short calls will not remain OTM in every case. The degree of ratio involved defines the risk. A 2:1 is quite risky, whereas owning 1,000 shares and writing 12 calls—a 6:5 ratio is much less risky, consisting of only 17% exposure and 83% cover. Similarly high cover ratios can be written with fewer than 100 shares as well. For example, a ratio write is created through ownership of 80 shares and one call; a variable form of this may involve 80 shares and two calls.

EXAMPLE OF THE VARIABLE RATIO WRITE WITH TWO STOCKS

The variable ratio write is better understood through demonstration. Among the 50 stocks in the sample, two were reserved for the variable ratio write: City Holding (CHCO) and Targa Resources (NGLS).

These two contain the following attributes as of the close of June 29, 2012:

Name	Ticker	July Ex-Dividend	Dividends Per share	%	closing price
City Holding	CHCO	July 11	0.35	4.23%	$33.69
Targa Resources	NGLS	July 19	0.62	7.10	$35.65

The dividend yield remains the primary focus of the dividend collar. In developing a variable ratio write, you accept a degree of risk in exchange for the creation of a net breakeven or credit from options. The idea is to monitor positions so that the current OTM calls can be closed before they go ITM. This is a reasonable expectation, given the three key elements: (1) the short calls are OTM; (2) expiration occurs within one month; and (3) the risk level is manageable and presents very little likelihood of exercise (which also is avoidable through closing before exercise becomes a problem).

The variable ratio write for each of these is created using the following calls:

City Holding (CHCO)
Jul 35 call = 1.45
Jul 40 call = 1.25
Targa Resources (NGLS)
Jul 35 call = 1.45
Jul 36 call = 0.85

Both of these will contain varying degrees of risk, depending on the number of contracts opened and the ratio itself. For example:

City Holding (CHCO)

Buy 400 shares @ $33.69	$13,476
Sell 3 Jul 35 calls @ 1.45 =	$435
Sell 2 Jul 40 calls @ 1.25 =	250
Total premium income	$685

This is a 5:4 ratio. The options expire in 21 days, but the higher-strike contracts are a full 6.31 points OTM. By tracking these until expiration, you can avoid exercise as long as at least one can be closed at a profit. This is a 5.1% yield in 21 days, or annualized: (5.1% ÷ 21) x 365 = 88.6%.

Targa Resources (NGLS)

Buy 400 shares @ $35.65	$14,260
Sell 4 Jul 35 calls @ 1.45 =	$580
Sell 2 Jul 36 calls @ 0.85 =	170
Total premium income	$750

The four 35 calls are ITM by 0.65 each; however, they are all covered and, in the event of exercise, will yield a net of 0.80 each (call premium of 1.45 minus exercise capital loss of 0.65, or a profit of $320. The short positions are 0.35 OTM. However, with a short period of time to go until expiration, chances are good that these can be allowed to expire worthless or closed if and when the underlying price moves upward. The "if expired" return is 5.7% ($750 ÷ $13,260). Annualized, this position creates a return of: (5.7 ÷ 21) x 365 = *99.1%*.

The variable ratio write does contain exercise risk; however, due to the use of two strikes, this risk is far smaller than the risk for the ratio write with the use of single strikes. However, the variable ratio write is left with downside risk. The breakeven is equal to the share price, reduced by the value of the call premium:

City Holding:

Original price paid for 400 shares =	$13,476
Breakeven value,	$31.9775 per share = –12,791
Net loss	$685
Option premium	685
Overall net profit/loss	$0

Targa:

Original price paid for 400 shares =	$14,260
Breakeven value,	$33.775 per share = –13,510
Net loss	$750
Option premium	750
Overall net profit/loss	$0

Expanding the Variable Ratio Write into the Dividend Collar

The rationale for the variable ratio write is carried over and applied in the creation of a dividend collar. This consists of several key elements:

1. Risks are built into the position, but these are manageable, especially compared to the structure of the one-strike ratio write.

2. Expiration occurs within one month, so you expect time decay to take place on an accelerated schedule.
3. As long as the higher strike is OTM, it is manageable, since the position can be closed if the underlying price begins moving upward.

It is possible, of course, for the underlying price to jump far above both strikes, in which case the risk of loss will be realized. Thus, to keep the variable ratio write dividend collar risks as low as possible, the ratio itself should be quite high (the higher the ratio, the lower the exposed portion and the lower the market risk). So with 400 shares in play, a 3:2 (six calls and 400 shares) is lower risk than a 2:1 (eight calls and 400 shares). However, a 5:4 (5 calls and 400 shares) is even less risky. The status of City Holding (CHCO):

Name	Ticker	July Ex-Dividend	Dividends Per share	%	closing price
City Holding	CHCO	July 11	0.35	4.23%	$33.69

Available options on City Holding as of June 29 were:

City Holding (CHCO)	Calls	Puts
Jul 35	1.45	
Jul 40	1.25	
Jul 35		1.45

A variable ratio write dividend collar can be created as a 3:2, based on the distance between the two call strikes. The 40 calls were 6.31 points OTM, so the position is structured as:

City Holding (CHCO)

Buy 400 shares @ $33.69	$13,476
Sell 4 Jul 35 calls @ 1.45 =	$580
Sell 2 Jul 40 calls @ 1.25 =	250
Buy 4 Jul 35 puts @ 1.45 =	−580
Total premium income	$250

In this example, the 35 calls and puts are the same price. Both were above the price of the underlying, so that exercise of either would produce a net capital gain of $524. So even a basic strategy would work with this underlying. The $524 is more than enough to absorb the transaction cost of all options involved (four calls and four puts). However, with the addition of two higher-strike calls, potential profit is increased. This is a low-risk strategy given the distance between current price and the higher strike.

In monitoring the overall position, when do you close the higher strikes? The overall breakeven is 1.935 points above the current value per share, so you will need to carefully track subsequent price movement of shares, with an awareness of the breakeven price:

Breakeven value, $35.625 per share =	$14,250
Less: Original price paid for 400 shares =	–13,476
Net	$774
Less: capital gain upon exercise	
Of either calls or puts	–524
Less: net option premium received	–250
Overall net profit/loss	$0

The three-month chart of CHCO shows the history of recent price developments (figure 10.1).

This chart shows that resistance remained in place over many months and more recently traded within the established range below resistance level. Toward the end of the period, however, support broke down and then began rising. This indicates some increased volatility in the price level, but based on the longer-term trend, exercise risk on the upside appears remote.

In the case of Targa, using strikes only one point apart increases the exercise risk. The underlying may more easily cause the exposed calls to move ITM with a relatively small point increase. For this reason, a less risky 5:4 variable ratio is suggested, with only one position in the higher strike. To review Targa's status as of June 29, 2012:

			Dividends		
Name	Ticker	July Ex-Dividend	Per share	%	closing price
Targa Resources	NGLS	July 19	0.62	7.10	$35.65

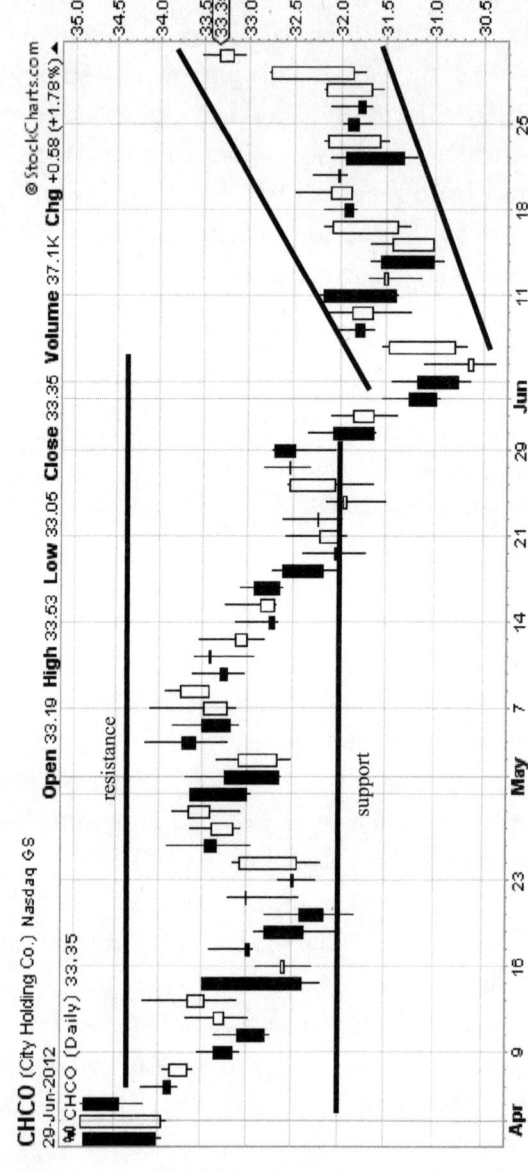

Figure 10.1 City Holding Co.
Source: StockCharts.com.

Option positions at the same time were:

Targa Resources (NGLS)	Calls	Puts
Jul 35	1.45	
Jul 36	0.85	
Jul 35		1.50

A variable ratio write can be created based on these price levels: Targa Resources (NGLS)

Buy 400 shares @ $35.65	$14,260
Sell 4 Jul 35 calls @ 1.45 =	$580
Sell 1 Jul 36 call @ 0.85 =	85
Buy 4 Jul 35 puts @ 1.50 =	−600
Net premium income	$65

The fact that the 35 calls were ITM by 0.65 at the time this position was opened, presents a more severe market risk than the previous example. Exercise of the four 35 calls or the four puts would create a net capital loss of $260 (0.65 x 4). As a consequence, the breakeven for this position is 0.4875 points *lower* than the current price:

Original price of 400 shares =	$14,260
Breakeven price, 35.1625 @ 400 shares =	−14,065
Net	$195
Plus: net premium income	65
Less: capital loss upon exercise	−260
Breakeven	$260

While the previous example of CHCO would be profitable under most price-movement scenarios due to the exercise profit, Targa's situation only serves to limit the net loss if the underlying price declines. In that instance, you earn the 7.10% dividend, or $248, and you can exercise the puts at the 35 strike and lose $260. This creates a net loss, so the upside exercise risk is not justified by either the level of downside protection or by the high dividend. The only way this strategy would work is if and when you are able

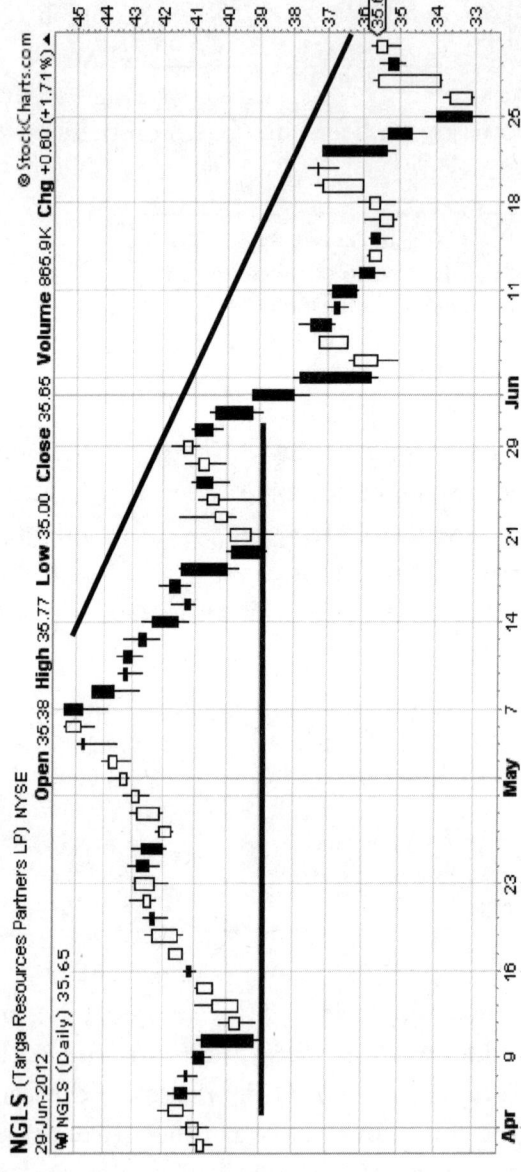

Figure 10.2 Targa Resources Partners
Source: StockCharts.com.

to close short calls at a profit even though the stock price rose without calls being exercised. This is a thin window of opportunity.

The three-month chart shows the underlying's price history (figure 10.2).

The chart displays considerable uncertainty. Established support was violated while resistance fell, an overall bearish trend. Even the most recent price level did not indicate a turnaround; however, by July 13, the price had risen to nearly $39 per share. This brings up a considerable exercise risk before the July 19 ex-dividend date, and with little time to react or adjust. The options all expired the day after the ex-dividend. The risks in this position did not justify a variable ratio write dividend collar for Targa even with its attractive dividend yield.

Assessing Strategy Risks

The variable ratio write dividend collar works in some situations. For example, the case of City Holding (CHCO) presented earlier in this chapter would have produced profitable outcomes upon exercise of either calls or puts. However, the addition of the higher-strike OTM aspect added an element of risk. In comparison, the Targa (NGLS) case could not produce a profitable outcome under any circumstances. Had the underlying price been lower than the applicable strikes, the outcomes might have been different.

This brings up the first point to be raised concerning risk for any positions subject to the basic dividend collar or one of the variations. A case that does not work today might work tomorrow or next week, and by the same argument, today's "perfect" dividend collar could be impossible to make work a few days later. Not only do proximity and prices change, making the comparison between value and strike different with each move, but the ever-changing implied volatility of every option makes the workability of a strategy dependent on the individual price relationships.

The strategy risk specifically associated with the variable ratio write dividend collar should be limited to the potential for exercise. If you cannot create a net profit upon exercise of the puts, then the downside protection is not risk-free but only serves to cap the maximum risk. This is not the intention of a dividend collar; it is meant to eliminate risk and to create a certainty of profits based on the proximity of price to strike, the moneyness of short calls and long puts, overall credit or debit, dividend yield, and time to expiration. With either the ratio write or the variable ratio write, you accept higher risks than with the basic strategy. As long as you understand those risks and are willing to accept them, you can create desirable variable ratio write conditions.

For the risk to be manageable, the put strike has to be at or above the current price of the underlying, or the net credit has to be large enough to offset a debit upon exercise of either call or put. In other words, if you suffer a net capital loss that absorbs or surpasses the dividend, then the strategy will not work. Elimination of downside risk is an essential starting point. For example, the CHCO version of the strategy was ideal because exercise of either call or put would create a net capital gain, and the net of options transactions was a credit. In addition, the large space between the current underlying price and the higher strike of the exposed short puts made the strategy attractive. As long as you are willing to undertake that added risk for the exposed short calls, the variable ratio write dividend collar can be very profitable.

In comparison, the Targa example demonstrated that the strategy cannot work in many situations. The greatest drawback with this one was that the call and put strikes were both lower than the underlying value. That meant a net capital loss would occur no matter what, and that the dividend income would not have been adequate to offset that net loss. It would make no sense to enter into a strategy in which a capital loss of this size would be a near certainty. If you would be able to close out some or all of the short positions at a net profit, that would still result in an overall debit due to the cost of the long put. So even with closing the short legs of the strategy, profitability was unlikely.

The benefit of analyzing both of these situations is that it demonstrates how the strategy has to be studied. You seek a situation like CHCO, where all of the elements are present: deep OTM call strike, short-term expiration, net credit on the options positions, capital gain in the exercise of either calls or puts, and the risk of the exposed short calls at a level you are willing to undertake. This does demand constant monitoring, of course, because you need to know when to close out the exposed short calls.

A cautionary word about rolling: Once you have opened a variable ratio write, what can you do if the underlying price begins to rise? The prudent answer is to close those exposed positions before they go ITM, and reduce the potential loss. Rolling forward is a desirable choice when you have a covered call strategy, but when you convert that to a collar and then add the ratio on the short side, rolling forward can turn a moderate strategy into a high-risk one very quickly.

If you roll your exposed calls forward and then the remaining covered calls are exercised, you end up having all of your underlying shares called away, and you end up with uncovered short calls. This, not downside risk, is the greatest risk to any ratio write. For this reason, you are wiser to close out exposed calls and take a small loss rather than rolling forward and creating a higher-risk position for yourself. Many traders roll forward, hoping that the underlying price will retreat and that those positions can then be closed or allowed to expire. However, this does not always happen. If the upside trend continues to move without any end in sight, you could end up in a very dangerous position. For example, if you have multiple uncovered calls as a consequence of rolling, you have not only defeated the original purpose of the collar (risk control or reduction), but you have also converted the positions into high-risk, uncovered calls.

The risk to this or any strategy is the aspect that has to be controlled and understood. Traders are accustomed to being concerned with downside risk and the consequence of paper losses. Even covered call writers might tend to ignore the possibility of upside risk, or exercise risk. A "covered call mindset" might be in effect even when you are creating a ratio write. Within this mindset you are content to accept exercise if the underlying price passes by the strike. Rather than roll forward to avoid exercise, you are happy to accept it and enjoy your exceptionally high covered-call income *and* the short-term capital gain on the underlying.

Once this mindset remains in effect but the covered call is expanded into a ratio write, you face considerably higher market risks. Now you could end up with exercise of the uncovered portion of the strategy, or rolling forward to create uncovered positions and no shares. This is one example of where options trades go wrong. So in trying to understand the entire scope of risk, look beyond the elimination of downside risk. With any ratio, the upside exercise risk can be more severe and more expensive.

The next chapter moves into a discussion of a form of the "collar" that is not actually a collar at all. Synthetic stock positions mirror changes in the value of shares of stock—one of each option representing 100 shares—and provide great leverage. A collar, strictly defined, is based on two different strikes, one each for the call and the put. In practice, most of the examples of the dividend collar will not be collars at all, but synthetics. The next chapter examines this variation of the strategy in detail.

CHAPTER 11

Modifying the Strategy with Synthetic Stock Positions

> Having a beard and wearing a shabby cloak does not make philosophers.
>
> Plutarch, *Moralia: Isis and Osiris*, ca. 95 AD

THE DISTINCTION BETWEEN A COLLAR AND A SYNTHETIC STOCK position is subtle. A collar usually involves two strikes, a short call, and a long put, both out of the money (OTM). A synthetic stock position is based on the same strike for both.

As long as either of these acts as desired, it does not matter whether the dividend collar gets established as an actual collar or as synthetic stock. The majority of examples used in the preceding chapters were synthetics. However, these earn the title "dividend collar" because they are different from the well-known collar. Rather than a collar between the two strikes and the stock, the dividend collar is a collar between stock/options on one side and dividends on the other. The stock/option side is devised to create a no-risk situation, so that traders can earn dividends without worrying about the underlying movement, and so that all outcomes are profitable. These outcomes include (1) being assigned through exercise of an ITM call; (2) the trader exercising the put to sell shares at the strikes; or (3) being assigned before the ex-dividend date and earning a capital gain on stock in place of earning the dividend.

The synthetic stock strategy is worth evaluating from a risk perspective on its own merit and without regard to dividend yield, and then to taking another look with that yield in mind.

The Nature of Synthetic Stock

The "synthetic" term refers to options that duplicate, or mirror, price changes in the underlying security. It involves two options, one call and one put. If the call is long and the put is short, the position is a synthetic *long* stock strategy. If the stock price rises, the overall value of the two options will track the underlying point for point. Simply owning a call will accomplish the same thing. The difference, however, is that synthetic stock costs little or nothing to open, and might even produce a net credit (at least before transaction costs).

Synthetic short stock is the opposite, a long put and a short call. This position is most advantageous when the underlying declines in value. In that case, the options track price movement exactly, and intrinsic value of the options will increase for each point the underlying loses.

Having short, uncovered options is a risky idea, however. But is it higher risk than taking a position in stock? No. In fact, synthetic long or short stock contains the identical market risk to that of owning 100 shares (for synthetic long stock) or shorting shares (for synthetic short). The primary difference is that synthetics can be closed, all or in part, to minimize losses while leaving the remaining leg of the position open. And if you are bearish, a synthetic short stock costs close to zero to open, but is less expensive and less complex than shorting 100 shares of stock.

An additional point concerning synthetic short stock: It contains an uncovered short call, meaning the potential market risk can be unlimited, just as it is with shorting 100 shares of stock. However, that short call can be covered if you also own 100 shares of the underlying. This not only eliminates the short call risk, but also sets up a synthetic version of the dividend collar.

Before examining how the synthetic short stock position works as part of a dividend collar, the long and short synthetics are worth examining. Synthetic long stock consists of one long call and one short put. The cost of the long call is offset by the premium you receive for selling the short put. On the upside, you enjoy unlimited potential profit. If the underlying rises above the call's strike, you will realize a net profit. When you just buy a call without any offset, your profit has to exceed the net cost of the call. For example, if your call costs 3, you have to get at least three points of intrinsic value in the underlying just to break even. With a synthetic long stock position, your net cost is at or close to zero. So any intrinsic value movement in the underlying is profitable.

The position also has unlimited risk. If the underlying price falls well below the strike of the short put, each point lost represents a loss in the short put. Eventually that position will be exercised and 100 shares put to you at the strike. But unlike shorted stock, you can roll the short put forward to avoid or defer exercise. You may also be able to roll forward and down to reduce eventual strike price loss. Breakeven on the synthetic long stock is going to be the strike plus posttransaction net paid for the overall position. For example, if you pay a total of 0.75 for the net long call and the short put (including transaction costs), your breakeven will be 0.75 points above the strike.

In a synthetic short stock position, you buy a put and sell a call. Thus, the breakeven and profit/loss zones are reversed. As long as you hold the short call, upside loss is in theory unlimited, just as it is for an uncovered call position. However, this risk is eliminated by ownership of the underlying security. So with a synthetic long stock position, it is not possible to cover the short put, but in the synthetic short stock position, ownership of 100 shares effectively eliminates the short-option risk.

SYNTHETIC POSITION EXAMPLES

One stock is examined as a candidate for a synthetic stock position, Legacy Reserves:

Name	Ticker	July Ex-Dividend	Dividends Per share	(%)	closing Price
Legacy Reserves	LGCY	July 26	0.56	8.95%	$25.01

Legacy Reserves reported their June 29 ending prices of options at the 25 strike as:

Expiration/Strike	Call	Put
Aug 25	1.15	1.60

LEGACY RESERVES

You could create a synthetic long or short strategy using these values, depending on whether you believe the company's stock price is likely to rise or to fall. As a variety of the dividend collar, examined later in this chapter, you could pick the synthetic short stock strategy, due to the combination of a long put and a short call (and the desirability of downside protection). But if you analyze the strategy without stock ownership, you could decide to open either a long or a short version of the strategy.

A synthetic long stock strategy based on Legacy Reserves would create a pretransaction cost credit of 0.45. The long call would cost $115, and the short put would yield $160, for a net credit of $45 before transaction costs. The outcome at various prices as of the expiration date would be:

Price per Share	Long 25 Call	Short 25 Put	Net Total	Stock Profit
$15	$–115	$–840	$–955	$–1,000
20	–115	–340	–455	–500
25	–115	160	45	0
30	385	160	545	500
35	885	160	1,045	1,000

The synthetic long stock position acts just like 100 shares of stock. The net difference between the change in the combined option positions, and the stock profit or loss is $45, equal to the original net credit (before transaction costs). This example demonstrates that the change in the options is the same as the change in 100 shares of stock. However, the synthetic stock position cost nothing to open (in fact it produces a small credit), so the leverage advantage is superior, while market risk/reward is identical to owning 100 shares of stock. The actual cost of opening a synthetic stock position will be the initial margin and maintenance requirements, factors that affect the number of contracts you can effectively use in this strategy. Because one side of the trade is short, it will require margin at the exercise price. The long side will require maintenance at 75% of the option's value. (To find out more about initial margin and maintenance, check the Chicago Board Options Exchange [CBOE, "Margin Manual" at http://www.cboe.com/LearnCenter/pdf/margin2-00.pdf).

A synthetic short stock based on Legacy is designed to perform best when the underlying price declines. The initial position creates a debit of 0.45 per share since the put is now long and the call is short. The outcome at expiration and at various price levels would be:

Price per share	Short 25 call	Long 25 put	Net total	Stock profit
$15	$115	$ 840	$ 955	$–1,000
20	115	340	455	–500
25	115	–160	–45	0
30	–385	–160	–545	500
35	–885	–160	–1,045	1,000

In the short version, the synthetic stock positions perform opposite of the stock price. So as the underlying price declines, the synthetic position moves upward in value, and as the stock price rises, the synthetics position loses. This equivalent of shorting stock is advantageous in the sense that it costs only $45 (plus transaction costs) to open, which is far cheaper than shorting stock, but market risk for both is identical.

THE SYNTHETIC SHORT STOCK VARIETY OF THE DIVIDEND COLLAR

The synthetic short stock example can work as a dividend collar if the underlying stock is also owned. This makes the short call risk-free since the call is covered; it also eliminates downside risk. Legacy's stock price was $25.01, versus strikes of 25. Dividend per share was 0.56, or 8.95%, a healthy yield.

The three-month chart for Legacy Reserves is shown in figure 11.1.

Note that the previous support was flipped and became the new resistance level, while a new, lower support was set, tested, and then held. This transfer of trading range provides some comfort that the newly set range has support both on the resistance and the support sides. When old support flips to new resistance, it often represents strength at the new top. As a result, it is more likely that the stock price will remain within this range or decline. In either event, the dividend collar is going to be profitable for Legacy, based on the pricing of calls and puts at the 25 strike.

An example of how this dividend collar would be established is:

LEGACY RESERVES (LGCY)

Closing price on June 29	$25.01
Dividend yield:	8.95%
Dividend amount per share:	0.56
Ex-dividend date:	July 26
Options expiring August 17	Aug 25 calls @ 1.15
(49 days)	Aug 25 puts @ 1.60

Actions:

Buy 600 shares @ $25.01	$15,006
Buy 6 puts @ 1.60	$–960
Sell 6 calls @ 1.15 =	690
Net options debit	$–270

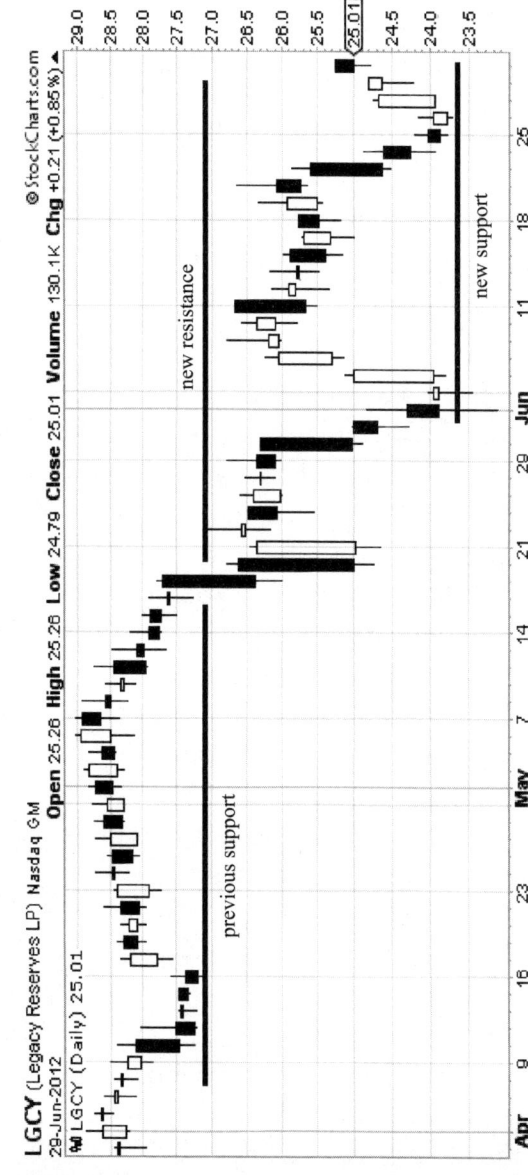

Figure 11.1 Legacy reserves
Source: StockCharts.com.

Outcomes:

Calls or puts are exercised, Net capital loss, 0.01 per share =	$–0.06
Estimated transaction costs: Stock (buy and sell)	–$ 18
Options: 12 round trips each, 24 total; (8.95 x 4) + (0.75 x 24)	–365
Net total losses	–$383.06
Net options debit, plus total loss	$653
Dividend, 0.56 per share =	$336

Because this example produced a net loss, it would not be a viable dividend collar. However, the five examples provided in the chapter examining the basic strategy were all synthetic short stock versions of the dividend collar. The practical effect of changes in call and put values mandates this in a majority of outcomes. OTM calls may profitable if the underlying price rises, since exercise would take place above the basis in the underlying. However, if the underlying price were to decline, the long puts could be exercised only at a price lower than the basis.

An exception is found when the original basis in the underlying was below the current price. For example, if Legacy had been purchased at $23 per share at the beginning of June, the end-of-June price of $25.01 represented a two-point net gain, or $1,200 for 600 shares. In this case, a dividend collar might be justified by the argument that the 8.95% dividend was desirable. At the same time, concern for the likelihood of a price decline could further justify the dividend collar as a means for (1) eliminating the downside risk below the current price and (2) earning the current dividend of $336. However, since it costs $653 to "buy" this level of protection, it does not rationally justify the position. A trader might be wiser to buy protective puts at a lower strike, write covered calls and accept the risk, or simply close the underlying position and take profits.

This demonstrates that when a dividend collar will not work, entering the position cannot be justified. This is especially true when an attractive dividend rate will produce a *lower* level of income than the cost of the dividend collar.

Epilogue: The Great Value in Patience

> Progress is man's ability to complicate simplicity.
> — Thor Heyerdahl, *Fatu-Hiva*, 1974

KNOWLEDGE, RESEARCH, ANALYTICAL SKILLS, AND PATIENCE— all of these are essential traits for successful options trading. But all of these are secondary to one unavoidable and necessary trait: self-discipline.

Knowledge is the usual starting point for a discussion of whether or not options are appropriate. Brokerage firms emphasize this on their options account questionnaires. The most important question on this form is related to the number of years the applicant has been trading, the types of trades executed, and the number of trades entered per year. All of this experience adds up to knowledge about the options market.

Research is a second essential trait. Just as a stock investor studies the multiple-year fundamental results and applies several important ratios, and just as the technical trader analyzes charts to time entry and exit, the options trader also needs to perform research. To the novice, this often is misdirected at trying to find the best-priced covered calls, meaning the richest premium. To these uninitiated new traders, the covered call is a simple "sure thing" method to generate income. They do not realize that those extra-rich premiums represent high volatility, and thus high market risk. The option premium is attractive, but the underlying price might be in great peril as well. So options traders need to combine knowledge with research to ensure that their trades are entered with full awareness of many kinds of risk.

Analytical skills are not the same as research. With research, you know what to look for and how to compare indicators among several underlyings to one another. Your analytical skills come into play when you know how to study the results of your research to compare not only the profit potential of a particular strategy but also the risks. Analytical skills take research a step beyond finding valid comparisons and enable you to make wise decisions based on an interpretation of your research.

Patience might be in short supply, but impatience is an expensive luxury for options traders. Even a strategy as profitable as the dividend collar is not always going to materialize when you are ready to get started. There might be extended periods of days or weeks in which no underlying produces the right mix of call and put prices at the most advantageous strikes, or for underlyings paying the most attractive dividends. At these times, waiting and doing nothing is the sensible and patient decision. But an impatient trader might not be willing or able to wait, preferring to do something in the desire to be "in the game" and willing to take higher risks just to make a move.

Self-discipline is the most difficult trait of all. It applies to both sides of the trade. You have to be patient to find the trade that works, that moment when the relative prices of calls and puts work just right, when strikes and current price have perfect proximity, and when the outcome either yields exceptional dividends or capital gains, all risk-free. However, self-discipline also applies to the other side of the trade. Once you have the position open, the sensible strategy is to wait out the ex-dividend date and then get out. This means accepting exercise of your short call that has moved in the money (ITM) or, if the underlying price has fallen, exercising your long put. In both cases, you leave the trade and begin looking for the next one. Some traders forget the simple "rule" of getting in and out in a short time frame, and decide to avoid exercise. The idea is that if the underlying price has risen, you can make more money by rolling the call forward and ending up with exercise at a higher strike. This contradicts the premise of the dividend collar. It ties up capital for a longer period, during which the underlying is not earning dividends (that will not happen for another three months), so you pass up more profitable opportunities. For many options traders, accepting exercise of a short call is very difficult, even if it is the most logical and reasonable step. Traders program themselves to set up strategies that include short calls, but then to dread the prospect of getting exercised. The call is ITM, so it means having shares called away below current market value, and that is difficult to accept. But self-discipline tells us to ignore this "greed impulse," stick with the strategy, accept exercise, and start the search for next month's attractive trade.

Even with these logical traits in place, though, you are going to run into resistance from other traders. The idea that risk is unavoidable permeates all trading markets. Suggesting that you can earn better-than-average yields while eliminating all market risk is simply not an easy idea to sell. Even with proof, you are likely to find yourself arguing with other traders on this point.

Hostility to This Strategy Based on Old Concepts of Unavoidable Risk

The strategy of the dividend collar is not as complex as some traders want to make it. This book included a study of 50 underlying securities with ex-dividends in July 2012, yielding 4% or higher annual dividend, and with options trading available. This field of 50 came from a total of 740 companies with 4% or higher dividends. Many of these paid dividends on an irregular schedule, or did not offer options. Among those remaining, only one-third on average had ex-dividend dates in July. This narrowed the field down to 50; however, only five produced the desired results. Four of these produced double-digit annualized yields, and one (Kite Realty; KRG) produced an annualized yield of 8.7%. So only 5 out of 50 in the study were profitable. And these were workable only given the proximity of price to the strike and the option values at that moment. The day before or the day after, an entirely different set of issues might have worked, and it is possible that none of these five worked profitably based on price changes. So there were only five, but you only need *one* per month.

The hostility to this strategy is due to the two claims made: (1) It is possible to earn annualized double-digit yields, and (2) this can be accomplished risk-free. The majority of traders understand that "risk-free" refers to market risk, or the risk of losing due to a decline in the underlying price, early exercise of the short call at a net loss, or nonexercise resulting in a net paper loss in the underlying.

The annualized double-digit returns are easy to explain, and the math is indisputable. If you can find an underlying every month with a current ex-dividend date, you have the starting point for the strategy. Every company that pays quarterly dividends is on an ex-dividend cycle, and there are four (Jan–Apr–Jul–Oct; Feb–May–Aug–Nov; and Mar–Jun–Sep–Dec). So each month you focus on those underlyings with ex-dividend dates within the coming 30-day cycle. You further narrow the search to those companies yielding 4% or more (this is the standard used in the book; however, an underlying yielding 2.5% or more also annualizes at double digits).

The 4% example is the best one to demonstrate how the double-digit annualized return works out. Each quarter, the dividend yield is 1% (4% per year). So if you can move in and out of positions so that you are stockholder of record each and every month, you will earn that 1% *every month*. If you hold the position open for 30 days exactly, this annualizes out to 12%.

This annualized example assumes two additional factors. First, the assumption is that you will earn nothing from the options trades or from capital gains on exercise of the underlying. In practice, a well-selected proximity in which strikes of both the call and the put are greater than your basis in the underlying will produce capital gains in addition to the dividend income. You may also gain from the net options if the initial trades produce a credit. These facts have been discounted for the purpose of focusing on dividends only. The exception: In those instances where the options trades or underlying trades produced a loss, these were deducted from the net outcome. The result was to then annualize the dividend yield minus the trading losses. In four of the five cases, the result remained in double digits.

The more controversial aspect to explain is how such trades can be risk-free. In the market culture of stocks and options, traders have been advised by professionals for years that risk is unavoidable and has to be *managed*. This is accomplished through diversification and conservative investment selection. But why manage risk if you can eliminate it? And why diversify if, in fact, you can set up a trade that eliminates all market risk?

The "perfect" dividend collar produces double-digit annualized yield *and* eliminates all market risk. For example, if you buy shares of an underlying at $38 per share and then set up a dividend collar with both the call and the put with 40 strikes, what are the possible outcomes? Whether your short call is exercised against you, or you exercise your long put, your outcome is going to be a 2-point net capital gain. This will be true no matter how high or how low the underlying price moves. When your call is exercised, the underlying will be above 40, but your capital gain will be the difference between the 40 strike and your $38 basis: $40 - 38 = 2$. If the price declines below 40 or remains below, you exercise your put and dispose of shares at 40; the same 2-point profit results. Meanwhile, you have earned the current dividend that annualizes to double digits.

The argument is offered that there is more to this picture than the obvious market risk. This is true. All traders face potential liquidity risk (in which case there is no market to enter the trade to begin with); knowledge and experience risk (in which case you should not be trading options and, certainly, your broker should not allow you to); and tax and inflation risk (which is going to be worse for lower-yielding strategies). So while there are many forms of risk that every trader faces, the plain truth is that the description of the dividend collar as a "no-risk" strategy is widely understood to mean no *market* risk.

The question remains: Can you really find trades for the dividend collar that will work? In the case study, out of the 50 underlyings with the ex-dividend in July, five candidates were located. For the sake of fair comparisons, the closing prices of stock, calls, and puts were used. In practice, you will more likely track prices in real time during the trading day, looking for the "sweet spot" when all of the prices align to create a desirable proximity, strike, and price. This does not happen on every trading day or for every issue you track, but it does happen.

A completely different potential is found for those issues purchased well below current price. For example, if you bought stock six months ago and it has gained eight points, you might want to protect your paper profits but ensure that you are likely to earn the current dividend; you might also be willing to dispose of shares at an identified strike of a call above the current price, or a put slightly below—in other words, creating a true collar, defined as consisting of an out-of-the-money (OTM) short call and an OTM short put. In this version of the dividend collar, you will find many more instances in which the premium for both the call and the put are quite close, because the strike prices of both will still produce a net profit based on your original cost of shares. This alternative allows you to have it both ways: eliminating market risk below the put's strike (and ensuring a net profit equal to the difference between that strike and your original cost), while paying for the long put with a short call (with that call at a higher strike that, if exercised, will produce a capital gain equal to the difference between the call's strike and your original cost), *and* allowing you to keep shares until you earn the current month's dividend.

This plan can have one of four outcomes. Your short call can be exercised and your shares called away at the strike; you may exercise your long put to sell at a profit; you may sell your put to take a profit in intrinsic value equal to or exceeding the loss in the underlying price; or the call goes ITM before the ex-dividend date and your shares are called away. In this last outcome, you get the capital gain but lose the dividend.

All four outcomes are profitable, and all eliminate the downside market risk below the long put's strike.

Whether the dividend collar is created all at once, or as a means for protecting the paper profits in long positions you already own, it does eliminate market risk while producing double-digit returns just from dividends. The capital gains likely to occur in properly structured versions of the dividend collar, or any net credit in the options, are acceptable outcomes given the overall net profit. The annualized yield assumption is based on a holding period of exactly one month (thus a 1% monthly dividend equals 12% annualized). In practice, the positions might be open anywhere from a few days to two months, all depending on when option expiration occurs in relation to the ex-dividend date.

A second argument against the position is based on the observation that, in many cases, the long put is going to cost more than the income from the short call. This is usually the case when the strikes are higher than current value, since the call will be OTM and the put will be ITM. However, taking a broader view, if the capital gain upon exercise of either option exceeds this net loss on the options, then the net between underlying capital gain and option cost will be positive. Traders need to analyze the entire picture, and not just an immediate debit from options trades. For example, if your call and put strikes are both 40 and your basis in the underlying is 38, does it matter that the long put is one point greater than the short call? Exercise of either option will produce a two-point capital gain, which more than offsets the one-point option debit. Incidentally, this would also cover all of the trading costs.

Alternative Method: Opening Segments at Different Times

The dividend collar as presented in preceding chapters was premised on the idea that you would open all three portions at the same time. So you buy stock, buy long puts, and sell short calls. This is a tightly restricted concept, and it works only in those few instances where all of the elements price out profitably, and when the price/strike proximity is also perfect.

The alternative strategy might be just as practical, especially for investors with a portfolio of long stocks. The scenario lends itself well to the elimination of downside risk via the protective put. For example, you have a portfolio with many stocks that you have owned for varying lengths of time. The market has enjoyed a healthy run-up, and many of your stocks have appreciated. Now you face a dilemma: Do you sell now and take profits before a correction wipes out your profits? Or do you hold on for the long term and live with the risk?

Below is a sample portfolio of five companies, showing all of the pertinent details and how a dividend collar could be structured (based on protecting paper profits earned over the long term, with prices as of July 19, 2012). In each case, dividend yield was above 4.5%:

Company and symbol	Current price	Basis	purchase date	dividend yield	per sh.	ex-date	options exp.	strike	$.
Altria (MO)	$35.66	$31.00	4/12	4.6%	0.41	9/13	Sep	put 33	0.25
								call 37	0.23
Conoco Phillips (COP)	56.24	44.00	10/11	4.7	0.66	10/19	Nov	put 52.50	1.60
								call 57.50	1.85
H & R Block (HRB)	16.63	11.00	11/10	4.8	0.20	9/07	Oct	put 15	0.60
								call 17	0.80
Leggett & Platt (LEG)	21.63	17.50	8/11	5.2	0.28	9/13	Sep	put 20	0.50
								call 22.50	0.55
Lockheed Martin (LMT)	88.13	67.50	9/11	4.5	1.00	8/30	Sep	put 85	1.80
								call 90	1.30

If you had purchased any of these companies on the dates indicated, current value would have represented paper profits. So the long puts effectively would protect most of those profits, and would be paid for by the premium from the short calls. In those instances where the options end up in a net debit (0.02 for MO, and 0.50 for LMT), the dividend collar still works. It provides protection against downside market risk. MO's debit is marginal and reduces the dividend only slightly. LMT cuts the dividend in half, from the 1.00 per share to the 0.50 loss on the option trades. Given this more severe cost (with the remaining profit mostly eliminated by trading costs), the only justification for the dividend collar in this case would be for the downside protection.

For LMT, an alternative would be to look at the variable ratio write version of the dividend collar. For example, the 92.50 calls were at 0.55. A ratio write could consist of an even split between these two calls, creating a net credit of 0.05 (1.30 + 0.55 – 1.80). This is a marginal credit and represents a degree of upside exercise risk. However, in this example of the dividend collar, you would assume that keeping the stock for the long term would be desirable, as opposed to the fast in-and-out of the alternate variety. This strategy, holding these positions until expiration, rolling forward and up, or closing at a net profit, are all viable alternatives to mitigate the added risk of the variable ratio write.

SETTING AND FOLLOWING YOUR OWN RULES

There is no single "best way" to execute a dividend collar. The strategy can be adjusted in many ways—the installment method, ratio write, variable ratio write, or synthetic stock—are examples. You can also use the dividend collar to protect established paper profits in long positions you have owned for many months or even years.

Another variation can be to close out the entire position on or after the ex-dividend date. As long as you own stock the day before the ex-dividend, you are the stockholder of record. If the position can be closed after that date has passed—meaning selling the underlying and the long put, and buying to close the short call—at breakeven or a small net credit, the dividend strategy can be used as a very short-term and profitable approach to trading. However, given the transaction costs, the ability to close all positions is going to be difficult to locate. It would require a bump in the underlying price with little or no change in the short call (or a decline in its value based on a decline in volatility). This is a possibility in circumstances when volatility has been exceptionally high due to unknown elements. For example, if an earnings announcement happens to occur shortly after the ex-dividend date, you might be able to take advantage of changing prices, especially when a favorable earnings surprise occurs.

For example, if the announcement exceeds expectations, and guidance for the future is also stronger than anyone thought it would be, the underlying price could get a one-day bump. At the same time, the unknown anticipation of earnings could have caused volatility to rise, and now that the announcement has passed, volatility is going to decline. This unusual combination could provide exactly what you want to see: a rise in the underlying price and a flat or declining premium in the short call. In this circumstance, closing out the entire position could produce a small profit.

This also sets up a different rule for your dividend standards. The previously proposed minimum of 4% annual dividend yield is based on the assumption that on average, the dividend collar will remain open one month. A 1% quarterly yield, earned every month, annualizes out to 12% per year under this assumption. If you set your standard at 10%, you can broaden the field of candidates to those issues with 2.5% or better dividend yield. If you are going to keep positions open only a few days, you can reduce requirements even further—and still annualize in the double digits. The problem here, however, is that it is not likely that you can repeat a short-term annualized return at all times. You certainly can time strategies to move from one ex-dividend date to another. However, this requires that price and strike proximity work out, and also that next-expiring option values also provide ideal conditions.

Remember, you only need one issue at a time to make this plan work. The liquidity of the market might not cooperate, and this is the reason for using the 4% and higher issues and basing the tests on month-to-month outcomes rather than on week-to-week possibilities.

If you do experience a very short-term holding period, annualized outcomes can be substantial even with relatively small dividend yields. The table below makes this point:

Open days	Yield	Annualized calculation
5	0.50%	(0.50 ÷ 5) x 365 = 36.5%
5	0.75	(0.75 ÷ 5) x 365 = 54.8%
8	0.50	(0.50 ÷ 8) x 365 = 22.8%
8	0.75	(0.75 ÷ 8) x 365 = 34.2%
11	0.50	(0.50 ÷ 11) x 365 = 16.6%
11	0.75	(0.75 ÷ 11) x 365 = 24.9%
14	0.50	(0.50 ÷ 14) x 365 = 13.0%
14	0.75	(0.75 ÷ 14) x 365 = 19.6%

So even if your yield is only 0.5%, holding periods up to half a month yield double-digit annualized returns. Based on this assumption, companies yielding a 2% quarterly return, held for 14 days, would annualize at 13%. If you were able to locate two (or more) companies meeting this minimum level, and you could roll into the next dividend yield twice per month, the 2% yield would be a profitable scenario.

The standard you set for yourself has to determine whether this is a wise move. Reducing the minimum from 4% (for one month) to 2% (for half a month) has the same outcome. By reducing the field, you broaden the candidates and increase the chances of finding an ideal situation, but the strategy then requires much more work.

In establishing your standard, whether based on a 4% monthly roll or a 2% half-month roll, what is the "ideal" candidate? Of course, the dividend level is only a starting point. You also need an ex-dividend date within a half month, and you will use options expiring at the next cycle. The proximity of price to strike also has to work. The very best proximity is going to be a strike averaging one point above the current price (or your basis), when the call and the put are approximately the same value, or even provide a small credit. This is an unusual situation because the put will be ITM and the call OTM, so it is more common for the put to be richer.

Furthermore, the bid/ask spread has to work favorably, and this requirement is going to reduce the number of likely candidates even more. In volatile markets, especially, the put premium is likely to be much higher than the equivalent call, so it is a difficult match to make. When you are able to find a viable candidate that is also ATM, you might have a chance of finding a working dividend collar candidate.

Another standard worth challenging is the selection of the option. The assumption in all of the tests has been that the next-expiring option is going to provide the best value for the dividend collar. This works in the sense that you want exercise, either imposed via the short call or enacted by your exercise of the long put. However, a dividend collar that is potentially going to be closed down soon after the ex-dividend date could be built using longer-term options. As long as the premium values work out, there is no reason that longer-term options with more time value should not be looked at as potential vehicles for the strategy. Although longer-term calls might be worth more than corresponding longer-term puts, it is more likely to move in the opposite direction. For the five companies used earlier in this chapter (MO, COP, HRB, LEG and LMT), all longer-term options than those analyzed provided a *worse* comparison than the next-expiring contracts (meaning long puts were more expensive compared to short calls). This is why the soonest-expiring contracts, with time value mostly gone or evaporating quickly, offer the best potential for profitable outcomes in the dividend collar.

Getting Away from the Love of Danger, Risk, and Complexity

The dividend collar does work, but its window of profitable outcomes is small. Many elements have to come together perfectly: distance between the ex-dividend date and option expiration, proximity between price and strike, and relative richness of short calls versus long puts. You can broaden your base by reducing the field of dividend yield and attempting also to shorten your holding period in order to approximate the double-digit annualized yields, but this requires much more work.

The strategy is very appealing to those "arbitrage junkies" of the market, traders who seek profits without risk on marginal trades. The dividend collar might be described as an arbitrage play, but it really is not. If the profit were to be earned from differences in long and short premium levels, it would be. However, the purpose of the options in this strategy is not to create profits but to eliminate downside risk at little or no cost net of trading expenses. Then the dividend yield accumulates risk-free. So it is not an arbitrage strategy, but the use of the underlying and its options to build risk-free dividend income on a monthly rather than a quarterly basis.

Among the criticisms of this strategy is the claim that short-term trading just to earn the dividend harms the market, especially the market for long-term value investors. The buy-and-hold group, this argument goes, pays the price that short-term traders exact from the market.

This is irrational. As long as you can find a seller of shares, willing to sell to you before the ex-dividend date, the auction market functions well. There is always a seller at a price, and as long as both the seller and the buyer are willing to execute at that price, where is the harm? The underlying company pays the dividend based on the number of shares outstanding, but that company does not care who owns the stock on the record date. The dividend is paid, whether to buy-and-hold retail investors, large institutions, or traders holding shares for only 48 hours. In any event, the dividend is not affected. If you do not buy those shares, someone else keeps them or someone else offers to buy them from the original owner. The dividend is paid out regardless.

The argument that short-term transacting of stock and options is somehow harmful to the overall market makes no sense. It is true that over several decades, the average holding period of stocks has declined. In 1945, the average holding period was over nine years. By 2012, that average had fallen to a few months. But what does this mean?

The change in the holding period is a reflection of lower costs of trading, the Internet and direct access to trading for all investors, and a better educated public. The explosion of the options market contributes to this trend as well, as investors and traders recognize the potential for profits that can be earned from short-term *trading* versus long-term *investments*. The value or importance of each is a matter of opinion, but whether you hold stocks for nine years or nine days, the holding period itself does not impact a company's share value. It only adds liquidity to a healthy trading market.

There is a danger, though, for options enthusiasts. Too many traders are attracted more to the excitement and complexity of trading, especially in strategies like the dividend collar, and less interested in the certainty and consistency of earning small profits from making wise decisions. The excitement and complexity are not problems by themselves, as long as you have also evaluated your decisions and understand risk levels. If you are willing to accept a specific level of risk, violating that standard leads to losses, and this is where so many options traders go off course. For example, if you open a ratio write and then roll exposed positions forward, and being exercised on the remaining covered call, you end up in the worst situation possible. In that case, being aware of risk would probably have told you to cover or close the exposed positions as the underlying began moving up, to avoid the increased risk. A wise trader recognizes this, but too many traders forget to constantly keep risk levels in mind.

The dividend collar is designed to generate exceptionally high dividend yield in the double digits, while eliminating market risk. This works only in a small number of cases and only when all of the elements come together so that the opportunity exists. It will not last, however, as volatility and put-call parity (the arbitrage element), all evolve. So today's "perfect" dividend collar might not be possible tomorrow, or even later in the current trading day.

The strategy is not designed as a solution to every investor's portfolio problems. It does point out why diversification is only necessary if you accept the traditional belief that risk is impossible to avoid. It also demonstrates that the inevitability of risk is not an absolute certainty. You do not have to manage market risk if you can eliminate it completely.

Notes

1 THE DIVIDEND PORTFOLIO, AN OVERVIEW

1. Fischer Black and Myron Scholes, "The Pricing of Options and Corporate Liabilities," *Journal of Political Economy* (1973): 81, 637–654—the paper was published at a time when calls were available on only 16 stocks, and no puts were available at all. The options industry had just started as a publicly available trading platform and, as a consequence, the assumptions made by the authors of this paper could not possibly anticipate how much this market has grown over the past decades.
2. The Dogs of the Dow system isolates the 10 highest-yielding companies among the 20 industrials of the Dow Jones Industrial Average. For 2012, these stocks, according to *www.dogsofthedow.com,* were

Company	Symbol	Yield
AT % T	T	5.82%
Verizon	VZ	4.99
Merck	MRK	4.46
General Electric	GE	3.80
Pfizer	PFE	3.70
DuPont	DD	3.58
Johnson & Johnson	JNJ	3.48
Intel	INTC	3.46
Proctor & Gamble	PG	3.15
Kraft	KFT	3.10

3. Vipal Monga, "J C Penney Makes Rare Dividend Cut," *CFO Journal,* May 15, 2012.
4. Sheyna Steiner, "CD Rates of May 17, 2012," *Bankrate.com,* May 17, 2012.
5. New York Stock Exchange Technologies.
6. Sal L. Arnuk and Joseph Saluzzi, "Why Institutional Investors Should Be Concerned about High Frequency Traders," http://www.themistrading.com, retrieved May 23, 2012.
7. Roger Blough, in *Forbes,* August 1, 1967.

2 Managing and Reducing Risk with Options

1. Philippe Jorion, *Value at Risk: The New Benchmark for Managing Financial Risk* (3rd ed.). New York: McGraw-Hill, 2006.
2. Paul Glasserman, *Monte Carlo Methods in Financial Engineering*. New York: Springer, 2004.
3. Espen Haug, *Derivative Models on Models*. Hoboken, NJ: John Wiley & Sons, 2007.
4. Seth Klarman and Joseph Williams, "Beta," *Journal of Financial Economics* (1991): 5(3), 117.

3 The Advantage of the Covered Call

1. To annualize return, the formula is:

   $((R \div B) \div H) \times 12$

   When
   R = return
   B = basis
   H = holding period (in months or partial months).

2. James B. Bittman, *Options for the Stock Investor*. New York: McGraw-Hill, 1997.
3. Marc Allaire and Marty Kearney, *Understanding LEAPS*. New York: McGraw-Hill, 2003.

6 Rolling the Stock Positions: Turning 4% into 12%

1. The Quotron system included magnetic tape sited at a brokerage, accompanied by desk units, keyboard, and a printer. The system recorded price data from a ticker line, from which brokers could enter a stock symbol or options symbol and get a quote. The original system listed the latest trade price, and did not provide price history. Brokers placing orders had to enter information, and someone on the exchange floor still had to receive and then enter the order. It was nothing like today's system in which the entire process is immediate and fast.
2. http://www.optionsclearing.com/.

7 Examples of the Basic Strategy

1. A synthetic short stock position consists of a long put and a short call with the same strike and expiration. It mirrors price movement in the underlying and works most effectively when the underlying declines. The major risk of the synthetic short position is the uncovered short call. However, when the trader also owns 100 shares of the underlying for each option call and put opened, it eliminates this risk and becomes a covered

synthetic short stock; it consists of a covered call and an insurance put, collectively costing little or nothing, or creating a net credit.
2. Fees are estimated based on Charles Schwab & Co.'s schedule: stock trades are $8.95 per trade; option trades are $8.95 plus 0.75 per contract. However, fees may vary even within a single brokerage. You might be able to negotiate reduced commissions for multipart strategies entered at the same time, so even a consistently calculated fee schedule will not apply for every transaction, and will be subject to different policies among brokerages. The examples assume round-trip costs for options on both sides, and this is very conservative. Either short or long positions may expire worthless, reducing the round-trip cost by half. However, in the event that a short or long position were subjected to a closing transaction, the estimated round-trip costs are the maximum fees likely to be assessed.
3. Net annualized return is based on dividend yield only. This excludes the net credit from stock and option trades, for which the minimum goal is breakeven. Any net credit (in this example, it was $247) is considered separate from the annualized net return from the dividend collar. If the total included income from options and stock trades, net return would be $237 + $991, or $1,228.

To annualize, divide the net return by the holding period (in this example, 49 days) and then multiply by the full year. The annualization may be performed based on days, weeks, or months. For example, using weeks:

i. $(1.9 \div 7) \times 52 = 14.1\%$.

Based on months, with 49 days rounded to 1.63 months:

ii. $(1.9 \div 1.63) \times 12 = 14.0\%$.

This return is also calculated based on the strike price; the return may be based on the purchased price of shares, current value, or strike. The same basis should be used in all instances to ensure consistency in outcomes.
4. In this case, annualized return is calculated on the basis of dividend income less the net loss on the stock/option trades. Although the previous example ignored the substantial net income, when a net loss is realized, reducing the dividend yield and then annualizing express the true net return. In this case, even with a net loss in the option trades due to transaction fees, the outcome is still in double digits on an annualized basis.

8 MODIFICATION: THE INSTALLMENT COLLAR APPROACH

1. For a free download of margin rules for all options strategies, go to http://www.cboe.com/LearnCenter/pdf/margin2–00.pdf.

9 EXPANDING INTO THE RATIO WRITE DIVIDEND COLLAR

1. To determine the cover rate, divide the number of 100-share increments by the number of short calls. The remainder represents the portion of the overall strategy that remains uncovered, or exposed. For example:

    2 ÷ 3 = 67% (exposure, or uncovered portion is 33%, or 1 in 3 options),
    3 ÷ 4 = 75% (exposure, or uncovered portion is 25%, or 1 in four options),
    4 ÷ 5 = 80% (exposure, or uncovered portion is 20%, or 1 in 5 options).

2. Increasing the number of uncovered contracts does not always represent *more* risk. For example:

    5 ÷ 7 = 71% (exposure, or uncovered portion is 29%, which is lower than the 3:2 ratio),
    6 ÷ 9 = 67% (exposure is 33%, the same as the 3:2 ratio),
    7 ÷ 10 = 70% (exposure is 30%, lower than the 3:2 ratio).

    In all of these instances, exposure is equal to or lower than the 3:2 ratio, with only one uncovered position. However, with all of these examples, three covered with two uncovered contracts will produce higher yields than a single exposed contract.

Index

Alternative Uptick Rule, 44
Altria, 116–19, 280
Ameritrade, 67
annualized return, 75–6, 79
asset allocation, 56–7
AT&T, 16–19, 96–7, 152, 203–9, 212–14, 216–18

Bank of America, 67
beta, 40–2
Black-Scholes pricing model, 10–15
Boyd Gaming, 70, 73–4
BP Prudhoe Bay, 231–9
breakeven rate, 23–5
butterflies, 108, 109–13

Caterpillar, 80, 81–3, 85
Charter Communications, 16–17
Chicago Board Options Exchange (CBOE), 39, 197
Citibank, 123
City Holding, 242–5, 253–8, 261–2
collar
   alternatives, 127–30
   appreciating, 133–4
   comparisons, 107–8
   entry and exit, 133–4
   features, 108–13
   ladder, 124–6
   modified, 130–3
   OTM structure, 126–7
   passive, 120–4
   protective, 133
   simplicity of, 115–20
Con Agra, 125
condors, 108, 113–15
ConocoPhillips, 20, 105, 128–30, 280
core earnings, 17–18

covered call
   annualized return, 75–6, 79
   exposure risk, 80
   if-called return, 76–7
   lost opportunity risk, 58, 80
   ratio write, 85–6
   return calculations, 74–80
   risk management, 80–5
   risks, 47–9, 63–6
   rolling stock strategy, 65–6
   static rate of return, 75, 77
   total return, 74–5
   underlying security, 66–74
   variable ratio write, 86–7
   variations, 85–7

debt ratio, 16–17, 69
Deere, 140, 143
delta, 37–9
dividend
   achievers, 17, 69
   aristocrats, 17
   discount model, 20–1
   Dogs of the Dow, 18, 23
   effect on option values, 10–13
   growth rate, 19–20
   growth stocks, 14–19
   irregular, 227–8
   noncash, 228
   perceptions, 7
   portfolios, 18–22
   risk, 7–8, 19
   skipped, 228
   yield, 8–9, 16–19, 22–7, 68–9
dividend collar
   appreciated stock for, 165–8
   basic strategy, 165
   candidates, 152–7, 172–4

dividend collar—*Continued*
  components entered, 168–72
  dangers, 284–6
  failed underlyings, 174–80
  hostility toward, 275–6
  ideal, 148–52
  installment, 180, 197–9, 202–12
  legged-in, 137–8
  opening in segments, 279–81
  portfolio management with, 160–3
  ratio write, 180–1, 212–21, 227–8, 237–41
  recovery strategies, 245–8
  reverse installment, 221–6
  risks (installment), 199–202
  risks (ratio write), 229–31
  risks (variable ratio write), 252–5
  rules, 281–4
  short-term, 137
  strategy selection, 251–2, 261–4
  successes, 182–95
  synthetic stock, 181–2, 265–72
  underlying, 157–60, 231–7
  variable ratio write, 181, 212–21, 242–5, 249–51, 255–61
Dogs of the Dow, 18, 23
Dominion Resources, 90–2
Dow Jones Industrial Average (DJIA), 18

earnings per share (EPS), 14
Eastman Kodak, 3, 25, 123
Eli Lilly, 95–6, 127
Enron, 3
Enterprise Products, 221–2, 225
e*trade, 67
exchange-traded funds (ETFs), 33–4
Exxon-Mobil, 20

Federal Funds rate, 11
Fidelity, 67
Firstrade, 67
Franklin Street Properties, 182–4, 193
fundamental volatility, 17, 144–8

gamma, 39
General Motors, 3, 25, 123
Google, 131–2, 138–9

H & R$ Block, 280
Hasbro, 154

hedge wrapper, 115
high-frequency trading (HFT), 26, 27–31
historical volatility, 138–44

inflation and taxes, 23–5
iron condor, 115

J.C. Penney, 19, 144–8
JPMorgan Chase, 29
Juniper Networks, 113–15

Kinder Morgan, 154
Kite Realty, 185–6, 193–4

Las Vegas Sands, 70–1, 74
Legacy Reserves, 270–2
Leggett & Platt, 280
Lockheed Martin, 280–1
long put
  alternative to shorting, 93–4
  backspread, 105–6
  collar component, 95–7
  downside protection, 89
  reverse hedge, 98–101
  short cover, 103–4
  straddle and strangle, 101–3
  synthetic short stock, 97–8
  workings, 89–94

married put, 92
McDonalds, 104
Merck, 18–19, 130–1
Microsoft, 116
MMM, 144–8

Omega Healthcare, 231–3, 236–7, 240–1
OPEC, 29
options
  Alternative Uptick Rule, 44
  asset allocation risk, 56–7
  delta, 37–9
  discipline risk, 2, 58–9
  discretionary account risk, 57–8
  disruption of trading risk, 57
  diversification risk, 56
  gamma, 39
  knowledge risk, 55–6
  long risks, 51–3
  lost opportunity risk, 58, 80

margin and collateral risk, 54
market risk, 33–43
risks, less obvious, 54–61
short differences, 46–51
short-selling risk, 43–6
spread and straddle risks, 53–4
tax risk, 59
uncovered, 49–51

pattern day trader, 54–5
PE ratio, 14–16, 68
People's United Financial, 186–9, 194
Pfizer, 18–19
Polaroid, 123

qualified covered call, 60

Research in Motion, 14–15
reverse hedge, 98–101
rolling stock, 135–7
Royal Bank of Canada, 221–6

Schwab (Charles), 67
Scott Trade, 67
Sears, 123

Securities and Exchange Commission (SEC), 44, 57
SPDR Gold Trust, 99–101
Standard & Poor's, 18, 40
synthetic short stock, 97–8

Targa Resources, 253–5, 257, 259–62
TD Waterhouse, 67
Teekay Offshore, 189–91, 194
trading curb, 57

Universal Corp., 166–8, 191–4

Value at Risk (VaR), 34–5, 40
Vanguard, 67
Verizon, 18–19, 97, 154, 156, 203–4, 209–12, 214–16, 218–21

Wal-Mart, 14–15, 140, 142
Walt Disney, 109–11
wash sale, 59–60
Wells Fargo, 67
Wynn Reports, 70, 72, 74

Yahoo, 138, 140–1